Shoot to Live

Presenting the Johnson Method of Musketry Coaching

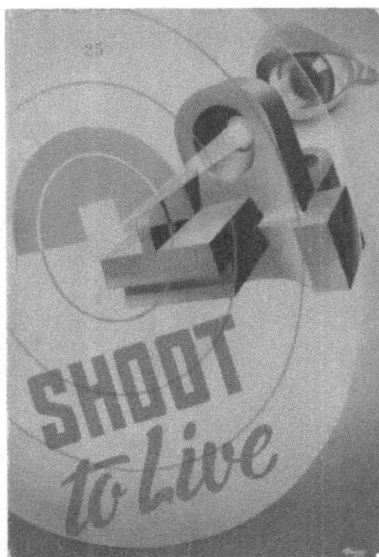

by

Stephen Johnson

Shoot to Live
Presenting the Johnson Method of Musketry Coaching
by Stephen Johnson

ISBN: 978-0-934523-91- 2

Editor @Middle-Coast-Publishing.com

INTRODUCTION

United States Rifle, Caliber 7.62 mm, M14

U.S. Army Basic Training, Fort Leonard Wood, Missouri - We were issued M14s, mine a Harrington & Richardson fitted with a synthetic stock. Other soldier's rifles were fitted with walnut stocks, Winchesters or Springfield Armory. Admittedly, prettier, but I preferred fiberglass furniture for the way it held zero better than walnut. In a sweltering classroom, Echo company Drill Instructors schooled us on dis-assembling and re-assembling the weapon, asserting an M14 is not a gun. It is a rifle, a firearm or a weapon. Never a gun, a word reserved for an artillery piece.

Rifles apart, laying on their backs in dozens of pieces on a table in front of us, we were told to put them back together as fast as we could. On the word go, it took me less than a minute. The DIs stared at me dumbfounded. I murmured that I had grown up with an M1 Garand, nearly the same as an M14.

Then we were instructed to forget everything our grandpas had ever taught us about shooting. That we were to shoot the Army way. I listened, casually.

The next day, with temperatures in the low-90s, were marched many miles down a hot and dusty road to the rifle range where we commenced to sight-in our weapons. We would to fire groups of three rounds at 25-yards.

DI Lyons looked at my first target and smiled, "Son, Army way or your way, keep doing exactly what you're doing." I had punched three bullet holes dead center in the target, patterned in a one-inch group.

For two years prior to going in the Army, I had spent every Thursday night with my Explorer Scout post, shooting: As a kid, post leader, Robert Reinhardt, had learned the Johnson method and passed on the knowledge base to us Explorer Scouts. After two years, I became quite good.

U.S. Army Expert Marksmanship badge

My personal Johnson Musketry method success story is not unique. There are thousands of case histories just like it. The point being, no matter how experienced a shooter, one can learn from the wisdom in this book. - Editor -

TABLE OF CONTENTS

Master Eye - Differences in Eyes - How to Remedy Eye Troubles in Aiming - Both Eyes Closed - Both Eyes Open - flinching - Use of Wrong Eye - Back Sight - - Optical Centre - How to Find and Use It - Looking Through Hear Sight - Sharp, Clear, Black, Square Front Sight - Focus - Sight Pictures - Field of View - Eye Distance - Moving Targets - - Service Conditions and Handicaps - The Front Sight Versus Target - Auxiliary Aiming Marks - Points of Aim - Precision of Aim - Blackening Sights - Equipment of Aiming and Use - American Sighting Bar - Australian Sighting Bar - Johnson Sighting Bar - Winter's Sighting Device - New Rules of Aiming.

TRIGGER CONTROL

Top Priority - Is 65% Important? - Needs Practice in Easy Doses - The Squeeze - The Slack - Testing Pressure - Direction of Trigger Movement - Place of Finger on Trigger - Application of Trigger Control - Wandering Front Sights - Follow Through - Checking Follow Through - - Calling the Shots - Checking Recruits' Trigger Control - Trigger Solitaire - Checking Front Sight - Coin Games - Recapitulation.

CO- ORDINATION

Combining all Five Basic Principles - Must Do All Automatically - Correct Use of Sandbag - Two- Foot Circle.

THE RANGE . . .

Preparation - Safety on the Range.

Except for Rapid Fire and Snap Shooting. the Instructional Phases conclude here. The following material is a guide to the coaches and not to be taught.

TARGET ANALYSIS

Each Bullet Hole Tells a Story - The Cause and Effect of Each Shot - Clues and Correction - Diminishing Area of Groups - Shapes of Groups - Sight Correction - Call and Check Card - Measuring Bullet Holes - Numbering the Shots - Language of Bullet Holes - Encouragement and Advice - The Completed Story - On the .303

Range.

DEDICATED
TO ALL RIFLE INSTRUCTORS
WHOEVER, AND WHEREVER, THEY MAY BE,
WHO WISH TO SUCCESSFULLY
TEACH OTHERS
TO STEER BULLETS.

Meet "Little Chief Wildshot" — The Musketry Gremlin

CHAPTER ONE

Introduction

SO YOU are the instructor who is engaged in teaching soldiers of the Canadian Army how to correctly shoot their rifles that they may efficiently diminish an enemy's strength and thus speed victory?

How successful have you been? We know how you have boasted to other instructors about the large numbers of recruits you have speedily passed through the mill in accord with the teachings of the musketry drill pamphlets and directives. You have told the troops everything the booklets have contained. You have carefully recited the drill.

But can YOU shoot as good a lecture as you can spiel?

Certainly you can shoot or you wouldn't be an instructor. But can you shoot *ACCURATELY* and understand *WHY*?

By shooting accurately, we mean dead in the centre of a target 99 times out of 100 shots. We will lay a side bet that with all your pamphlet prowling you can either explain in logical detail how and why you get good scores or you are exaggerating your own rifle prowess. If you don't know what gives perfect target results you don't know shooting and cannot teach it. You stand a chance of winning the "Order of the Bengal Lancers" for being a better talking marksman than a practicing one.

On the other hand, if you will settle your mind down to getting rid of antiquated ideas about shooting and study, instead, the simple but scientifically developed methods explained in succeeding chapters, your record of successful musketry instruction will startle you.

Good musketry cannot be taught by long-winded lectures that are mildewed with age and given in a sing-song, memorized manner. Neither can you teach it without knowing the reasons why certain desired results are obtained.

Shooting is fun—not hard work. That is, if it is good shooting and most soldiers want to be good shots. They are not wearing battle dress just for the privilege of lugging a Lee Enfield around for ballast. They want to be able to kill the enemy and then get back to the "little woman" at home. But soldiers are human enough to sit through a dry lecture dreaming of what the cook will have in the dinner stew unless you can capture their enthusiasm with interesting, logical instruction.

Thus, to be a good coach, you must first be a good rifle shot yourself. You cannot afford to be careless. The boys you train are going out to fight while you give fighting instruction at home. If one of your candidate's names appears on a casualty list, blame yourself—don't curse the enemy. That boy would probably not have been a casualty had he been properly taught to shoot accurately. Remember, one bullet, perfectly fired and confidently delivered, can beat any foe.

Your first job, after reading this handbook, will therefore be to get out onto the range and learn to do everything it teaches. You must shoot perfectly and prove with your bull's eyes that you can. If you cannot shoot, then you cannot interest Private John Quincy Buck to shoot, nor can you deride these new methods of teaching, just because they differ from old and long-used systems.

The responsibility is ALL YOURS.

Before delving into a discussion of proper and effective teaching methods, your attention is called to SAFETY. The old bromide, "I didn't know it was loaded!", does not rate in musketry. *EVERY RIFLE IS LOADED UNTIL YOU HAVE SATISFIED YOURSELF OTHERWISE. If, while you are instructing, a soldier is wounded by rifle fire, don't call it an accident.*

You could be charged with attempted manslaughter if you were a civilian. Accidents are only caused by carelessness and any in YOUR class will be YOUR CARELESSNESS.

In wartime, good musketry resolves itself into shooting and killing the enemy—not shooting the gas. If you listen to canteen conversations you will hear plenty of men who, at the gulp of an ale, can tell you how good they are at hitting the bull's eye. Maybe they have scored a few good shots in their day but can they prove it at a rate of 99%? Every red-blooded Canadian regards himself as an ace marksman. If he never had a rifle in his hands before he joined the Army, he knows it is very simple. To him it is just a matter of picking up that old Lee Enfield, selecting a target and jerking the trigger.

So what happens?

Farmer Jones over in the next county is asking "whoinell" shot his brindle cow. The know-it-all soldier has only a blank target, his shoulder or arm is sore from the rifle's recoil, and his pride is so injured that he hates his rifle, his instructor, the Army and HIMSELF.

On the other hand, a properly taught recruit would not have been allowed onto the range until he had mastered the fundamentals of Position, Holding, Breathing, Aiming and Trigger Control. When that recruit did reach the range he would have a confidence that he could shoot accurately because that was the only way he had been taught.

Good shooting is nothing but the simple and complete mastery of the five prime essentials: *POSITION - HOLDING - BREATHING - AIMING* and *TRIGGER CONTROL* which are then all tied together by *CO-ORDINATION.* A soldier, to attain this mastery, must have *THOROUGH* and *ENTHUSIASTIC COACHING* in all these. He must know what every step means and why it has been taken. He must be convinced that each phase of training is a vital part to the eventual result.

No special aptitude is necessary in learning to shoot. Good marksmen are not born as such. No specially-perfect physique is required and only average intelligence and willingness is expected. The soldier must be keen enough to accept the methods of attaining good marksmanship through conscientious practice. To reach the goal that has been set he will see that with a sensible application to the business of correctly learning the values and reasons for good shooting, it will be easy. It will be much easier and much more natural than some other aspects of his military training.

You may ask, "Why does this new policy in teaching musketry come up now when the old, established methods served us for years? In other words, why change at this stage?"

These are logical questions. The Canadian Army of 1914-18 was credited with being one of the finest shooting formations of all the British Armies but the modern Canadian Army does not command such honours. Nazi battle records captured in North Africa praised the sniping abilities of the New Zealanders. Then what is wrong with the Canadians?

Either we have become careless in our shooting or our training methods need modernizing to meet the current trends of war. If Canadians are to succeed, the Maple Leaf brand of shooting must be perfected. One rifleman, given the right opportunity, can decide a war with a well-placed bullet and YOU might be the lucky man.

War has no Hollywood-directed dramatics. The demands upon each individual rifleman crop up without warning. The enemy, who is not as well equipped as you, knows that he is out to kill you or die in the attempt. Your number is on his bullet and his number on your bullet. You can win the duel by beating him to the well-executed draw or you will be his victim. There is no time to discuss these factors with him. It is either a case of shooting accurately and immediately or of being a casualty.

A British rear guard was slogging over a bridge spanning the Corinth Canal in Greece, in the dark days of 1941. Royal Engineers who were engaged in mining the bridge were forced to flee from their task before affixing all detonators. Nazi paratroops showered down upon the bridge area in hot pursuit of the Tommies. The Germans frantically sought the TNT so that their pursuit of the British would not be impeded.

Lieutenant Rawlinson, Engineer officer, lay in a slit trench watching the feverish hunt of the Germans. He saw one of the cigarette-sized detonators dangling from a thin wire against a concrete abutment. Carefully aiming his rifle, he fired. The bridge was wrecked, the canal was choked with dead or drowning Germans and the withdrawal of the British troops to waiting warships was assured.

United States Marines will tell you about the Gopher who was the best shot the Japs had ever put up against the Leathernecks. The action in which the Gopher performed was on Peleliu, in the South Pacific. He operated on Bloody Nose Ridge, which was honeycombed with connecting caves and tunnels. He would pop out of a hole, fire his rifle and then disappear. While Marine marksmen hunted him, he would appear at another hole, fire his rifle and then disappear. He killed 87 Marines, each with a perfectly-aimed shot in the head.

Eventually, Marine marksmen were so placed that they covered all the holes in the ridge. When the Gopher popped out, on another deadly mission, he was killed—with a perfectly-delivered Marine bullet in his head.

The enemy fights for keeps and war is changing in order to keep up with its own demands. It is therefore obviously imperative that Canadian soldiers meet the challenge with accurate fire from their basic infantry weapons. Infantry instructors must be prepared to teach in terms of accurate yet maximum fire power. It is not claimed that the methods described in detail in the following chapters are the best, but they are far better than any others we have been able to muster or offer and their complete application will guarantee the results desired.

It is not intended that the steps outlined herein be memorized and then

4

recited as mechanically as a phonograph recording. Rather, it is suggested that the instructor apply the material contained in this handbook to his own words. If you, as the instructor, have proven to your own satisfaction that the doctrine of good shooting as described, is effective, you will be able to enthusiastically lecture, accordingly. Your class will then capture the spirit and through practice attain consistently accurate sniping skill.

Much stress is placed upon the sequence, or order, of the material offered. Just as you crawled before you walked, walked before you ran and ran before you gained that sense of rhythm which is dancing, so must you study musketry step by careful step, until each is taken confidently and automatically.

The various phases of the training as outlined under the headings POSITION, HOLDING, BREATHING, AIMING, TRIGGER CONTROL and CO-ORDINATION have been presented in the sequence which practice has proven capable of producing the best results. Each chapter has been broken down so that the recruit may be taught, step by step, how to shoot properly. Each phase of the training comes in its logical order. To further assist you, illustrative material accompanies the text.

The story, presented in sequence, leads to the eventual steadiness of the rifle long enough for a bullet to be sped toward its target. The phases might be more clearly described as being relaxed position; scientific resting of the rifle on the body structure; steadied breath control; the correct use of rifle sighting devices and perfect trigger squeeze.

Baseball and golf provide good illustrations. In either one, you know that if you are to achieve good results, a comfortable stance (Position), a proper grip of the bat or club (Holding), a momentary but not strained breathing pause as the ball is struck (Breathing), your eye on the ball (Aiming) the perfectly struck ball (Trigger Squeeze) and the automatic use of all these together (Co-Ordination) are required.

All of this sounds mechanical and it should become mechanical, or automatic through practice. The methods outlined in succeeding chapters are the pet secrets of the crack shots and after they have been mastered, soldiers, thus trained, will be able to shoot accurately and as easily as they button their shirts.

Older methods of teaching musketry stressed aiming and avoided the intricate but necessary study of what leads up to the science of good shooting. That science has been so developed that now it can be discussed—which is this handbook. The training offered is thus streamlined enough to encourage a practical approach to the theories of musketry. Yet it is simple enough that the average soldier is assured of mastery of the art.

Any normal person can quickly learn good shooting; that is if he has been properly taught. Good teaching doesn't call for a recitation of the various parts of a rifle. If you are learning to drive an automobile, you don't study the names and functions of every gadget in the motor and transmission. All you are interested in is what makes the car go and stop. Musketry is similar. Soldiers want to shoot their rifles, not pull them apart. A set-screw's name is much less important than the operation of firing a bullet so that it hits the target toward which it has been steered.

The good instructor, therefore, should teach proper musketry fully, yet

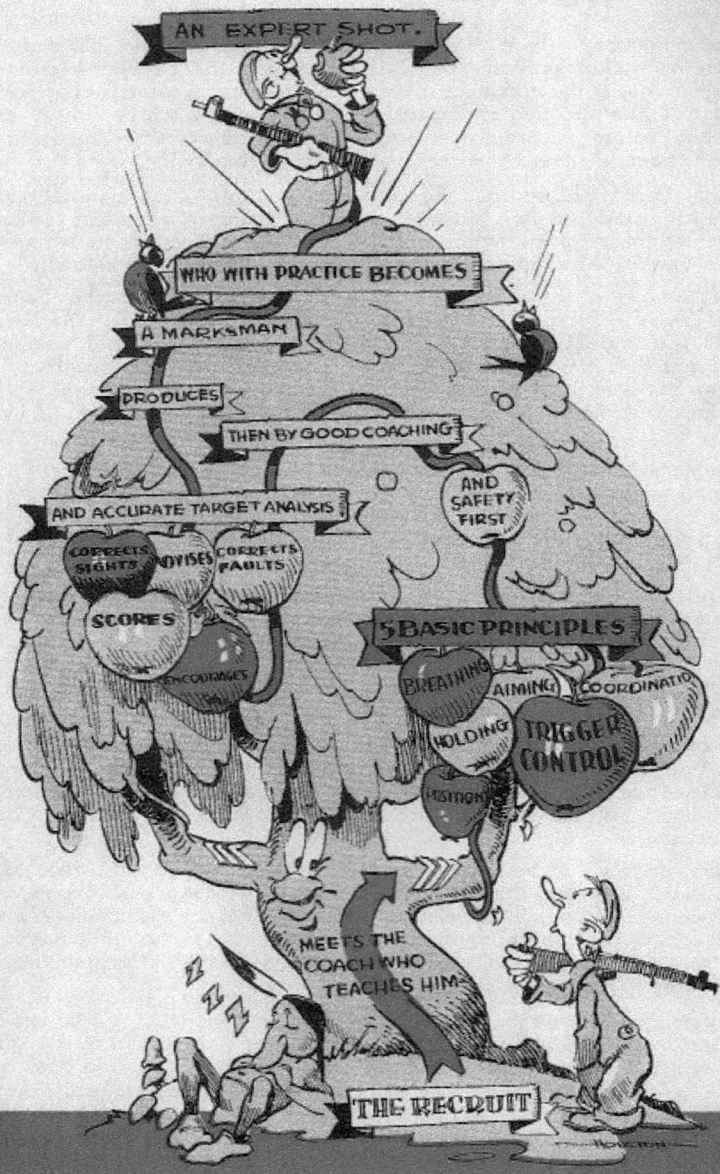

quickly and clearly. He should never be a "show-off" by using words, or terms, which are beyond the understanding of his class. He should not browbeat nor ridicule his men. He once was a "dumb" beginner himself. He should teach a phase of a lesson and demonstrate it. The recruit should then imitate that demonstration and practice it until it has been mastered and fully understood. Then, and then only, should the next phase of the course be approached. As the instruction unfolds itself the recruit will see how each phase ties into another to become a complete and confidence-inspiring whole.

The successful coach studies his class carefully, as a football coach studies his beefy linemen and temperamental halfbacks. The boxer with poor training and little confidence is a certain loser when compared with the cocky one. Therefore a pat on the back, a kind word and ready co-operation on the part of the instructor will produce eager and efficient marksmen.

The instruction outlined, herein, is not for just a chosen few. It should, instead, be the keynote for every Officer, N.C.O. and soldier in the Canadian Army—including the natty lads of the Royal Canadian Army Cadet Corps. Nor is the matter, herein, restricted to rifle fire. The expertly-taught rifleman possesses the basic principles which will lead him to effective use of all small arms. If Canadians can restore their reputation as a nation of ace marksmen, war mongers will think twice before getting us onto any future battlefields.

What will be the results of this new method of teaching musketry? The confident, well-trained rifleman will be automatically able to stalk the enemy and "erase" him. He will know that his perfectly controlled weapon will prove more than a match for the enemy machine-gunners and snipers because with an economy of ammunition and effort he can pick off an enemy quickly and at will. He is a triple-threat which the enemy can neither readily counteract nor comprehend.

Because he can hit a target at 200 yards with consistent effectiveness, the well-trained Canadian rifleman can deal with practically every circumstance of battle. He will be able to win his own war, in his own way, and his nation will be rightfully proud of him.

For the purposes of this instruction all references and illustrations concern right-handed recruits, but should a soldier be left-handed or able to shoot somewhat better from his left shoulder, the instruction can easily be adapted to his needs.

. . . AND NOW WE'RE GOING TO TEACH YOU HOW TO SHOOT!

CHAPTER TWO

Position

GOOD position in successful shooting becomes a matter of placing the recruit into a restful, relaxed position from which he can establish the foundation for good marksmanship. The prone, or lying, position is rated as the best because it provides that solidness and comfort which induces precisely accurate fire. Note the similarities to artillery pieces portrayed on the opposite page.

When the recruit first takes his properly-fitted rifle and lies upon the ground or floor, nine times out of ten he will show a tendency toward bad shooting habits.

The instructor should not scold him but, rather, carefully and kindly correct those faults, step by step, and encourage him to practice each step carefully. As each phase of the training is taught, its value will be proved in comfort and in confidence. Bad shooting habits cannot be tolerated.

You cannot teach a recruit, with a few curt orders, how to hold his rifle. He may insist upon being shown how and why he should take a position or do thus and so. He can be shown by the professional interest which you take in him.

If he were to go to the medical officer with a sore throat he would have confidence in being cured because of the M.O.'s patient but expert approach, diagnosis and treatment. You, too, must approach patiently and scientifically the musketry problems peculiar to each individual whom you instruct.

It will not be necessary for you to teach the recruit the mechanics of horizontal or vertical triangles referred to in this chapter. They serve as a means for you, the instructor, to so adjust the individual pupil to correct position that he may engage in good shooting.

This is where coaching begins and the kindly manner in which you apply the proof will encourage him in his endeavours toward becoming a marksman of merit.

Keep your recruits OFF THE RANGE until they have mastered the fundamentals of good shooting. Encourage them to practice while in barracks or off duty.

You may have to repeat your lessons several times in teaching an individual to acquire correct shooting position but the time and effort will bring rich dividends.

FIG. 1

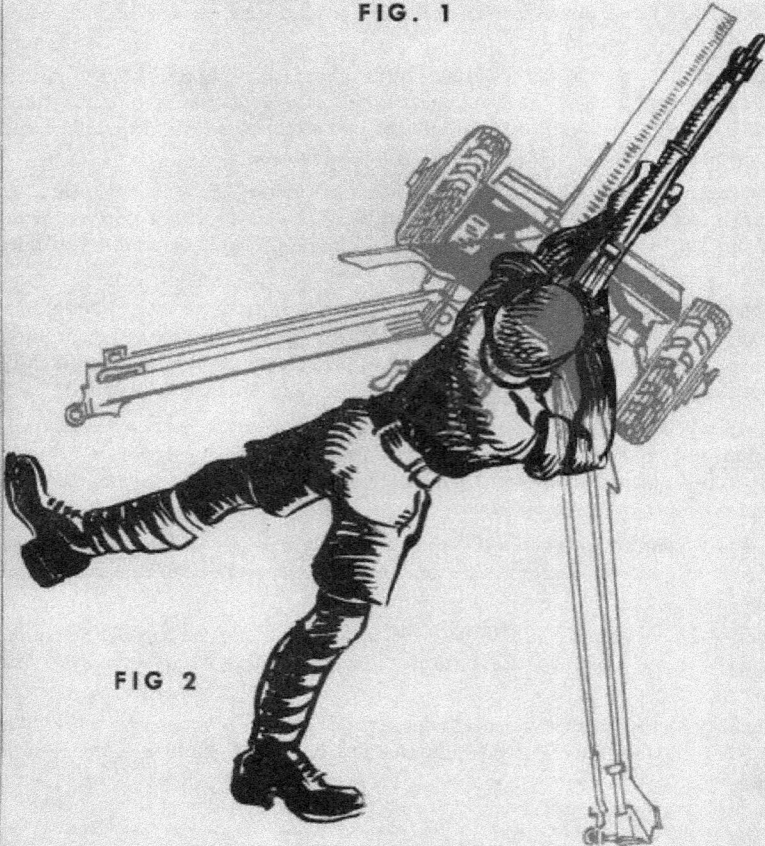

FIG 2

10

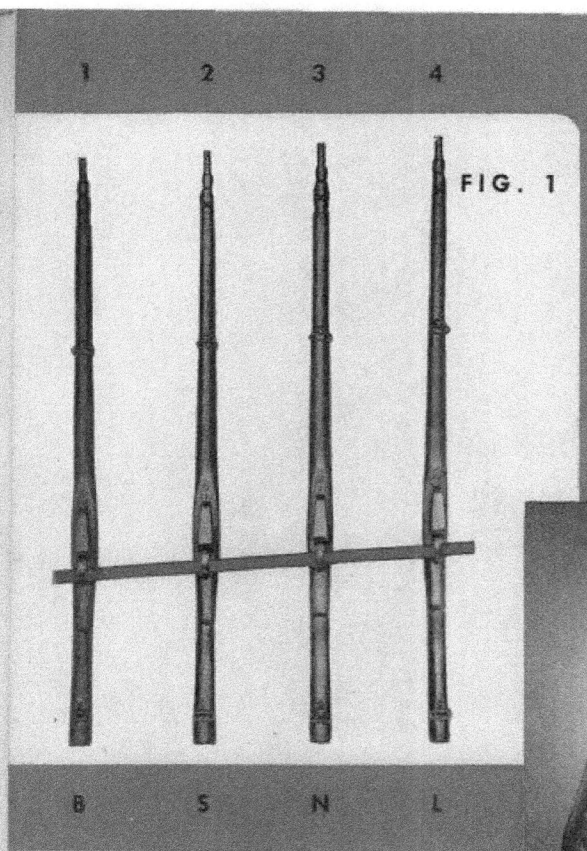
FIG. 1

FIG. 2

| 1 | 2 | 3 | 4 |

| B | S | N | L |

BUTT LENGTHS

THE Canadian Army rifle is made available to troops in four butt lengths. The varying differences in the lengths of arms and fingers naturally imply that the rifle which is comfortable for one person is uncomfortable for another.

Instruction of a recruit should not be commenced until he has been properly fitted with a rifle. Figure 1 above shows the comparison of butt lengths while Figure 2 gives the location of the markings which are "B" for bantam, "S" for small, "N" for normal and "L" for long.

Figures 3 and 4 opposite show the natural position of the right hand when the butt is placed in the crook of the elbow for measuring purposes. It will be seen that the wrist must be kept straight—not bent—and that if the rifle action is cocked, the trigger should come approximately midway between the first and second joints of the index finger and NOT on the tip of the finger.

As there are exceptions to the usual physiques, adjustments may necessarily be made by the instructor to insure that each recruit is as well fitted as possible. Moreover, there may be some recruits, whom you have fitted, who will require additional changes of rifle butt later.

11

FIG. 3

FIG. 4

12

THE LEFT ELBOW

THE instructor will quickly appreciate that to the right-handed person the left forearm is the pillar of bone upon which the rifle must solidly rest while the left elbow is the pivot upon which the whole position of the marksman depends and revolves.

As the recruit takes his prone firing position, with his properly fitted rifle, the initial stress must be placed upon the exact location of the left elbow.

Proving the position of the elbow, you can remove the magazine and the bolt from the rifle and vertically slip a lath or yardstick down through the space. If the elbow is in the correct position, there will not be more than one and one-half inches from the inside of the elbow's point of contact with the floor and the point of contact of the vertical stick. Note Figure 1 opposite.

You can check the position from side views as shown in Figures 2 and 3.

FIG. 1

1½″

FIG. 2

FIG. 3

14

THE HALF ROLL

THE correct position of the left elbow is sometimes difficult for some recruits to reach. They will have a sideways slope to their left forearm no matter how much they grunt or stretch. In cases of this sort, you should have the recruit make a so-called Half Roll over onto his right side while keeping the right elbow stationary, and the rifle pointing upward. Remember—this is only a partial roll. The recruit should then pull his left elbow well in toward the centre of his body, then roll back into firing position. This method tends to release some joint in the shoulder which will permit the marksman to get his left elbow farther under the rifle and at the same time ease some of the tension upon his arm and shoulder muscles, which are somewhat taut at first.

In some cases, there still may be a bit of strain along the left arm but practice will loosen these muscles. Figures 1, 2 and 3 below, demonstrate how to use the half roll to assist in getting the left elbow closer to a direct position underneath the rifle.

FIG. 1

FIG. 2

FIG. 3

15

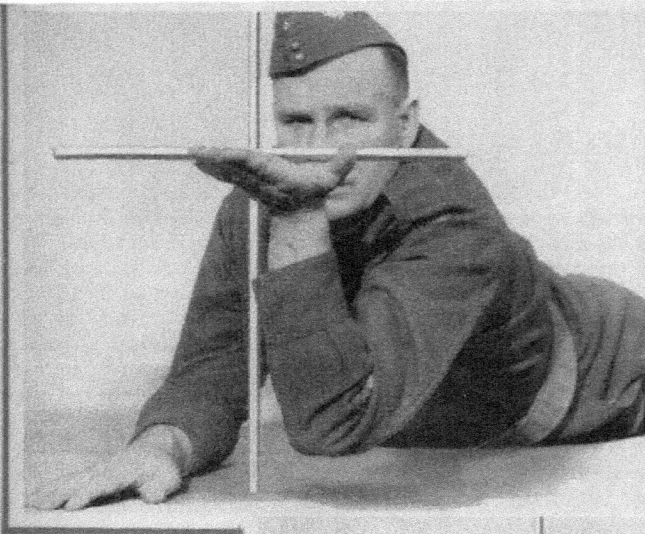

FIG. 1

FIG. 2

THE FLAT HAND METHOD

ANOTHER effective means of acquiring the proper position of the left elbow and known as the Flat Hand Method is to have the recruit hold his left hand level. By that we mean *level*. If you were to place a spirit level on the hand the bubble would be plumb in the centre. The elbow should be about three or four inches from the floor. See Figure 1 above.

The recruit will quickly see that he cannot get his hand to flatten out level, unless his elbow is pulled in to the right. When he does get the elbow well in towards his body the hand will be level. Then have him lower the elbow to the floor with his hand still level. See Figure 2. By this time he should have an appreciation of the position the elbow and arm must take and he naturally is able to understand the strength which the position implies.

Now hand him his rifle and check the stick through the bolt-space of the magazine again. The elbow will be within that one and one-half inches of the stick.

16

IMPORTANCE OF THE LEFT HAND

H AVING established the correct place for the left elbow and forearm, the top of the pillar (the left hand) takes on a vital role. Note Figure 1 below and you will see the rifle lying across the heel of the left hand. The axis of the rifle bisects the angle formed by the lines running from the centre of the wrist to the thumb and third or fourth fingers.

This is the perfect groove, because the weight of the rifle is directly above that solid upright of bone. The rifle is now the girder lying balanced across the sturdy upright.

To attain this solidness, the centre of the wrist should be directly underneath the centre of the rifle. This is almost bound to occur if the recruit has been carefully taught the flat-hand method of adjusting his elbow into position. His left hand should also be as far forward of the magazine as comfort will allow. In fact there should be a clearance of at least the width of one finger between the wrist and the breach-cover staple on the lower side of the rifle.

The rifle should rest well down in the hand—right in the groove—so that it permits a firm but not too tight grip of the rifle. A grip that is too tight tends to promote tension and discomfort.

After the recruit has attained this position, the instructor will see that as in Figure 4 opposite, the rifle rests in a cradle and points toward the centre of

FIG. 1

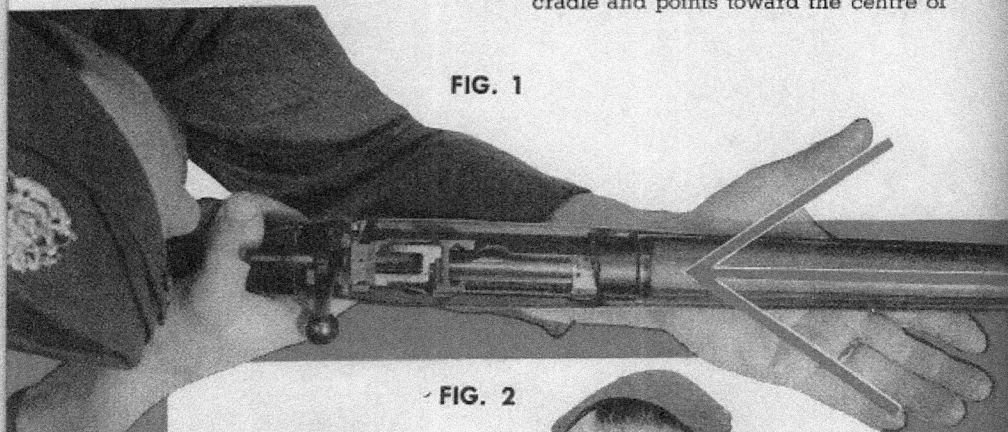

FIG. 2

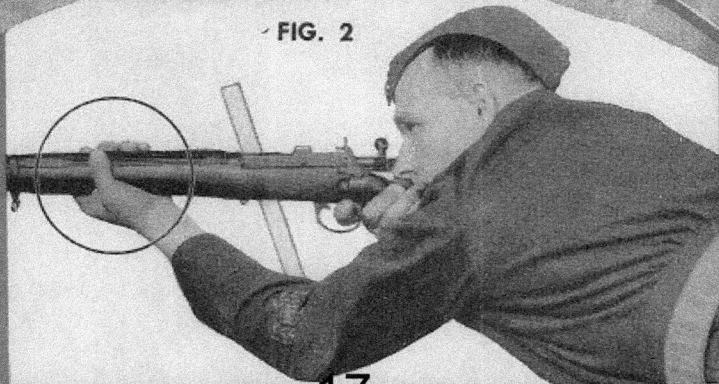

17

the target when the recruit's breath is briefly held. The recruit will also see some progress in his training.

You can test the steadiness of the recruit's position by having him rest the rifle upon his open palm. If the rifle remains steady and apparently in its proper position, then the left elbow, arm and hand are doing their work properly. It will thus be seen that there will be no need for a tight grip which would only increase unwanted tremors of the body. If the rifle is not steady, then you should check back upon the position to ascertain wherein the fault lies.

Looking at the left hand (Figure 3) as it clasps the rifle, you will note that the fingers curl up and over the handguard so that the fingers and thumb almost, but not quite, touch. All parts of the inner surfaces of the hands and fingers should grasp the handguard without bending or straining the fingers or permitting light spaces between them and the rifle.

Let us check that hand for angles. The properly resting rifle will look exactly like Figure 1, when opened and viewed from above. It will look like Figures 2 and 3 when viewed from the sides while closed. As shown in Figure 4 it will appear to form a cradle or cup that virtually shouts solidness when seen from in front.

Should the recruit have long fingers, like those of a pianist, let him wrap them around the upper part of the handguard even to the extent of blocking out his vision toward the front sight. This can be corrected later. At the moment, the insistence is upon the proper placing of the left elbow and hand.

In this position, the left hand's job is merely to hold the rifle firmly and draw it backwards to the shoulder. This is frequently referred to in later chapters as "Backward Pressure."

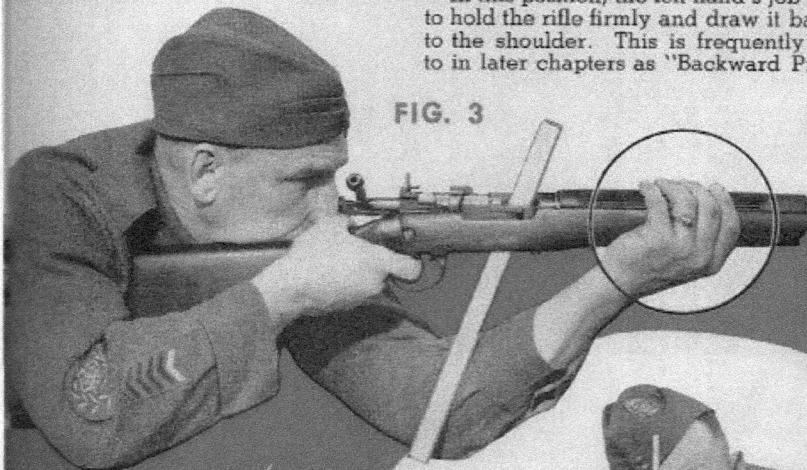

FIG. 3

FIG. 4

18

THE RIGHT HAND

THE right hand, which does all the trigger squeezing, is nevertheless important to the correct position of a rifle when accurate shooting is sought. It is the top of the third leg of the tripod formed by the left forearm, your prone body and your right forearm.

The right hand should clasp the small of the butt so that the thumb nearly touches the rear of the cocking piece when the action is fully cocked. The forefinger or trigger finger should be around the trigger so that it is between the first and second joints or creases. The thumb should overclasp the small of the butt with the second, third and fourth fingers gripping the butt from below and across the small of the butt. The recruit is now gripping the small of the butt just as he used to grip a toy pistol when he played cowboys and Indians. See Figures 1, 2 and 3 opposite.

Some recruits may not, however, attain this perfect grip too easily. So have the recruit place his hand upon the small of the butt and slide it forward until it touches the rear of the cocking piece when it is cocked. Then have him grip the small of the butt as in Figure 2. Now the index finger is in position to reach around the trigger with the slack taken up. His second, third and fourth fingers should be pointing upwards grasping the rifle across the butt.

Here the recruit must take firm grip. It must be solid enough that the tendons on the back of the hand will stand out more than under normal conditions. A good test of this would be for the instructor to have the recruit remove his hand from the small of the butt after a period of gripping it and show that his fingers are flatter and whiter than normal.

This grip does not need to be so tight that the hand will ache, yet it should be firm enough to steadily hold the rifle and exert its required backward pressure against the shoulder.

THE BUTT GRIP

WHEN it comes to the matter of proper grip of the rifle the old bugbear about differences in the physiques of soldiers again appears. Observe Figure 4, which illustrates a firm grip. If this cannot be attained readily, ask the recruit to hold the butt against his shoulder and then raise the right elbow slightly from the floor as shown by the dotted lines in Figure 4.

Now let him take the grip as illustrated and then lower the elbow without relaxing the grip. He will see how the elbow falls into the correct position.

As he becomes accustomed to the proper grip, this raising, gripping and lowering of the elbow will become less and less necessary until it can be abandoned.

19

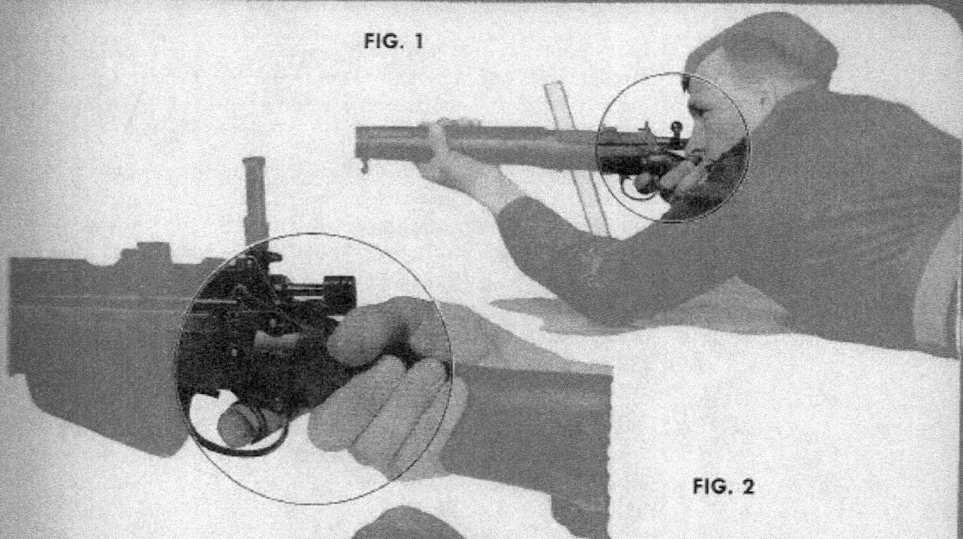

FIG. 1

FIG. 2

FIG. 3

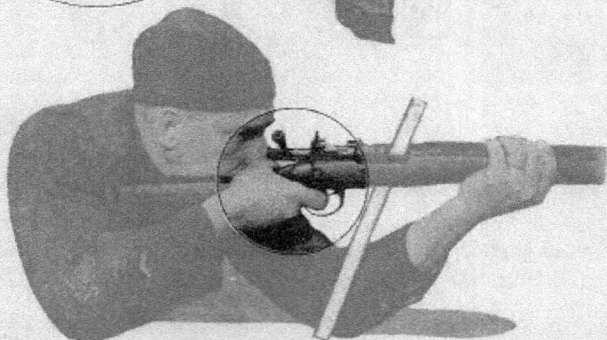

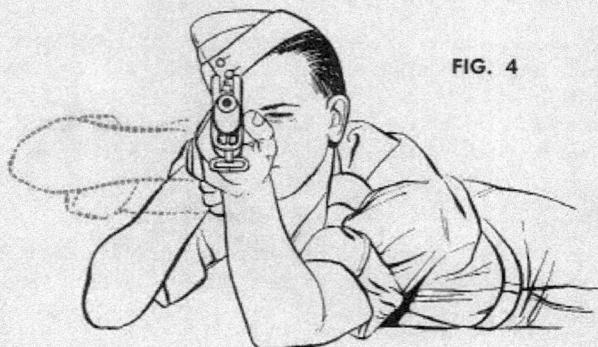

FIG. 4

20

THE HORIZONTAL TRIANGLE

HERE is where the professional comes into the picture. The recruit has done everything he has been told to do. But is it correct? Let's check, not by telling the recruit exactly what is being done, but by indicating in an expert manner that you are proving the correctness of his position, which is merely the means by which the body and the rifle are lined up together.

In achieving this perfect position, the body, the arms and the rifle form triangles the shape of which, when adopted by the recruit, will prove the correctness of his position. They will be the Stop-Go signals by which you will measure his progress.

Incidentally, the axis of the rifle is that imaginary line which runs through the centre of the weapon. It will frequently appear in subsequent chapters and sub-topics.

With the recruit in the prone position you have taught him to take, stand over him and with your eyes almost closed visualize the flat or horizontal triangle formed by imaginary, straight lines connecting the two elbows and the centre of his body. The centre of the body is that point directly beneath the spine and where the chest meets the floor. See Figure 1, opposite.

Now, if the recruit has religiously followed your previous instruction, the sides of that triangle will be almost of equal length. If he has not the proper position, the triangle's sides will be irregular in length. But again, if he is in correct position with his head on top of and against the butt, the triangle will be well nigh perfect.

You as the instructor, however, cannot just judge the correctness of position too much by casual observation. So you prove to yourself, by using chalk marks, how correct the position is—and at the same time prove to the recruit that you are taking a personal interest in him.

One chalk mark is placed just inside the left elbow where the bone touches the floor (see Figure 2 opposite). It can be labelled "LE". "RE" would similarly be inside the right elbow with "CB" marking the location of the centre of the body where it touches the floor. Now mark "BUTT" directly beneath the end of the butt, "MAG" directly beneath the magazine and "MUZ" beneath the end of the muzzle.

Ask the recruit to get up from the floor and with a yardstick or other straight edge join up LE, RE and CB and there you will have the recruit's horizontal triangle. If the rifle has been correctly held all three sides will appear equal.

Now join up BUTT, MAG and MUZ and if the position has been correct BUTT will be in the middle of the side of the triangle RE—CB.

Let us further prove this position. Draw a line at LE at right angles to the

21

rifle's axis. It should not go more than one and one-half inches before meeting the line BUTT—MAG—MUZ. Odd but true, that distance is the same as the distance between the elbow and the yardstick inserted through the open magazine.

Should it be that these proofs do not work out, corrections can now be made. If the left elbow is not in its proper place, now is the time to use it as a pivot and shift the body around until the left elbow is in correct position, under the rifle. The right elbow may have to be moved in or out to make further adjustment, or it may have to be moved forward or back but the left elbow is the all-important member. It is the key to the whole story.

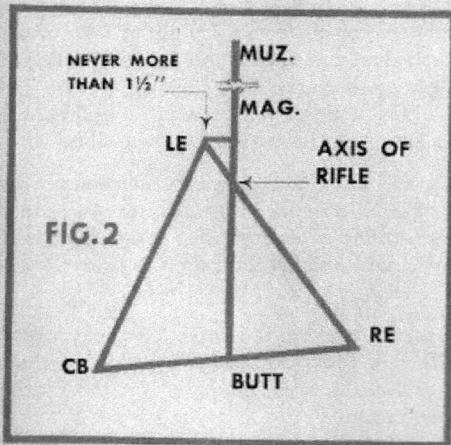

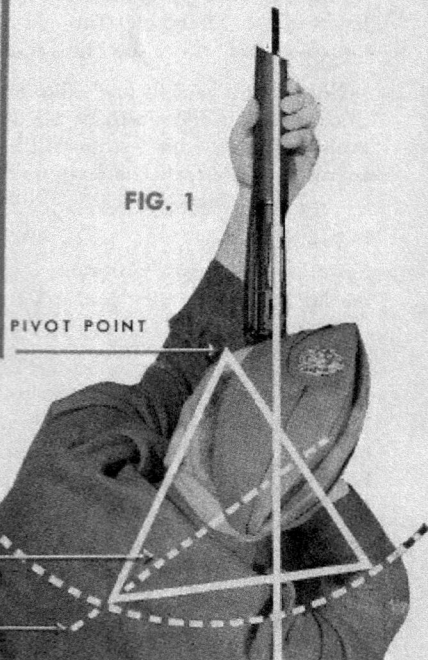

FIG. 2

NEVER MORE THAN 1½"

MUZ.

MAG.

AXIS OF RIFLE

LE

CB

BUTT

RE

FIG. 1

PIVOT POINT

PATH OF AUTOMATIC ALIGNMENT

HORIZONTAL TRIANGLE

CENTER OF BODY

THE VERTICAL TRIANGLE

WITH professional flare you are now commencing to impress your recruit. You now introduce a Vertical Triangle as further proof of correct position. This Vertical Triangle is not really what its name implies because it is oblique or sloping. Get down in front of the muzzle and look under it toward the tripod-like support which the recruit is giving to his weapon.

Visualize a line which will connect the inside of the two elbows and then two more lines which will extend slopingly upwards from each of the inner sides of the two elbows until they meet at the point of the grasp of the rifle. There you have your Vertical Triangle. If you wish, you can use laths upon the floor and along the inside of the forearms to further establish this triangle. Note Figure 1, opposite.

Now if you will refer to the illustrations below you will see that Triangle 1 is high and unstable caused by the elbows being too close together forcing upwards the apex of the triangle and permitting side motion if a rifle were held.

The illustration of Triangle 3 shows a low, flat, weak triangle which means that muscles and not bones are holding the rifle, thus permitting vertical motion.

Triangle 2 illustrates the normal position which is an equally-sided vertical triangle of strength.

The recruit at this juncture rightfully asks why this stress upon triangles. You can demonstrate the normal position to him by having him sit (just behind the left hand) upon your properly-held rifle. You can hold his weight and he will see the strength of the position. See Figure 2A.

But if he has a low triangle, pressure of your thumb and first two fingers will push the rifle from his grasp as in Figure 2B.

A high vertical triangle can easily be moved sideways as in Figure 2C.

The correct vertical triangle is shown being tested for strength in Figure 2D.

No. 1—HIGH   No. 2—CORRECT   No. 3—LOW

FIG.
2A

FIG. 1

FIG.
2B

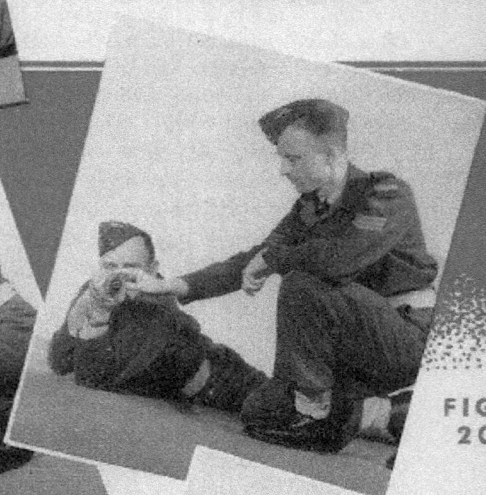

FIG.
2C

FIG.
D2

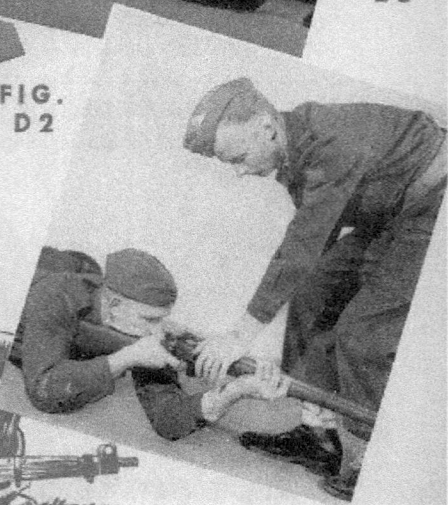

24

THE HIGH RIGHT SHOULDER

UPPOSING your recruit has a high vertical triangle. What is the cause? Most likely it is because of an improperly-placed right elbow and this can be readily spotted by you. See Figure 1, below.

The shoulders should be almost level as in Figure 2, opposite. They cannot, in most cases, be positively level but they can be mighty close to it, which will suffice. Why has a man a high right shoulder? It is because his right elbow is too close to the body forcing the shoulder upwards from four to five inches.

Instructors should look at the shoulder level as it is almost as vital to good shooting as the perfectly placed left elbow. You have shown him the means by which the right hand has gripped the small of the butt. Now to insure that the right elbow is in perfect position as third leg of the tripod formed by the centre of the body and the two arms, have the recruit move his right elbow out from the body until the shoulders are level and there it will serve its purpose as a substantial support for the rifle.

Too much stress cannot be placed upon the fact that the right shoulder must not be humped if good musketry results are to be attained. Get it down now and Private Buck will benefit by your insistence and kindly coaching.

HEY, SARGE!
IS THIS WHAT
YOU CALL THE
HALF-ROLL?

BODY SLOPES

A RECRUIT, in order to follow your direction in respect to correct position, may get himself all tensed up into unnatural slopes and angles. It will, therefore, be necessary to check his position so that he may be comfortable and relaxed.

Observing Figure 1, you will note the sharp angle or slope of the back. This abruptness has likely been caused by a high right shoulder or a high vertical triangle, which can be corrected by altering the position of the right elbow. A body slope that is low or flat, as in Figure 2, will not permit the strength of the position he seeks. This is caused by a low vertical triangle. If it is low, move that left elbow more beneath the rifle and bring the right elbow slightly closer to the body.

Proper body slope, a smooth curve as shown in Figure 3, indicates a proper vertical triangle and that means also a proper horizontal triangle and correct position. You see, now, how one phase of this course ties in with the other?

By now you have, or should have, the recruit in a perfect firing position but you want to make certain again that the left elbow, which is the key to the entire position, is in correct place.

You open the bolt of his rifle, drop a lath through the magazine opening, so that it touches the floor and is *ABSOLUTELY VERTICAL*. If you can place more than two fingers between the bottom of the stick and the elbow's point of contact with the floor he has lost the position of his left elbow and should bring it in again.

27

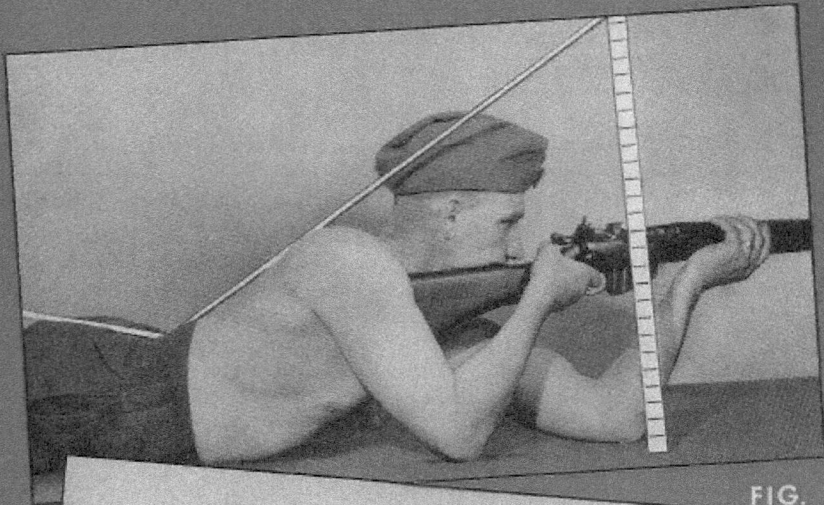

FIG. 1

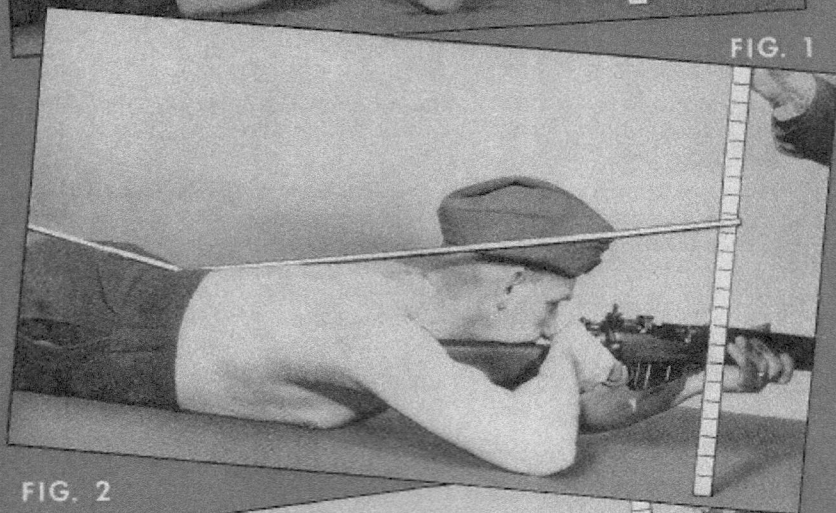

FIG. 2

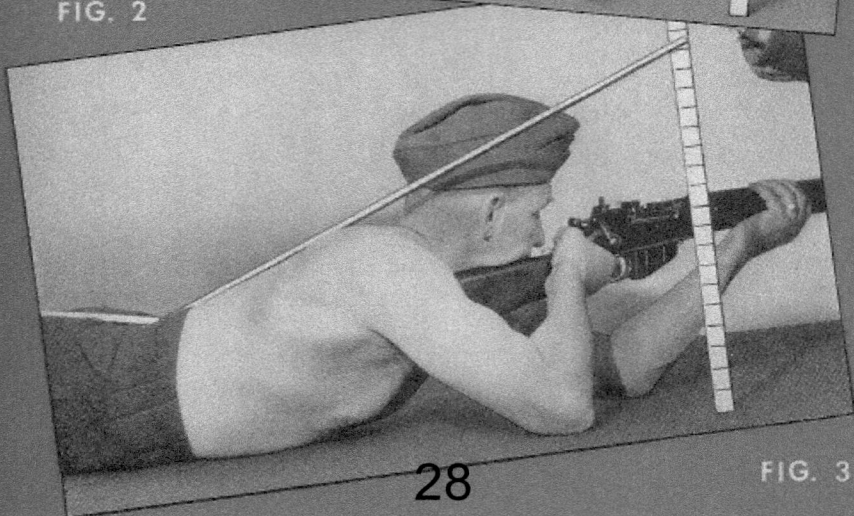

28

FIG. 3

OBLIQUE BODY ANGLES

YOU know that the body must be at an angle to the rifle if it is to be held properly. The left elbow must be well out in front of the right elbow and under the rifle. The right hand must firmly grasp the small of the butt and the trigger. The butt must be against the shoulder and the head on top of, and against, the butt. Your recruit cannot do all these things and lie directly behind the rifle. Instead, his body must be at an angle to the rifle and this is known as the Oblique Body Angle.

The size of this angle depends upon the physique of the recruit. IT CANNOT BE STANDARDIZED. It should measure somewhere between 30 and 45 degrees to his line of fire—the axis of the rifle.

The angle of the body to the line of fire should be established while the recruit is in proper position as outlined previously in this chapter. The wider the angle, the closer the eye will be to the rear sight or aperture sight, a factor the importance of which will make itself increasingly apparent.

THE INSTRUCTOR DOES NOT TEACH OBLIQUE ANGLES TO THE RECRUIT. He uses the methods of determining those angles as a means of checking and adjusting the position of the recruit so that the body angle is in proper relation to the line of fire and suitable to his physique.

After observing Figure 1, opposite, demonstrate oblique body angles by selecting two laths, a ruler, chalk and a protractor. Ask two men to assist you in measuring the angles of the recruit. Have one man hold a lath along the barrel, or axis, of the rifle and have the other place the second lath along the centre of the back and head of the recruit. This lath will represent the centre of the body.

Now, measure the angle formed by the two laths. Measure the distance between the two elbows, by drawing lines at the contact points of the two elbows at right angles to the axis of the rifle. Also measure the distance from the pupil of the recruit's eye to the aperture sight.

What do these measurements establish? By noting the table (Figure 2, opposite) you will see that as the body angle increases, the left elbow is farther forward than the right elbow and more easily placed directly underneath the rifle. The distance between the eye and the rear sight has been decreased.

Thus you will be able to determine the correct placing of the recruit's elbows and to either increase or decrease the distance from his eye to the rear sight.

It is advantageous in aiming, to have the eye as close as possible to the rear sight. Yet it cannot be so close that the face will be struck by the rifle's recoil.

By using the oblique body angle method, you can advise him as to the correct position his body should take. The average angle is approximately

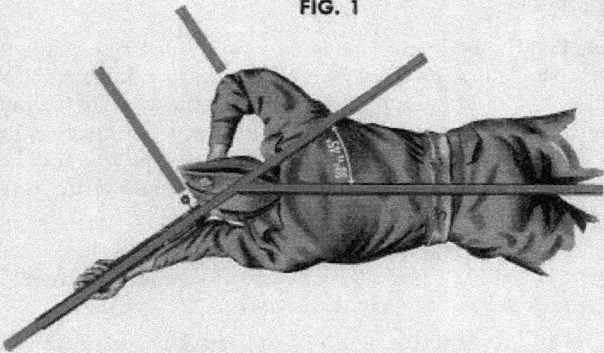

FIG. 1

FIG. 2

OBLIQUE ANGLES	LEFT ELBOW IN FRONT OF RIGHT ELBOW	DISTANCE OF EYE FROM SIGHT
45°	14"	
40°		
35°		2¼"
30°		
25°	11¼"	
20°		3½
15°		
10°		
5°		
0°	4⅗"	6"

OBLIQUE BODY ANGLES—Continued

35 degrees, as the bulk of recruits range between 30 and 40 degrees. However, the closer he can come to an angle of 45 degrees, the farther his left elbow will be ahead of the right one and the closer the eye will be to the rear sight. If he is dangerously close to that rear sight, decrease the angle. If he has difficulty getting his left elbow under the rifle, increase the body angle.

FIG. 1
MINOR ADJUSTMENT

FIG. 2—MAJOR ADJUSTMENT

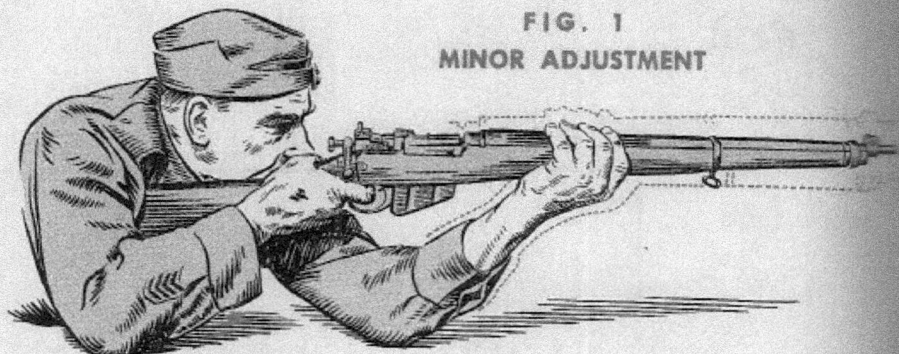

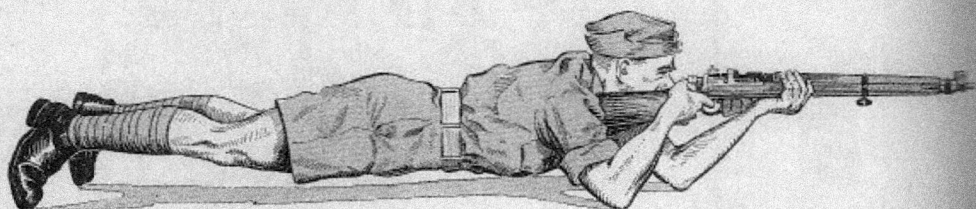

MAJOR AND MINOR ADJUSTMENTS

IT WILL be found necessary to raise or lower the rifle in order to aim at higher or lower targets. These changes in elevation can be effected by either Major or Minor Adjustments without shifting the solid position which you have already taught the recruit to maintain.

If the recruit wishes to make a large change in the elevation of the rifle's muzzle, he should be taught to dig his toes into the ground and inch himself forward without changing the position of his elbows. In this way he forces the butt of his rifle slightly upward, which in turn forces the muzzle down. The muzzle can be raised by using a reverse movement. Note Figure 2 above.

The Minor Adjustment is made by raising or lowering the rifle by sliding the left hand forward or backward as required. This will adjust the required height of the front sight according to the needs of accurate aiming. See Figure 1 above.

It can now be seen why some distance between the wrist and the magazine was insisted upon, because these minor adjustments cannot be made it if is tight against the magazine.

31

LEGS, FEET AND HEELS

LEGS should be well apart, so they may serve as the support or trail of your well-positioned rifle. Legs that are well apart give the sturdiness to the rest of the body that your position demands and usually adds to the comfort of the recruit.

Toes should be pointing downward and out from the body, with the heels as close to being flat as possible. Some physiques cannot get their heels flat onto the ground and if they cannot do this they SHOULD NOT BE FORCED by insistence to do it. You should never stand upon a recruit's heels in order to get them flat as this will be extremely painful and will reflect upon his shooting. Merely get them as flat as possible.

When he gets onto the battlefield and the enemy bullets start to fly, your pupil will get his heels down.

POSITION CHARTS

THE CHART on the opposite page has been designed to show, as graphically as possible, the various methods of checking a marksman's proper position.

If recruits are as close to the correct position as their physiques will permit, they will naturally attempt to get closer through continual practice.

By using these charts, which should be distributed to the recruits, they will be able to check each other's style of position against the illustrations. Two men, for instance, can work together in barracks to improve their musketry. By this time their interest in good shooting should be so keen that they will welcome a chance to do some homework.

While one assumes the firing position, the other can check it against the chart by viewing the marksman from above, from in front and from each side.

The points to be stressed are listed alongside the chart and the critic can check each, quickly.

The chart should not be used, however, until after the recruit has been thoroughly taught the correct position.

The correct position may appear to be awkward at first due to muscles being put into new and unaccustomed uses but this condition will be quickly overcome.

It must be remembered by instructors that the correct position can never be absolute because what may be satisfactory for a stout man will be difficult for a tall, thin one.

If you have mastered your own position in accord with this chapter and you have assured yourself that the student marksmen of your class have achieved similar perfection, proceed to the next phase of instruction in good musketry.

> *If a man has not acquired perfect position, then this chapter should be restudied and its recommendations implemented before he is permitted to undertake additional phases of this training.*

POSITION CHART

FRONT VIEW

1. Notice triangular position of elbows
2. Right elbow fairly well out from body
3. Left elbow almost underneath rifle

VERTICAL TRIANGLE

VIEW FROM ABOVE

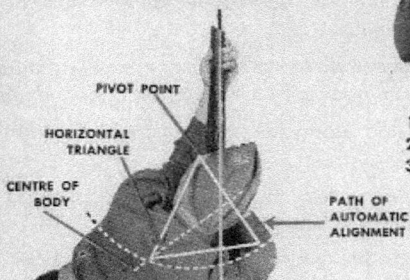

PIVOT POINT

HORIZONTAL TRIANGLE

CENTRE OF BODY

PATH OF AUTOMATIC ALIGNMENT

1. Rifle well down in palm of left hand
2. Notice position of left hand, and
3. Position of head on butt

BACKWARD PRESSURE

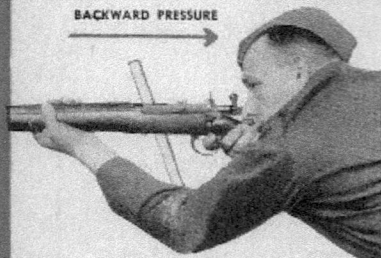

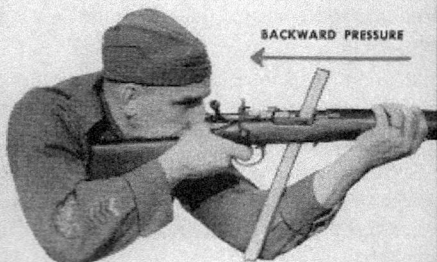

RIGHT SIDE VIEW

1. Rifle pulled well back into shoulder
2. Notice low position of butt,
3. Pressure of chin on butt, and
4. Firm grip of left hand

BACKWARD PRESSURE

LEFT SIDE VIEW

1. Rifle well down in palm of left hand
2. Notice position of fingers on butt,
3. Position of forefinger around trigger, and
4. Low position of firer

34

CHAPTER THREE

Holding

"HOLDING" a rifle is a frequently misused expression because actually a rifle should not be held. It should, instead, rest upon the bones of the body to secure that stability which is so necessary.

The use of brute strength in clutching the weapon only aggravates a condition which the recruit is trying to avoid. Yet it is that condition which causes the rifle to be unsteady.

Tensed muscles pass along vibrations which the rifle naturally picks up. The more tension or strength used in gripping the rifle usually means more vibration. Relaxation is, therefore, the answer.

Adoption of proper position assures the marksman's comfort and encourages relaxation. In other words, it means that the rifle is pointed with the whole body and not just with the strained muscles of the hands and arms.

Just as an artillery piece consists of a barrel and recoil mechanism mounted on a carriage, so does the Rifleman function. His muscles are the recoil apparatus and the bones of the arms and hands form the rigid carriage.

The left arm should provide a perfect V-shaped support under the rifle while the right elbow is located so as to give it firm but bracing support to the body.

The recruit should concern himself with making certain his position is such that there is no muscle strain of any sort in his arms. That position will be gained through the careful adoption of the correct position outlined in the preceding chapter and will be ONLY that position.

A correctly-held rifle doesn't kick

DO YOU SUFFER FROM UNNECESSARY RECOIL?

HOLDING—Continued

Every beginner has been faced with the EXASPERATING PROBLEM OF KEEPING THE RIFLE STEADY LONG ENOUGH TO SEND A BULLET SPEEDING ON ITS WAY. Usually the muzzle of the rifle circles and zig-zags all over the range and the more he grimaces and grips in trying to hold it still the more it jumps around. Practice of proper position is the prime cure.

If you can check the before and after results, you will see that at least one quarter of the movement has been lost in your adoption of the proper position, religiously practiced.

When it comes natural for a recruit to assume the proper position, his dancing rifle has quietened down. Proper holding, equally well practiced, will slice another quarter off the unsteadiness total.

By the time the course is finished the newcomer to the field of perfect musketry will be able to nick the heart of a bull's eye every time.

BONES versus MUSCLES

YOU will recall that in the preceding chapter you, as the instructor, proved to the recruit the strength of a perfectly-acquired position, by sitting upon a rifle when it rested upon solid bone. Your recruit was amazed at the strength provided by the vertical position of the left arm. When the recruit held his rifle in a low vertical triangle, with the left elbow out of its proper place, you were able to force it downward with your two fingers and thumb because he was attempting to support it solely by means of strained muscles.

Referring to the illustrations accompanying this phase of "Holding," note the strength provided by the bones as compared with that of the muscles. In Figure 1, opposite, the solidness of the weight resting squarely upon the upright stick is obvious.

In Figure 2, you will notice, in the left picture, that the soldier has his left elbow out from underneath his rifle and that the muscles must be holding it in place. In the opposite picture, he is shown with the correct position—a perfect, vertical triangle and the rifle is solidly resting upon the bones of the upright forearm.

If X-ray photographs of the two arms, shown in Figure 2, were to be obtained, they would reveal, as in Figure 3 (left), the off-centre effect of incorrect position with no support upon which the rifle may rest, except the trembling, strained muscles. Now compare this with the upright pillar of bone established by the correctly-placed left elbow (Figure 3, right).

37

FIG. 1

FIG. 2

DON'T HOLD IT WITH YOUR
MUSCLES

SUPPORT IT WITH YOUR
BONES

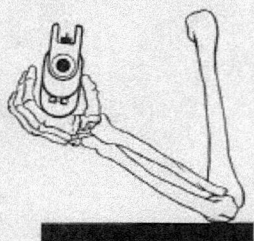

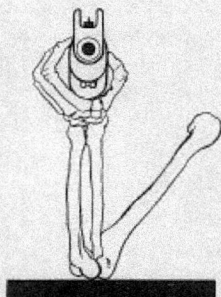

FIG. 3

FIG. 1

FORMING A BRIDGE TRUSS

THE engineering principles, manifest in the construction of a bridge, serve as an ideal example of the soldier seeking that solid foundation of bone upon which his rifle is to rest.

You will recall that steel girders rise up V-shaped, from the abutments of certain bridges, so that they carry the weight of the structure solidly. Note the illustration, above.

These V-shaped, solid, weight-supporting girders serve the same purpose as your two arms. The elbows are at the base and the weight of the body and the weight of the rifle are evenly supported by the V for strength and firmness, formed by the bones of the upper arm and forearm. See Figure 2, below.

FIG. 2

39

THROUGH PROPER INSTRUCTION IN HOLDING
THE TRAINED COACH CAN OVERCOME THE
PUPILS' FEAR OF RECOIL

A SCAFFOLD OF BONES

THERE are 206 bones in the human body and they all serve as a scaffolding to support you and your rifle, in that co-ordination that is known as good shooting.

To prove this, your attention is called to Figure 1, below. Using laths to represent or demonstrate the position of bones, we place one along the inside of the left forearm of the recruit, who is in proper prone firing position. It will extend from the point of contact of the hand with the rifle, down to the elbow.

Now place another lath from the shoulder to the elbow, along the inside of the upper left arm. This portrays one of the V-shaped supports for your rifle to rest upon.

Next place a lath along the outside of the right forearm, from the top of the hand to the elbow and another lath from the outside of the right shoulder, to the elbow. There you have a second V-shaped truss.

Then, just to bring these two trusses together, you place another lath across the shoulders so that it meets the tops of the laths, which rest alongside the recruit's upper arms.

The arms and the upper body now appear to give almost complete and co-related support to the rifle, like so many girders of a well-constructed

FIG. 1

41

bridge. The only place where the support is lacking, is an inward pressure at the butt. A final lath, slanted from the floor to the left side of the head, will naturally represent the pressure exerted by the chin against the butt, thus completing the picture of a solid structure. This last lath is the counter brace which steadies the bracing of the right forearm.

Note Figure 2, below, where the body's bones are likened to a solid block of timber, bolted to the floor, while in Figure 3 the "rifle" is supported by a scaffolding attached to that block in much the same manner as your bones support it and as you demonstrated to your recruit by means of laths.

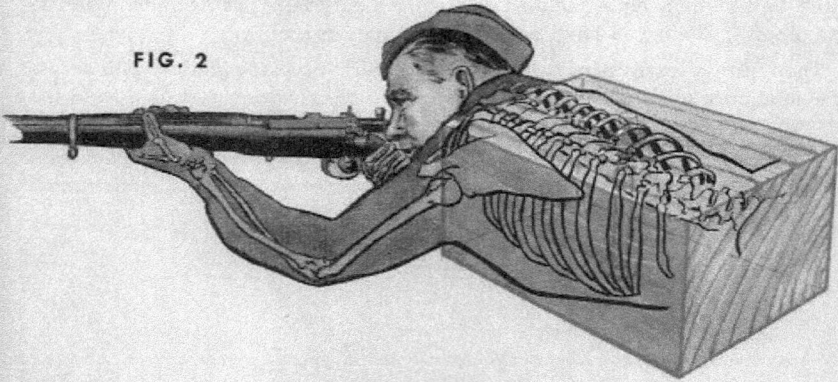

FIG. 2

FIG. 3

VIBRATIONS AND TENSIONS

A COMMON tendency on the part of many recruits is that of gripping the rifle with brute force and determination to hold it still by muscular effort. The more they grip and grimace, the more taut the elastic-like muscles become and these in turn quickly pass their vibrations into the rigid rifle and the muzzle starts to dance around.

No amount of muscular effort will correct this condition.

As much stress has been placed on the correct resting of the rifle upon the framework of bones, you will find that your recruit will feel that as he has such a solid position he can improve it still further by a tight grip. But his muscles cannot do the work of his arm bones in holding a rifle still.

You will note that the muzzle of his rifle is showing much movement. You should insist that he relax himself, so that all undue pressure is eliminated. Naturally some pressure is required, in order to keep the rifle in position, but he does not have to go to extremes, because the effect will be lost in the vibrations passed from the tensed muscles to the rifle.

All body vibrations cannot be totally eliminated but by a reasonable amount of relaxation, the vibrations will be reduced to a minimum.

It is best to watch your recruit, as he lies in firing position, for it will be your sole means of determining whether or not he is tightening his muscles. If it is difficult for him to appreciate the vibration effect of tight muscles, ask him to raise an arm so that his hand hangs limply downward from the elbow, while the upper part of the arm is parallel with the floor. He will see very little tremor in his fingers.

Let him raise his hand up to his face, without changing the position of his upper arm, and he will note tremble in his fingers. Now, if he will clench his fist, he will see a marked increase in the tremble.

By this it is not meant that limpness is the solution to good shooting. Some muscular effort is required in holding the rifle but certainly this effort need not be excessive.

> *In all phases of musketry training, the instructor who encourages his men to be calm, collected and not excited or under tension is the one who produces the best shots.*

43

HEAD AND CHIN

NOW that the solid truss work has been built for the structure which will firmly carry the rifle, one important span is required to finish the job and it must drop perfectly into place so that it will bind together the trunk of the body, the V-shaped supports of bones and the rifle.

That needed span is the head and it forms the keystone around which the entire rifle-firing structure has been organized.

The head must fall into the place provided for it. Hence, the recruit should be impressed with the fact that his neck muscles must be relaxed so that the head will naturally fall forward upon the butt and rest there comfortably.

Just as relaxed muscles have been stressed in earlier phases of this training, so must your pupil be impressed with the weight of the head and its effect upon good shooting.

If the upper body is allowed to sag freely forward without muscular effort, so that it will rest solidly on top of the butt, its steadying effect will immediately become apparent.

There it will serve as the clevis which attaches the barrel of the artillery piece to the carriage and recoil mechanism.

"RELAXATION"

44

HOW TO PLACE THE HEAD

THE HEAD must fit into its proper place, however, when it falls forward. This place is determined by the recruit taking up his prone firing position and placing his chin over and upon the top of the butt (Note Figure 1, below).

Without drawing his head away from the butt, he should cause the chin to move over and down the inside of the butt, as in Figure 2, until the right eye is in direct alignment with the aperture of the rear sight (See Figure 3).

If this has been done properly, the chin will be firmly pressed against the butt so that it seems to be a part of the butt itself—just as if both were bolted together.

But the chin cannot be permitted to fall too low. A brake must be applied and this is done by a sideways pressure of the chin and cheek against the butt at the precise moment the eye is opposite the aperture of the rear sight.

This halts the downward movement of the head as it sags forward against the butt. Frequently this is done by stopping the downward movement at the slight hollow which runs along the lower side of the chin. This hollow may vary according to the contours of various faces but in most cases it can be readily determined.

It is imperative that the pressure of the chin, imposed by the weight of the head, be sufficient to serve as a counter brace to the supporting effect of the right forearm and also be a means of keeping the eye in place so that it can see through the rear sight.

The eye must be as close to the rear sight as safety will permit. If too close, it might be struck by the rear sight when the rifle recoils.

The solidness imposed by the head resting on top of and against the butt will permit the head to ride with the butt, when the rifle recoils upon being fired. Both should react as one.

FIG. 1   FIG. 2   FIG. 3

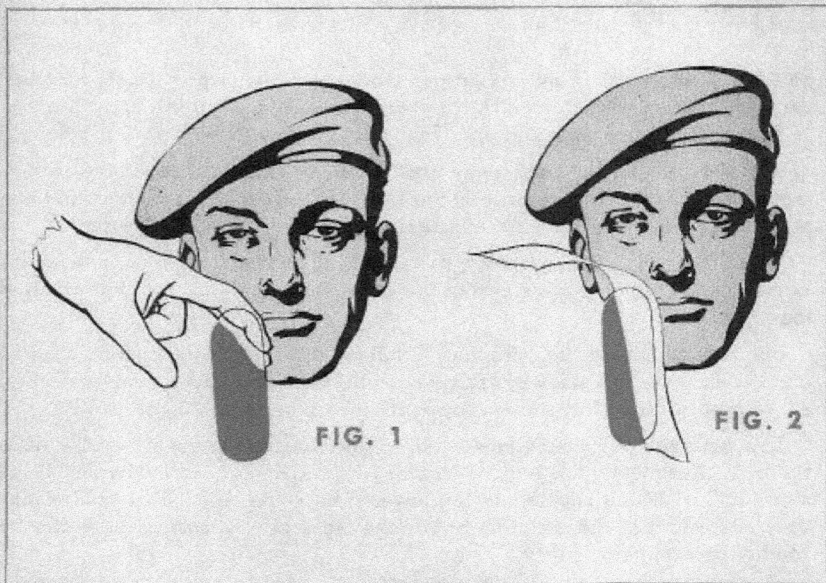

FIG. 1   FIG. 2

TESTING CHIN PRESSURE

IT IS NOT intended that the pressure of the chin against the butt should be excessive. Otherwise unnecessary strain will cause the unwanted tremors of the head to be imparted into the rifle just as too tense a grip of the rifle causes tremble.

There are two methods of teaching chin pressure and they should be carefully shown to the recruit so that he may get the feel of the pressure you exert upon your rifle and then compare it with his own pressure.

One method is to have him place his first and second fingers along the butt of the rifle, which you are holding, at the point where your chin should press against the butt (See Figure 1, above). Slide your chin over and down against the butt and his fingers and as he draws the fingers away he should feel the pressure which you are NORMALLY exerting.

Another method of checking would be to place a folded strip of paper, about twelve inches long, between the cheek and the rifle (See Figure 2). Have the recruit withdraw the paper by means of short, sharp, directly-upward tugs and he will note how the paper crackles because of the normally-exerted chin pressure.

HEAD IS KEYSTONE

Y OUR recruit will now see that his head has become the keystone which completed the solid arch of bone (See Figure 1, opposite), upon which the rifle is firmly but comfortably resting.

It has the steadying effect of a sandbag which will bind the entire rifle-holding framework tightly together as if it were precisely fitted and perfectly welded.

It has rolled forward just as a sitting sleeper's head falls forward. (Note Figure 2, opposite). Neck muscles are relaxed and the head rests upon the pillow which is the butt.

At least one third of the head will overlap the butt, insuring proper position of the head and also insuring correct chin pressure.

THE SHOULDER

T HE greatest bugbear in shooting is fear of the rifle's recoil hurting the shoulder. The so-called "kick" has been over-rated, largely because the novice rifleman has heard, so many times, that a rifle has a terrific recoil which will hurt him. In his effort to avoid a sore shoulder, he sacrifices shooting skill.

Instructors must appreciate the serious responsibility of seeing to it that each recruit has his rifle against those muscles and not against bone, as the success of this training depends largely upon the removal of recoil fear from the minds of the troops.

Watch out, however, for suspender buckles or other hard objects which might spoil the effect of the muscle pad.

> *The proper location of the rifle against the shoulder muscles, and not against solid bone, reduces the effect of the recoil to a minimum that is noticeable and certainly never injurious to the soldier.*

47

FIG. 1

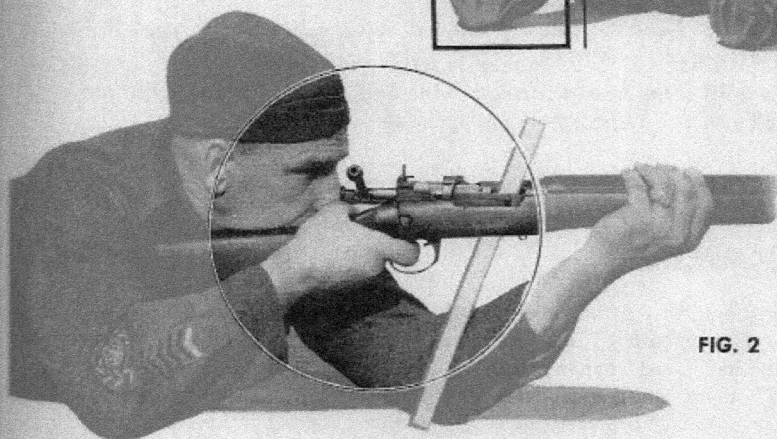
FIG. 2

48

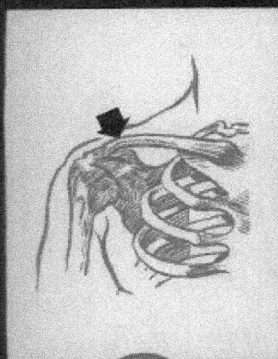

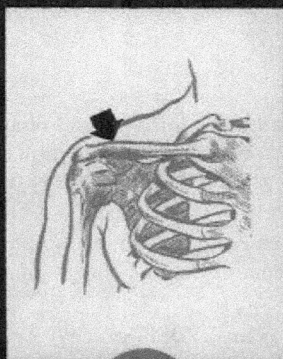

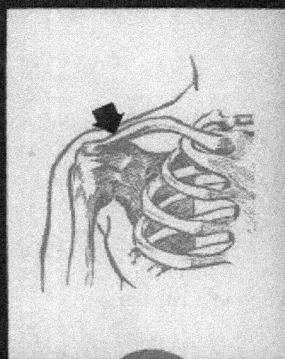

FIG. 1   FIG. 2   FIG. 3

COLLARBONES

T O DETERMINE the proper location of the rifle, it is first necessary to study the recruit's collarbone structure, so that in placing the rifle against the shoulder he will avoid having any part of the butt resting against solid bone. The recruit should be stripped to the waist, in order to clearly understand your demonstration.

If there are several members in your class, you will be able, by tracing collarbones with your fingers and coloured chalk, to determine their shape and type. You will learn whether each collarbone examined is slightly curved as is the normal type shown in Figure 1; or whether it is a low, flat bone as shown in Figure 2; or a highly-curved one as in Figure 3.

It will be of help for the entire class to observe these three types of collarbone structures, which may be demonstrated with a horizontally-held ruler upon the chalked outline of the collarbone. Each man should know what type of collarbone he possesses and the instructor must be thoroughly satisfied that he does know it.

Now call the attention of the class, to the fact that forward parts of the collarbone structure are only thinly covered with skin and are not protected by blow-absorbing flesh or muscle. A blow struck against such a bone would bruise the skin and probably injure the collarbone. That is why football players wear those big shoulder pads.

You can effectively demonstrate this to your recruit, by tapping the collarbone structure with your finger or knuckle. Your recruit will feel the solidness of the thinly-protected bone and hear the ringing sound of the tapping. He will also appreciate that a rifle's recoil would injure the unprotected collarbone.

MUSCLE PADS

OBSERVE next, that the recruit has a large pocket of muscle directly below the collarbone. Digging around with one's fingers it can be quickly and clearly located. Find it for the recruit and let him feel it. This muscle pad is the area upon which the butt must rest. See Figures 1 and 2, below.

It will be noted that the rifle, in resting against that pad, is virtually leaning upon a cushion of muscle, as comfortably as if it were sitting upon a pillow of sponge rubber.

The instructor MUST (This is an ORDER) *clearly point out, personally, to each recruit, the exact location of that muscle pad so that each recruit will know precisely where it is.*

What does this muscle pad do?

It serves as the cushion for the recoil. It is the spongy shock absorber that prevents injury and dispels fear of the rifle's kick.

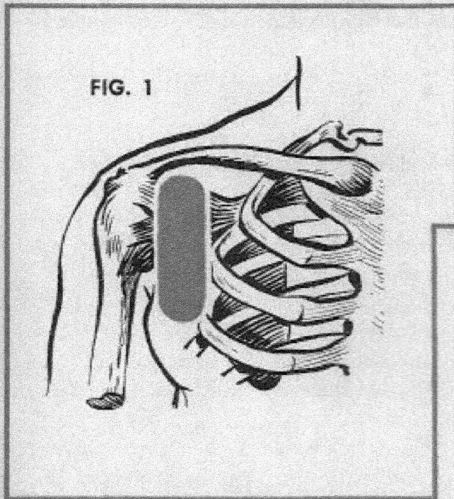

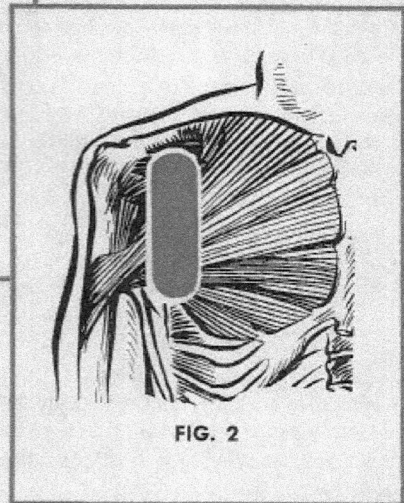

FIG. 1

FIG. 2

50

PLACING THE RIFLE

INSTRUCTORS may now teach the recruit (who is still stripped to the waist) how to get the rifle onto this shoulder muscle pad.

With his right hand, have him slip the butt plate into the hollow of the shoulder so that it rests upon the muscle pad. This should be done while the right elbow is raised, to enable the right hand to take a solid grip of the small of the butt (Note Figures 1, 2 and 3, opposite).

He should now drop his right elbow into its proper position and allow the head to slide into place so that the cheek provides the firmness against the stock, that is required (see Figure 4.)

This little trick of slipping the butt into the muscle pad, while the weight is carried by the left elbow, is a secret of good shooting and its importance is such, that it should be used each time the recruit assumes his firing position.

The recruit will see that the butt plate is—or should be—well into the pocket of muscles and NOT against the collarbones, or the arm muscles.

He will probably also see that when he raised his right elbow to assist him in placing the rifle, the muscle pad was extended so that he could place the butt more accurately.

This factor is particularly helpful to soldiers who are of slight build and who sometimes experience difficulty in the proper placing of the rifle.

Check your recruit by chalking the end of the butt and placing it where he considers the muscle pad is located.

Now have him remove the rifle, and the chalk mark on the skin will show exactly whether or not the rifle was properly placed on the pad where it belongs.

This sure-fire method of checking will be appreciated by the recruit, who by now, will consider that you are looking out for his own personal welfare. It will impress upon him the fact that there is a correct way in which to avoid injury from the rifle's recoil because what you have taught him is sensible.

Have your recruit practice this placing of the rifle until he has the natural "feel" of the butt plate against the cushion.

Get the rifle-placing habit.

PLACING THE RIFLE

FIGURE 1

FIGURE 2

FIGURE 3

FIGURE 4

AMOUNT OF BUTT ON MUSCLE PAD

TO INSURE that the recruit places his rifle correctly on the muscle pad and not on the collarbone or the arm bones, have him adopt the correct position and lower his rifle. Now stand over him, insert a finger under his collarbone and with your other hand raise the heel of the butt until it touches this finger. Observe the illustration, below.

You can also check the amount of butt in contact with the muscle pad by running your thumb up the butt plate from the toe, to the point of contact with the body. If your recruit is a plump lad there will be more of the butt plate covered by muscle than what you may find with a soldier of slight build.

Types of collarbones also affect the amount of butt which a soldier can rest upon his shoulder muscle pad.

Obviously, the greater amount of butt plate upon the muscle pad, the greater the resultant cushion effect. It is only seldom that all of the butt will rest upon the pad. There are so many differences between physiques that as long as your pupil has as much, as possible, of the butt properly located and NONE of it on the collarbone, he will be safe from hurt shoulders caused by recoil.

The inserted picture (left and below) of the butt plate shows approximately the amount of butt plate (red area) which rests upon the muscle pad of soldiers of normal physique and collarbone structure.

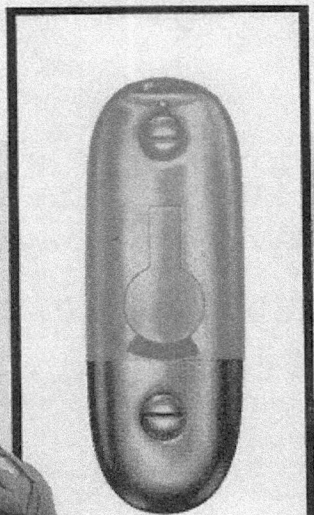

53

CONTROL OF THE RIFLE

WHEN the trigger is squeezed, the resulting explosion creates so much pressure that all of it cannot chase the bullet on its flight to the target.

Thus, there is a tendency for the explosion to react upon the rifle so that the weapon "wants to go some place" to escape the blast. But it has little opportunity to do so because it cannot leap nor lurch if it is properly held.

Of course, if it cannot go forward, or down, or to either side, it will want to rear backward and that is its recoil.

Later in this chapter, the movement of the rifle upon discharge will be fully discussed.

The hands, as they hold the rifle, the weight of the head, the chin pressure and the pad of muscle in the shoulder, all unite and co-operate to arrest the recoil.

But this control can only be effective if it is done in such a way that each controlling agent does its full duty—nothing more nor less. Too much backward pressure by the hands, or forcing the head forward onto the butt of the rifle so that more pressure is built up than is normally apparent in the weight of the head, would spoil the effect of other control.

Control your rifle in the normal manner, doing everything that you are expected to do and doing it well, but don't strive toward one operation to the exclusion of all others.

SNUBBING EFFECT OF THE HANDS

YOU HAVE told your recruit to firmly grasp his rifle, yet without gripping it so tightly that body tremble would be passed into the rigid weapon.

It is natural for him as he lies in normal position to draw the rifle back into the muscle pad snugly. He knows, by now, that this pressure against the muscle pad assists in keeping the rifle firmly placed there. He does it naturally—or at least he should. This is a factor which the instructor should carefully check upon.

While the rifle is correctly held, the two hands serve as snubbers when the recoil occurs. To demonstrate this, place your hand upon the barrel of your recruit's rifle and move it backwards about two inches toward his shoulder.

As you do this, call the recruit's attention to the fact that his hands absorbed much of the movement. He will thus appreciate what happens during the recoil process, when the rifle's backward movement is partly arrested by this snubbing effect, of the two hands.

54

CHECKING BACKWARD PRESSURE

NATURALLY, the correct amount of backward pressure exerted by the hands, in drawing the rifle into the pad of shoulder muscles, must be determined for the benefit of the recruit.

The instructor should take the correct firing position, then have the recruit place a lath upright directly in front of and one-half inch beyond the muzzle (See Figure 1, opposite). Now warn him to observe the forward movement of the muzzle as the backward pressure is released.

He will note that the right hand is released first from its grasp of the rifle which will, however, remain still.

When the second step is taken by opening the left hand flat, the rifle will be forced forward, along the open palm, by the reactionary effect of the spongy shoulder muscles. It will travel approximately one-half inch and will likely touch the upright lath. See Figure 2. The demonstration should be given several times, so that the recruit will see exactly the effect of the backward pressure.

Then have the recruit try the experiment while you hold the lath. Don't permit him, however, to force the rifle forward by any movement of the shoulder. In other words, he must not nudge it forward. It must glide ahead as a result of releasing the pressure against the muscle pad.

Have him practice this checking experiment until he is thoroughly accustomed to the proper amount of backward pressure required.

FIG. 1

FIG 2
56

FIG. 1

FIG. 2

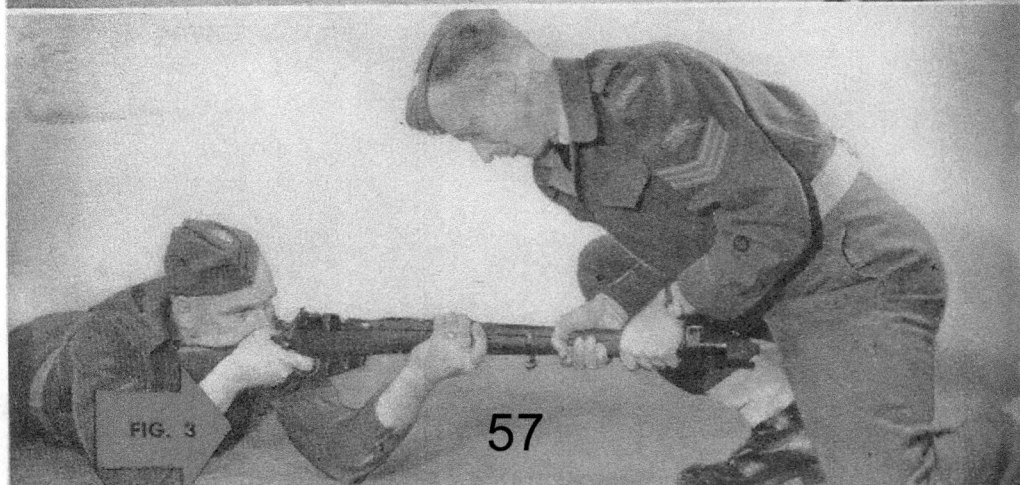

FIG. 3

57

SOLID HOLDING

THE RIFLE must become just as much a part of the soldier as his arm or leg, if he hopes to become a good shot. There must be co-operative teamwork between him and the weapon, if the bullets he fires are to pierce the centre of the target.

Your attention is called to the demonstrations illustrated in Figures 1, 2 and 3, opposite. In Figure 1, you will be able to show your recruit that while he is in proper firing position you can take his leg and with a steady push, or pull, shift him around. If the recruit is holding his rifle properly, it will be so much a part of him that it will move with the push or pull, also.

Using a steady, straight and forward pull (not by jerking or drawing, up, down or sideways) bring his rifle forward toward you. His entire body will move with the pull if his grasp of the rifle is solid. Note Figure 2.

Reversing the procedure, as illustrated in Figure 3, shove (or attempt to) the rifle directly backwards. You will find it exceedingly difficult to budge the soldier. If he does move with the shove, it will be very slight.

Thus a solidly-held rifle cannot be dislodged. It has become every bit as much a part of him as an arm or leg and working in unison with the body is as solid as a block of granite.

BLOW versus SHOVE

THE SECRET of good holding in rifle-shooting so that recoil is arrested, amounts generally into transferring the blow of the recoil into a shove. If you walk up to someone and deal him a punch on the shoulder, he will go down with a sore chest. But if you place your fist against his shoulder and then shove, his muscles will naturally react to absorb the pressure. He will not be hurt.

Note Figure 1, opposite. Where the shoulder of the man on the left has been dealt a hard blow—just like the shoulder of a man, whose loosely-held rifle has recoiled. The man on the right, however, by the correct use of backward pressure and muscular absorption is transforming his blow into a harmless shove.

The comparison is probably not quite so marked, as in Figure 2, which shows a prize fighter's punch on the left as against the feminine hand (right) which shoves aside the wolfish Canuck.

Beginners may acquire all of the tricks of proper position and holding but, because of fear of recoil, will pull away from the rifle at the moment the trigger has been squeezed. That movement causes the solidness of the position to be lost, gives the rifle a chance to wind up a haymaker and also swing off the target.

Have your recruit keep the solid position and drum into him the fact that in correct holding there can be no blow from recoil.

ROLLING WITH THE SHOVE

IF YOU stand up to the batter's box and the pitcher whips the ball directly to your head, you duck out of the way. If the heavyweight boxer was to send his big fist out in the general direction of your nose, and you saw it coming, you would let your head instinctively go back to ride the blow (See Figure 3, opposite).

The same thing applies in rifle shooting. You have taught your recruit that his cheek and head must be virtually bolted to the rifle butt. It naturally has to come back when the rifle is fired, so if your head is placed right it will come back too—IF the muscles in the back of your neck are RELAXED.

It won't come back far. In fact it will only ride as far as the butt travels and then return to its normal position.

This movement, on the part of your head, further arrests the recoil. There will be little noticeable feeling to the action and you will be keeping your eye always at the same distance from the rear sight.

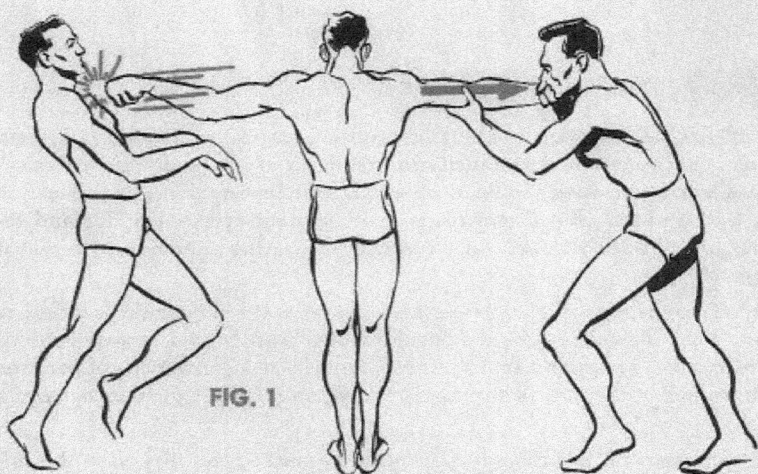
FIG. 1

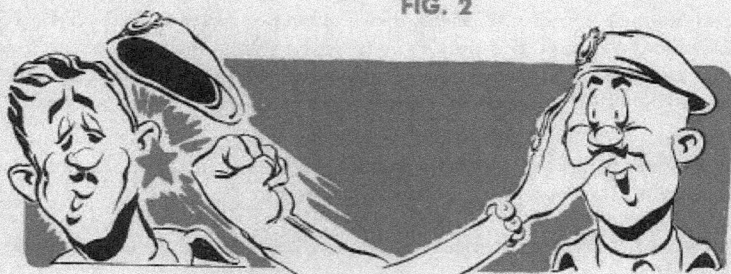
FIG. 2

FIG. 3

60

FAULTS AND REMEDIES

A NUMBER of faults in holding, sometimes develop whereby the firer becomes slightly hurt. If these are not corrected quickly, your recruit may develop that curse of good shooting which is flinching.

A swollen lip is sometimes caused by the knuckle of the thumb striking the lip when the rifle is fired. To correct this condition, one or several of the following remedies may be applied:

1.—Decrease the oblique body angle so that the head and the eyes will come farther back on the butt, to increase the distance of the eyes from the rear sight;

2.—Have the recruit ride the butt, or increase his chin pressure, so that he will ride with the butt during recoil;

3.—Increase the backward pressure of the hands so that the butt will be more firmly in position on the shoulder muscle pad;

4.—Move the right hand closer to the cocking piece so that it will not strike the face;

5.—Check the butt length of the rifle. A longer and more correctly-fitted rifle may be needed.

6.—Increase the grip of the hands upon the rifle;

7.—Encourage the soldier to roll with the blow.

There have been occasions when the thumb knuckle has struck the firer in the nose causing it to bleed. This is usually the result of very loose holding and can be corrected by the remedies outlined for the swollen lip. Stress, however, is again placed upon solid holding.

A cut chin is usually caused by long fingernails, of the right hand, cutting the chin. The cause of this can be traced to the head resting stiffly against the butt so that when the recoil comes it does not ride with the butt as if both were bolted together. Instead, the butt and the right hand move past the chin thus permitting long fingernails to lacerate the lower part of the soldier's face. Here, again, the remedies outlined for swollen lips will apply, together, with a careful trimming of fingernails.

> *If a soldier gets hurt, blame the instructor first.*

MOVEMENT OF RIFLE UPON DISCHARGE

UNDER the sub-title "Control of the Rifle," at page 53, the movement of the rifle upon discharge was mentioned. There will be movement of the muzzle immediately you send your bullet on its way. The direction that movement takes and the distance it travels are ideal indications upon which you can check the correctness of a rifleman's position and holding.

As the force of the explosion will follow the course of least resistance and when the good marksman is solidly holding his rifle in the cushion of shoulder muscles, there is only one direction the rifle muzzle can take.

The rifle is not weighted down on top of the barrel, and the butt, while resting against the muscle pad, still has no support directly beneath it, so the rifle's movement is naturally upwards. See Figure 1, opposite.

This natural, upward movement is slight but it occurs AFTER the bullet has departed from the muzzle.

If the rifle moves either sideways or downward, there is faulty holding.

As you observe the recruits upon the range, you will be able to spot this movement upon discharge and if it is anything but upwards, then the Holding and Position of the rifle are faulty and should be promptly corrected.

This movement amounts to little more than a slight "bounce" upwards, of the barrel and then it should settle back into its normal position.

The observant recruit, at first, will feel a disappointment that the rifle moved at all and he will think that because it went upward that he missed the target.

The instructor should pat this boy on the back because he is shooting properly, he is observant and he is certainly watching his follow through.

Much of the foregoing deals with what actually happens on the range. As your recruit has not been permitted to reach the range as yet, it may appear to be premature to discuss this phase of holding here.

It is, however, important to discuss this topic with your recruits so that they may be properly appraised of all these little tricks of a rifle when it is discharged. It is also important because the recruit feels that now you are getting him closer to the day when he gets onto the range and puts into actual practice all that you have taught him.

Encourage your recruits
to be observant.

63

FIG. 1

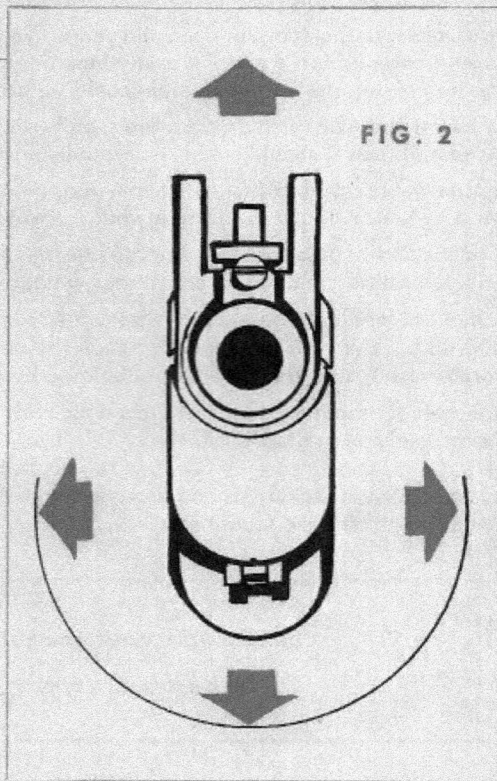

FIG. 2

Summary

HOLDING cannot be over-stressed because it provides much of the insurance against recoil.

If you, Mr. Instructor, have impressed your recruit with the fact that good position taken with good Holding will not only minimize recoil until it becomes a mere shove and that both, together, will assure him of better scores because of the removal of unwanted vibrations, you will have accomplished much toward bringing that boy close to shooting perfection.

This is very important because it scatters from his mind old ideas and bad habits about shooting. If properly presented it should remove his fear of the rifle's kick and if you have done your job efficiently he should commence to see the objective of your teaching because through acceptance of logic he now understands the reasonableness of what he has been shown.

Thus it would be well to just check back on these phases of his instruction:

1.—Have you sold him on the use of bones instead of muscles so that he provides a bridge truss or scaffold of bones which arrest vibrations and tension?

2.—Does he know how to place his head and fully appreciate the work it does when the chin pressure is applied?

3.—Is he so well aware of the muscle pad below his collarbone that he automatically places the butt of his rifle upon that pad and not upon bones?

4.—Does he understand how his two hands serve as snubbers when backward pressure is applied?

5.—Are you satisfied that his head will roll with the shove of the butt when the rifle is fired?

If your recruit is perfect in these fundamentals he may be taken to the next phase of this course. Don't proceed unless both you and he are perfectly satisfied that he fully understands all you have taught him about Position and Holding. He should be given ample opportunity to practice what you have taught so that his acceptance of it is correct and automatic.

Remember—

If the FIRER hasn't

LEARNED

The INSTRUCTOR hasn't

TAUGHT!

CHAPTER FOUR

Breathing

THE successful marksman has been compared, in previous chapters, with the carriage and recoil mechanism of an artillery piece. But the field guns have no pumping hearts, no intricate and sometimes balky nerve systems, no straining, trembling muscles, no breathing apparatus nor pulsing arteries. YOU HAVE ALL OF THESE.

Brother, breathing rhythm is as essential to good shooting as Position and Holding. It has been estimated that 95 percent of Canadian Army riflemen do not breathe properly while using their rifles and as a consequence, their scores are not as good as they are capable of producing.

As your recruit has slowed down the movement, or "dance", of his rifle by correct Position and Holding, so can he further slow it down by proper Breathing habits.

Correct breathing resolves itself into relaxed, normal breathing interrupted by a heavy, normal sigh just before firing. This sigh is naturally followed by a pause in breathing — *a brief period when you virtually DO NOT BREATHE* — and it is during that pause that your rifle is steadiest, thus giving you the opportunity to squeeze the trigger.

It is not suggested that the sigh should be one of weariness or exasperation but rather one of those heavy, normal sighs which one probably gives fifty or sixty times a day, probably in place of a cuss-word.

The instructor should show his recruit exactly how breathing affects the control of the rifle. He will see that if he is breathing normally, while in the prone firing position, every breath he takes causes the rifle to move up and down.

This is only natural because of the fact that he and his rifle have become a part of each other. Yet, when the normal rhythm of breathing is interrupted

by the natural sigh, the rifle remains most steady in that momentary dead pause which follows the sigh.

This is the point in breath control which, if the rifle is correctly positioned, held and aimed, that the trigger should be squeezed. It is this point at which the rifle's movement has been reduced to almost a dead stop.

The illustrations opposite show the three common types of breath control in shooting. "A" portrays that type of soldier who takes a deep breath, filling his lungs. His muscles are all tensed up and there is bound to be body tremble and strain.

Panel "B" illustrates the normal breathing, which is the natural sigh. The lungs are neither over-inflated nor are they deflated excessively.

Panel "C" shows what has happened when the natural sigh has been taken but with an ADDITIONAL and FORCED sigh, causing too much air to be expelled from the lungs. The lungs are virtually gasping for air and body trembles are bound to result.

Muscular strain, imposed by faulty breathing, is never apparent when the normal, relaxed, comfortable sigh as in "B" is taken.

HOW TO DEVELOP SIGH AND PAUSE

THE PROPER shooting sigh by the recruit is made by taking two or three breaths that are deeper than usual and then releasing the air in a slightly audible manner. (Be sure you, the instructor, can hear it).

It is not meant that more air than the normal amount should be forced from the lungs but, rather, just the amount which would be released if a heavy sigh were given. As in other phases of good musketry, the natural functions of the body are always the best.

The musketry class can learn proper breathing by holding the breath for periods of 30 seconds. This is accomplished by asking your recruits to close their eyes and with the class members taking deep breaths in unison, you can clock them off at five-second intervals until thirty seconds have elapsed.

Ask them to mentally note their reactions as to comfort, then proceed to have them expel as much air as convenient from their lungs and clock them again. Now have them take a heavy sigh and pause for another thirty seconds.

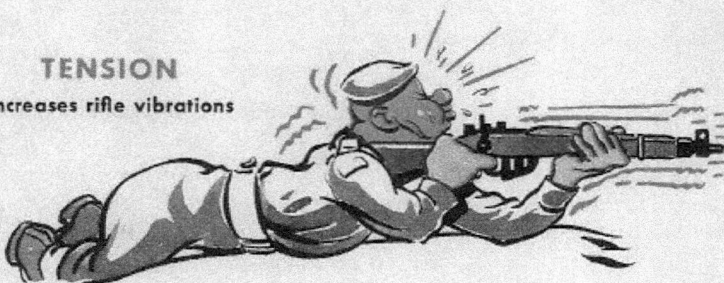

TENSION
increases rifle vibrations

A

NO SIGH

Lungs fully inflated

Breath held

Result:
strain and tension

UNNATURAL

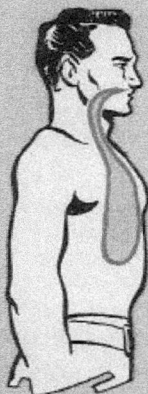

B

NORMAL SIGH

Lungs partly deflated

Breathing momentarily
suspended

Result: relaxation

NATURAL

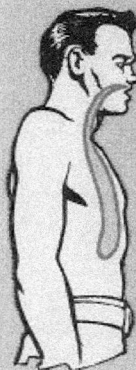

C

NORMAL SIGH *PLUS*
FORCED SIGH

Lungs fully deflated

Breath held

Result: strain and tension

UNNATURAL

RELAXATION
decreases rifle vibrations

A vote of the reactions, experienced by the class, should reveal better than 85 percent preference for the pause when the lungs are normal. It is recommended that between phases of this demonstration, that you allow your class members to rest so that normal breathing rhythm may be restored before attempting a new phase.

To fit the sigh into marksmanship, the recruit only has to momentarily stop breathing, immediately after he has given the sigh and to pause long enough to squeeze the trigger.

Have your recruit assume the firing position and indicate to him the way the three types of breathing habits affect his rifle's steadiness, when it is pointed at the target. He will readily see that the normal way, with the sigh, causes the rifle to visibly rest much steadier.

You can check the recruit's breathing habits by watching the rise and fall of the muzzle, by watching the movement of the small of the back or by feeling, with your hand, for any tension or tautness in the back. It will be easy to determine whether the muscle action is tensed or relaxed. The muscles of the back should be relaxed.

A piece of white paper placed upon the bayonet of the recruit's rifle will demonstrate to him the rise of the muzzle with the exhale and the fall with the inhale. Those movements are caused by the action of the chest in breathing and are relayed into the rifle.

Some times it is necessary to take a minor adjustment to the rifle's position after the exhale or sigh, by sliding the left hand forward, or backward, to correctly reach the elevation upon the target, which you desire.

Should, however, a soldier feel that he cannot get his shot away during that brief, breathless pause following the sigh, he should not endeavour to force himself. He must take a few normal breaths to rest himself and then try the shot again.

Instructors should check upon all recruits, at all times, to insure that they are not tightening up their muscles in acquiring this shooting sigh. Any unsteadiness that is apparent can be corrected by a patient coach who keeps insisting each pupil should be fully relaxed.

Eventually, through practice, the recruit will be able to approximate the expert's 10 seconds interval between the sigh and the squeeze of the trigger. This, of course is the maximum time expected of a sigh, when normal targe firing is being done. It would be appreciably shorter under battle conditions or in rapid-fire shooting.

TENSION versus RELAXATION

BY NOW, the recruit understands that steadiness, comfort and correct breathing deserve his full attention before starting the bullet on its way to the target.

He will see that in attempting to hold his breath too long, his muscles will tighten up; he will get red in the face; he will commence to shake and his rifle will dance. Hence, tension must give way to relaxation.

The instructor should synchronise his breathing with that of the recruit. If the soldier's breathing, while he is in firing position, is not correct, then the coach will note from his own uncomfortable breathing, timed to the recruit's, that it is wrong. The coach will know that if he is uncomfortable in following an unnatural breathing tempo, then the recruit must be uncomfortable, also. If this condition prevails—and it will be quickly noticed by the observant coach—then the recruit is holding his breath too long. This is a common fault.

If the recruit holds his breath longer than 20 seconds, stop him and insist that he start over again after a few deep, restful breaths. If necessary, let him bring his rifle down from the firing position, for a brief rest.

77

You have probably observed theatre audiences which became so intensely interested in the dramatic developments of the play that they virtually stopped breathing. When the climax of the moment had passed and the heroine had been saved from the designing clutches of the villain, there was an audible sigh from the audience. This is exactly the kind of a sigh you will want from your recruits.

The recruit is similar to a theatre audience in his reactions while shooting. He is inclined to become so interested in some of the phases of good marksmanship that he will forget to breathe. This will only cause him to be uncomfortable and unwanted tremors and tightness will result.

Proper breathing, when firing, is not difficult. If carefully taught and practiced, the soldier will learn it is the normal and comfortable experience which he will want to adopt.

He will note, too, that as his breathing is done properly while shooting, he will lose the tension and instead acquire the relaxed, normal and comfortable pause good marksmanship requires.

BREATHING AND AIMING

CORRECT breathing is always accompanied by its twin—proper Relaxing. Together they will reduce the tremors of a front sight of a rifle at least 30 percent.

If the front sight is wobbling or dancing, despite proper position and holding, then something is wrong with your recruit's breathing or he is holding himself all tightened up like the core of a golf ball.

Have your pupil resume his firing position and aim his rifle at a target. Now if he will watch the reaction of his fore sight upon the centre of the target and take a deep breath, he will note that the muzzle has lowered. See Figure 1, opposite.

As the breath is exhaled, the foresight will naturally return slowly to the mark again and it will be more steady than it was before, owing to the relaxation introduced into the body reactions by the sigh which was taken—or should have been. See Figure 2.

A recruit should not be allowed to restrain his breathing until he becomes uncomfortable. He should, instead, experience the natural, deep sigh. If he fails to experience it, he should be given a rest before trying it again.

THE COACH MUST INSIST UPON AN AUDIBLE SIGH BEING GIVEN. IT IS THE SECRET IN CHECKING PROPER BREATHING.

This type of breathing is not done instinctively by the student marksman but it is not difficult for him to learn and this can be done by concentration, practice and good coaching until it becomes a habit.

FIG. 1

FIG. 2

AUTOMATIC ALIGNMENT

THE TERM Automatic Alignment means that if a rifle is properly positioned, held and steadied by correct breathing habits, it will be dead upon the target to which it is pointed.

By that, it is inferred that if you had three targets in front of you and you wished to fire at either the right or left one, instead of the centre target toward which the rifle is pointing, the change could be made around the pivot which is your left elbow.

The artilleryman can shift the horizontal direction of his field piece by wheels and gears but if he wants to make a major shift he has the trail lifted and swung with the gun carriage's wheels serving as the pivot until the desired direction is attained.

To the recruit, this change is as easily made by shifting the body so that it pivots around the solid, upright, left forearm. This means of automatic alignment keeps the marksman's body and rifle directed upon the selected target as rigidly as a field piece. Note Figures 1 and 2, opposite.

The correctly held rifle comes to rest upon some target. To make it coincide with the target which you want to hit, you must shift your whole body and rifle together so that the rifle will naturally come to rest in the direction of the selected aiming point.

Far too many recruits entertain the viewpoint that if a new target is selected, all that is required is to shift the rifle so that it points in the desired new direction. This calls into play unnecessary muscular effort.

A recruit cannot shift his rifle from one target to another, properly, without altering his whole body direction around that left elbow pivot. If muscles are used, instead of this pivoting method, good position, perfect holding and proper breathing rhythm are all lost.

Your recruit must learn that he and his rifle are wedded and welded and as one moves, so must the other. He should be so thoroughly taught this phase that once having spotted his target, he will, through sheer force of habit, so adjust his body that when he aims his rifle at the target, no muscular effort will be required to register it perfectly.

A pitcher facing third base can instinctively whip around and nick a runner off first base. He knows exactly the direction his throw will take. He knows the first baseman will be ready to take the catch. He knows exactly how his feet must be placed in order to deliver the throw. The same things should apply to your recruit, so that he will automatically and instinctively place his body in order that the rifle may be pointed directly toward the target.

When his body is in alignment, with the target and he raises his rifle to the firing position, it should point precisely to the spot where he wants it to point. When he can do this, he will not have to rely upon unsteady muscles.

73

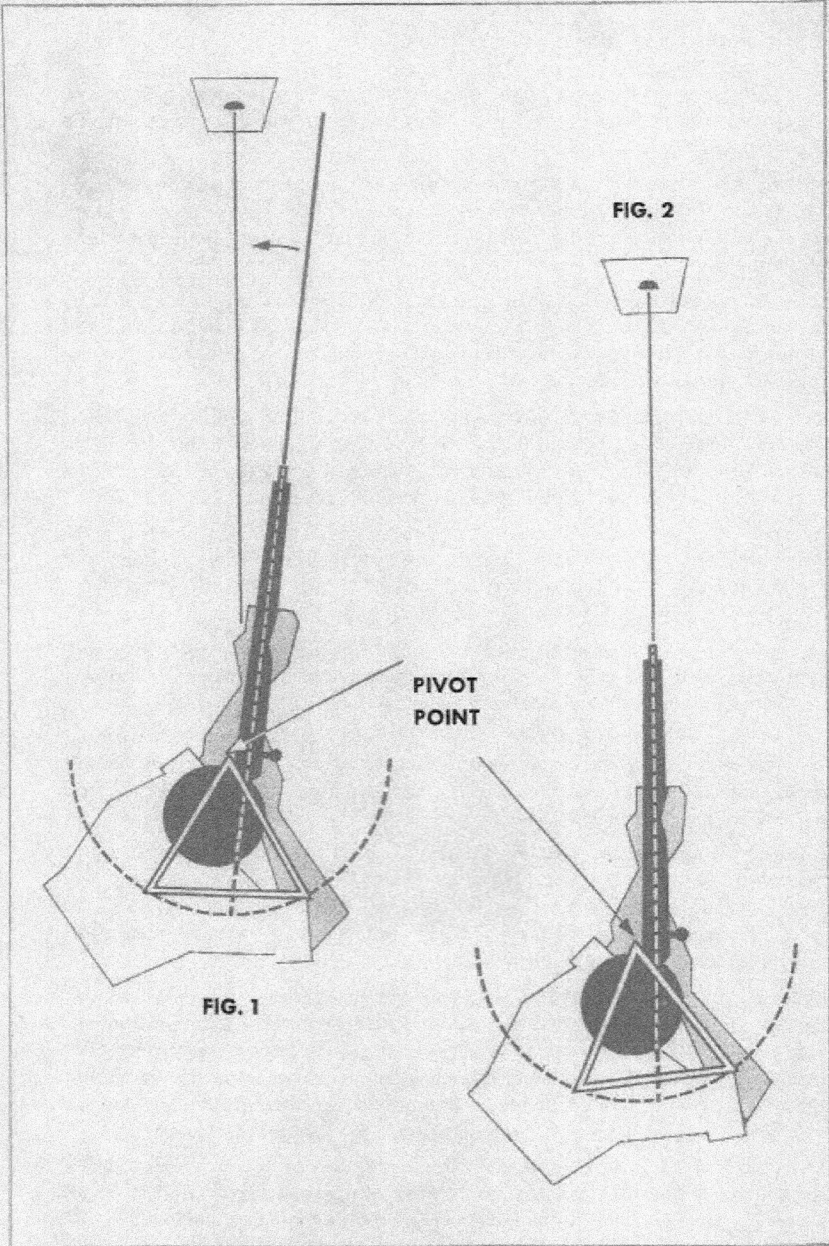

PIVOT
POINT

FIG. 2

FIG. 1

An easy demonstration would be to place a carpenter's square upon a flat surface and aim one end of it at a target. Place your thumb upon the angle. (See illustration below). Now select a new target and by moving the second leg of the square, swing the whole instrument so that it is aimed at the new target. The point where your thumb has rested has performed the same function as the left elbow pivot.

The major value of automatic alignment, in war, is that the soldier who uses it, knows he can take his "stance" in shooting each enemy and that he will get that enemy with one shot and no alibis. Automatic alignment, as a worthwhile shooting habit, is the secret of successful rapid-fire and snap shooting.

**THIS IS
AUTOMATIC
ALIGNMENT**

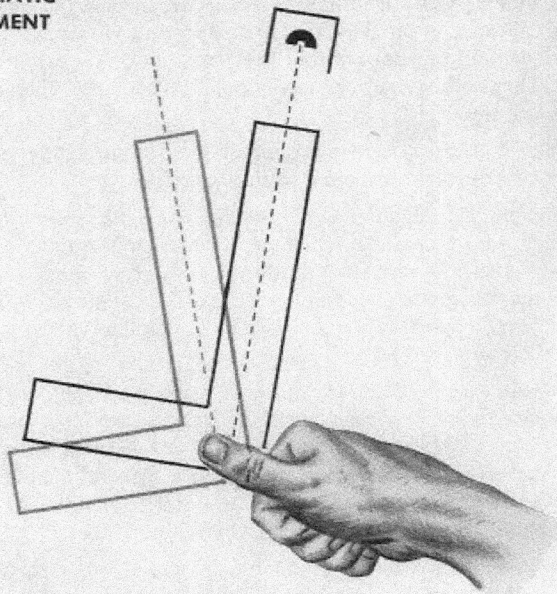

75

CHAPTER FIVE

Aiming

WHEN steering a bullet to the centre of a target, the recruit must aim his rifle perfectly. But he will grasp the lessons of Aiming ONLY if he has mastered the preceding factors of Position, Holding and Breathing. He cannot hope to aim correctly if he has not learned those lessons well.

Many would-be marksmen have been taught the theory that the open sights on rifles are still the best. The open sight is as hopelessly out-dated when compared with the peep sight, as the horse and buggy is in transportation when lined up alongside a supercharged, twelve-cylindered automobile.

There are many people who have become accustomed to open sights upon early model rifles or upon their favourite sporting weapon. They will brag loudly and lengthily on the fact that they can get better results with their V-shaped or U-shaped back sights than is possible with the peep sight. It is an old and silly argument.

It is possible to do good shooting with the open sight *but you can get a far greater degree of accuracy with a peep sight.*

Reasons for much of this discussion as to the merits of each type, lie in the fact that many people have grown so accustomed to the open sight they have ignored the peep sight and know nothing at all about what it will do. They do not know the mechanics which make it the more accurate sight to use. And although ignorance may be bliss, it is also a very serious rut for any progressive instructor or soldier to get himself into.

The peep sight assures accuracy and increased speed in shooting an enemy. War is an emergency in which arguing over the relative merits of various sights or of using musty or erroneous methods of steering a bullet instead of the logical and natural methods, amounts to a form of sabotage to the war effort. The enemy does not want the Canadians to be crack shots, yet he stresses the musketry training of his own soldiers.

There are hard-to-convince persons, however, who insist that one must look at the back sight, then move the post of the front sight up so that it is in the dead centre of the U-space of the rear sight. Its top must be level with the top of the U. They say it should be right under the bull's eye. But here the law of optics raises a big argument.

Observing the diagram of the eye, shown in Figure 1, opposite, you will note the elliptical or oblong shape of its lens. Now turning to the upper illustrations in Figure 2, it will be seen that the lens assumes a thick shape when the eye is focused upon the back, U-shaped sight which is approximately one-half a yard from the eye.

In the second illustration of Figure 2, the lens becomes thinner when focused or directed upon the front sight which is one yard distant and still thinner when concentrated upon the target which is 300 yards away (third illustration).

Observing the bottom picture of Figure 3, you will see a composite eye lens embracing all three previously-shown shapes. To the right is a composite view of the back and front sights and the target.

In other words the eye CANNOT AT THE SAME TIME, FOCUS CLEARLY UPON THREE OBJECTS, ALL AT VARYING DISTANCES. It is possible to see each one individually without delay in shifting the eye focus from one to the other but the three cannot be seen at one and the same time with the necessary clarity that good aiming demands. Thus, later on, the merits of the peep sight, which overcomes this bit of optical gymnastics, will be discussed.

There will be those soldiers who will look through the peep sight and complain that they cannot see the target. This can usually be blamed upon faulty concentration. If the soldier, thus complaining, were to look at some Parisian postcards in the peep machine of a penny arcade, he would see everything portrayed. The closer he gets to that peep hole the more he can see. The farther away from it, he is, the less he can see. Try your recruit looking through a hole in a piece of paper and he will learn the advantages.

In the Army, as elsewhere, there are show off types who will pick up a rifle and because of a special aptitude or skill, place five shots in the centre of a bull's eye and then hand the rifle to a recruit and expect that he will get the same results.

Just because one man wears size eight boots is no reason why the whole Canadian Army should be equipped with that size of footgear. Each rifle must, first of all, fit the recruit as to length of butt. If the recruit then does everything you have taught him to do and finds that his five bullet holes are clustered on the target but not on the bull's eye, his rifle needs some sight adjustment so that it will be fitted to his eyesight. But when that rifle is so adjusted that the recruit can register high scores, his bunk-mate cannot hope to shoot accurately with it—nor will anyone else. Rifles must be fitted to the person and the person to the rifle just like a tailor-made Sunday suit of clothes.

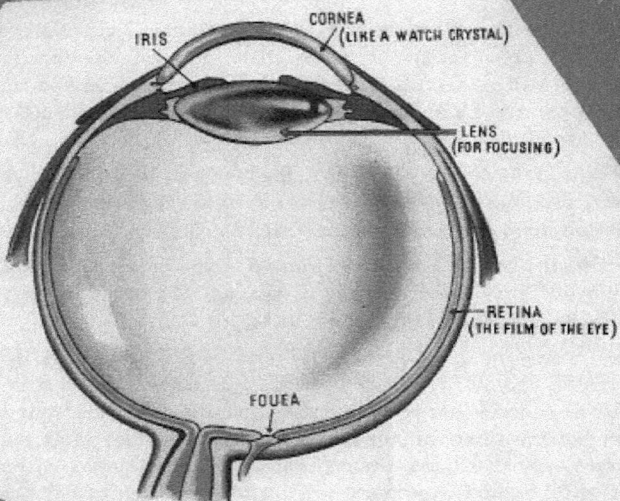

IRIS

CORNEA
(LIKE A WATCH CRYSTAL)

LENS
(FOR FOCUSING)

RETINA
(THE FILM OF THE EYE)

FOUEA

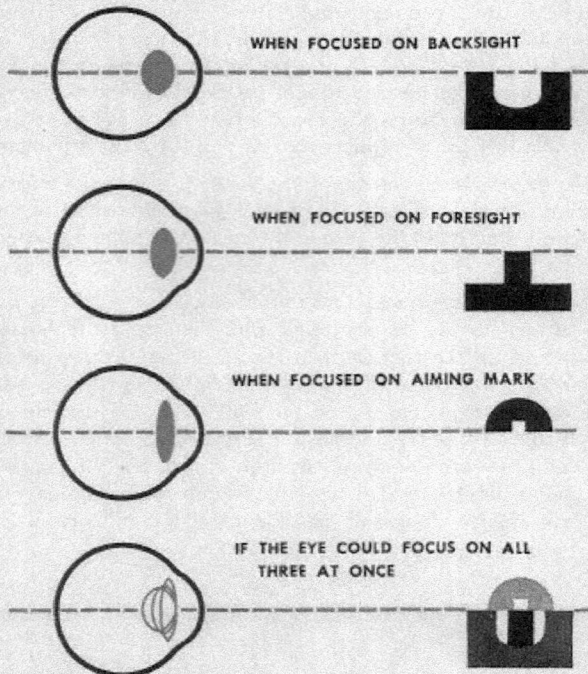

SHAPE OF LENS

WHEN FOCUSED ON BACKSIGHT

WHEN FOCUSED ON FORESIGHT

WHEN FOCUSED ON AIMING MARK

IF THE EYE COULD FOCUS ON ALL
THREE AT ONCE

78

In the past, aiming has had all the stress of musketry training. Aiming is actually the least important of the five Basic Principles of good shooting. Trigger Control comes first by being THIRTEEN TIMES AS VITAL TO GOOD SHOOTING as Aiming. Moreover, Position, Holding and correct Breathing are from two to three times as important as Aiming.

If the essentials to good shooting are followed religiously, then aiming will select its own groove with a minimum of teaching, practice and effort. It will come to the recruit as natural as the correct use of the handlebars when learning to ride a bicycle.

There is an amazingly large number of people who suffer from a hallucination or pet alibi that they cannot shoot accurately because they have eyes that are not good enough for precise aiming. These people are guilty of carelessness. If they have been accepted by the Army for service, they can see well enough to shoot.

If they can spot a neatly-turned pair of female ankles at 100 yards, they can certainly see a target's aiming mark. Alibis sound very foolish in shooting because they show lack of a determination to learn.

PERFECT AIMING IS UNQUALIFIED

NOW that all of the ancient, out-moded and less accurate methods of aiming have been discarded from your endeavours to instruct soldiers as expert marksmen, it should be stressed that there is only one kind of aim — PERFECT!

Aiming has no qualifications such as fair, good or better. It is either PERFECT or it is BAD. Your recruit cannot expect that he will get away with much canteen gloating over registering five scattered shots on a target. Bullet holes must ALL be within the centre of the target. The more your pupil is taught that perfection in shooting is the only thing worth striving for, the better shot he will be.

The Canadian soldier is entitled to the assurance that every bullet he fires will register another name on an enemy casualty list and keep his own hide intact. He must gain that assurance by being thoroughly proficient with his rifle, which is still the most effective of weapons. You, as the instructor, will be the means by which he will win that assurance.

LONG FINGERS

SOME recruits have long fingers like those of a pianist or surgeon. In the chapter on Position and under the subtitle "Importance of the Left Hand" the instructor was told to teach his class how to grasp the handguard of the rifle with the left hand, so that the fingers curled upward and over the rifle.

The long-fingered gentry are going to be stymied in aiming, unless those parts of the fingers, which block the line of vision between the two sights, are shifted.

Figure 1, below, shows some of these longer-than-normal fingers around a rifle handguard. Figure 2 shows them now out of the eye's road. The tips are sloping so that they are down on the handguard and pointing slightly toward the butt of the rifle.

This may, in some cases, cause a small space between the handguard and the small and third fingers but this can be overlooked as long as the rifle is resting UPON THE HEEL OF THE HAND, while the left elbow is beneath the rifle.

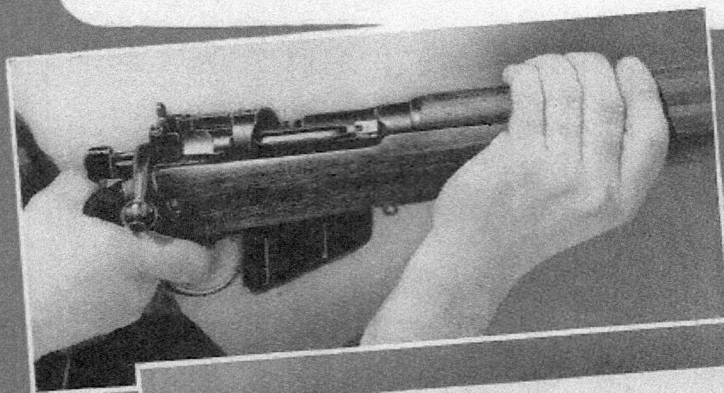

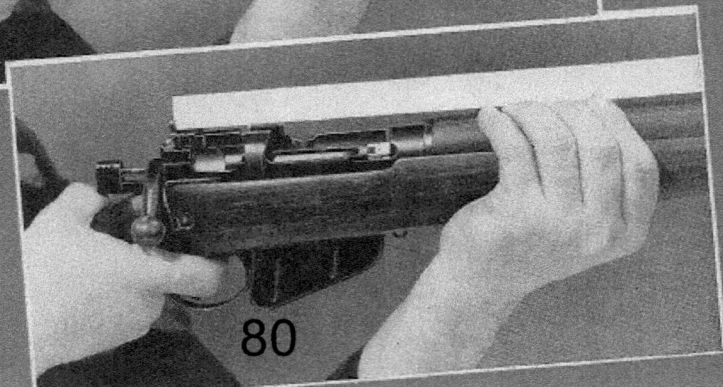

80

EYES AND AIMING

THE PERSON who uses his right hand more than his left one, usually has a slightly larger right hand than its mate. If a person is left-handed, that one will be the larger hand because of its additional muscular development. It comes to be known as the Master Hand.

Oddly, without the knowledge of most of us, one eye is used more than the other and without borrowing any fancy phrases from the mystery thrillers, it is known as the Master Eye.

To learn which eye is the Master, have the recruit select an object at least 30 feet distant, which can be clearly seen. Then, using a finger ring or similar small circular object, have him hold it up in front of his eyes, at arm's length and pointing toward the distant object.

With both eyes open, while looking through the ring, he will be able to see the object framed inside the ring. Should he close his left eye and look through the ring with the right one he will either see the object inside the ring or it will be outside the frame. By trying the left eye, while the right one is closed, the opposite of what was seen when the right eye was open, should prevail.

The eye that sees a selected object within the ring without the ring having been moved in order that it be framed as it was when both eyes were open, is the one that is "on the beam". It is the Master Eye.

If a baseball pitcher was prevented from playing just because he was a southpaw, the howl of disgust from the bleachers would echo for years. Then, why should a hard, fast rule be applied to marksmanship, that all left-handed people be compelled to shoot right-handed?

And if the Master Eye happens to be the left one, why should the full value of that eye in focussing be lost in such an important duty as shooting the enemy?

As far as good marksmanship—and that is what is wanted—is concerned, if a recruit's right eye is the Master Eye and he is right-handed, he would shoot that way. If he has a left Master Eye and is naturally left-handed, he should shoot as a port-sider.

If, however, the recruit is right-handed and has a left Master Eye (or vice versa) you should use common sense to determine whether he should shoot right- or left-handed. He will quickly learn either way. The test should be: "Which way will most efficiently permit him to kill the enemy?"

Changes may be required in the recruit's shooting habits or in his tendencies to adopt certain habits. He may be imbued with the fact that although left-handed he must shoot right-handed. The instructor should assist the recruit during his first interview. As it is a matter of life and death to him the recruit deserves the kindly help and patient experimentation which you as a coach can give. It may not be necessary for you to explain to him why his shooting habits are being checked but if he is able to acquire a confidence with the shooting side that suits him best he will be a much keener student.

81

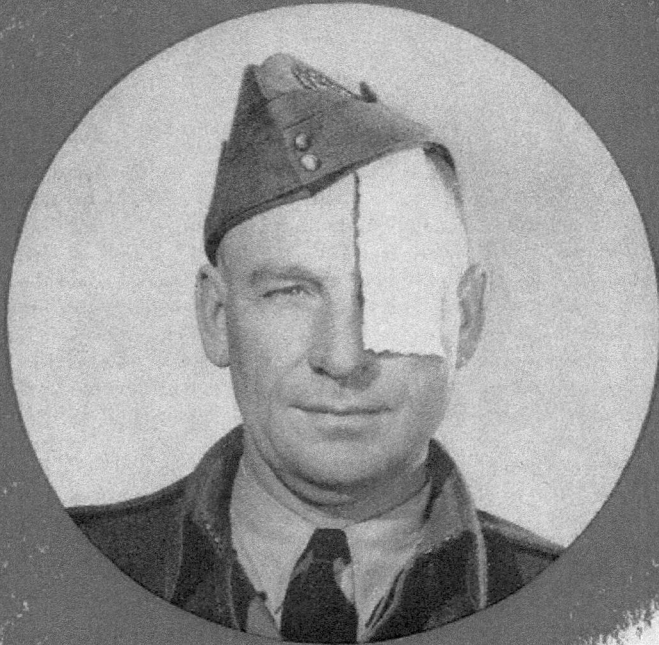

EYES AND AIMING—Continued

No two persons can satisfactorily wear the same glasses or spectacles. Just as glasses are ground to fit the individual whose eyes have been tested for them, so are people's eyes different. One person does not see precisely the same as his brother or neighbor.

When four marksmen of equal ability fire the same rifle at the same target, the bullets of each firer will be clustered in four different zones of the target. Yet, only the bullet holes of the soldier to whom the rifle was fitted, will be parked on the bull's eye. In other words the rifle was fitted to one man and not to the others.

The old-fashioned armourer may adjust a rifle's sights so that they are mechanically perfect but because of the variations in individual eyes, few, if any marksmen can shoot accurately with it. Emphasis placed upon the sameness of normal sight is not only erroneous but harmful. You, the instructor, cannot too severely criticise a recruit's shooting skill if his eyes do not see exactly the same as your own.

Some people cannot close one eye while sighting. Whether their eye lids are just plain stubborn or the eye does not want to miss anything, the lids just will not close, one at a time. When an instructor meets a recruit with this handicap, he should place a card or similar cover over the eye which is not the Master Eye. See the illustration, above.

The recruit should then practice with this card until he learns to concentrate along the barrel with his Master Eye. Even if the secondary eye is open behind the card it will not matter. After a recruit learns this factor of concentration he will be able to get along without the card and with both eyes open he can shoot well.

The Master Eye MUST be the one used in looking THROUGH the rear sight to the front sight.

Keeping both eyes open, in shooting, is no sin. There may have been a time when it was considered the acme of musketry mistakes to keep both eyes open but many of the world's best shots unconsciously have both eyes open by the time the trigger is squeezed. Note the illustration below.

It is not recommended that the recruit be taught to open both eyes, but neither should he be discouraged to avoid keeping them open if he unconsciously does open them. The important thing is that he see clearly through the peep sight.

EYES AND AIMING—Continued

The soldier who shoots right-handed and whose left eye is the Master Eye should not be allowed to push his head over the top of the butt so that he may use his Master Eye. The obvious thing would be for him to change over to left-handed shooting.

A similar change would be required of a left-handed recruit with a right Master Eye. Note the illustration above of the right-hander trying to use his left eye, in sighting. The marksman is apparently uncomfortable. Moreover, in this position he is apt to be hurt when the rifle recoils.

The cancer of musketry is that fear of recoil which causes the recruit to tightly close his eyes, grit his teeth and tense his muscles just before the trigger is squeezed. He acts as if he were setting off a Big Bertha, or about to have a tooth pulled without an anaesthetic.

Yet, this condition, known as flinching, is far too common among would-be marksmen. It is one of the chief causes of poor shooting and it is nearly as hard to cure as cancer, once it develops.

The soldier with fear of recoil suffers from false impressions of what recoil is. He is to be pitied. No one can ridicule him, or get tough, and expect that the fear will be dispelled. He must, instead, be patiently taken back over the phases of Position and Holding and he must be convinced by logic and demonstration of the mechanics that produce and minimize recoil. His fear will melt if the instructor's kindly and patient approach to the problem has been sincere.

In the chapter on Holding, much space was devoted to collarbones, muscle pads, and other aspects of arresting recoil. These things were introduced to help instil in the mind of the recruit that recoil can be controlled. It is the instructor's sacred duty to see that no recruit goes on the range with even the slightest fear of recoil.

This counts most when the first ammunition is fired. If you have failed in your early teaching you may have ruined any chance of your pupil attaining a shooting skill. He has the cancer of musketry and it may develop to the point that, for want of confidence and proper training, he will be killed in battle because he is unable to use his rifle effectively.

Teach and preach recoil control before the recruit reaches the range. Let it become a legend with him that he won't be hurt. Remind him also, that you have been trying from the first to insure against his being hurt. It will produce good results. The illustration below shows "flinching."

THE BACK SIGHT

HAVING found the Master Eye, the vision is directed along the top of the rifle's barrel. But the question of how to use the peep sight becomes a factor which frequently changes the whole viewpoint of Aiming. As previously indicated, many people expect the sight to be either V- or U-shaped, like the old, open-sighted rifle. The peep sight thus appears too involved to these persons.

Why has the old type sight been scrapped in favour of the peep sight? It is simply because it was found that better shooting could be assured, if the marksman looked THROUGH the sight and not AT it.

You will recall how the lens of the eye was obliged to take a fantastic series of shapes in order to focus upon the rear, open sight, the front sight and the target. The peep sight eliminates the first sighting problem because the eye does not look at the back sight but THROUGH it.

In your early days, you doubtless looked at fancy pictures of your forefathers. They were tinted up and were usually placed in circular frames of deeply-carved gilt-painted wood. About the only thing those frames ever caught was dust, because the eye always automatically centred upon the stern features of the old beezers. You didn't pay any attention to the frames, at all. The frames merely helped you to find the centre of interest, which was the face of your grandpappy.

So it is in shooting. The peep sight is the frame that helps you to find the centre of interest, which is the fore sight.

Your recruit, having learned automatic alignment and major and minor adjustments for elevation, now raises his rifle so that the front sight is right on the centre of the aiming mark. If he is looking AT the rear sight, he only sees a piece of gun metal with a pin-sized hole in it.

But if he looks THROUGH it, from a point as close to it as safety from recoil will permit, he will find, with concentration, that a tiny fish scale or disc of light is apparent.

The best way for the recruit to see this would be for him to hold the rifle up to the light as in Figure 1, opposite. The rifle should be reversed so that the butt points to the light and the aperture in the rear sight is completely filled with light from the sky.

The closer he is to that minute hole in the rear sight, the smaller the disc of clearer light becomes. See Figure 2. The farther back from the hole that he locates his eye, the larger the disc becomes until it fades away.

Actually this disc of light is the eye's vision concentrated into a funnel of sight and pointed in its natural and perfectly centered direction. Surrounding it is a halo of haze.

Now that the recruit has found the fish scale of light, let him reverse his rifle to the natural firing position. Then let him find that disc again and having found it bring the tip of the front sight up into it from the haze. See Figure 3.

He will immediately note the sharpening up effect (see Figure 4), as the front sight is in that fish scale of clarity. He will find that it appears to be as sharp as a razor's edge. It will be square. He will see, also, that he does not have to look for the centre of the back sight. He will, instead, find it automatically because now what he seeks is the sharp, square and clear shape of the front sight.

He will know that his vision, the rear sight and the front sight are in perfect alignment.

He will also note that the size of the disc of light is regulated by the distance between the eye and the aperture.

Make sure the recruit understands and uses the Optical Centre of the Back Sight at All Times.

FIG. 1

OPTICAL CENTRE

WHAT YOU SEE

FIG. 2

AT 2½″   AT 3½″   AT 4″

ITS USE

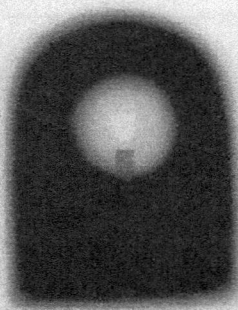 

FIG. 3   FIG. 4

88

THE BACK SIGHT—Continued

The eye looks THROUGH the rear sight so that the vision is condensed down to a single, straight stream, directed onto the front sight so that the latter is seen as a clear, sharp, square picture while the target rests in the background of the picture. The all-important factor is in seeing that the tip of the front sight is SHARP. Then everything else in Aiming becomes secondary.

The motorist driving down a busy street looks THROUGH his windshield. He doesn't look at it, admiring the dust spots or the stickers. If he didn't look THROUGH it he would either spend much time in hospitals or more time explaining to judges.

Thus the backsight serves a similar purpose to the windshield. It is something to see THROUGH. The Master Eye picks up the disc of light, which is the optical centre of the back sight, with ease. This optical centre when directed upon the front sight serves as a major aid to good aiming because it will always be perfectly in the centre of the rear sight. It will be mechanical because if you look through that sight, the vision is automatically cut down to a tiny pencil pointing from the centre of the back sight to the TIP OF THE FRONT SIGHT.

It is therefore essential that if there must be a concentration of vision upon the front sight, there must also be a concentration of mental effort.

The recruit must be encouraged to exclude all distractions and instead, focus upon that tip of the front sight. The eye will assist him in this because if it is focused completely upon one thing it cannot see several others.

Every time the recruit picks up his rifle he does not have to seek out the optical centre. Having once found the fish scale of light and having seen what it does toward making the front sight stand out clearly, square and sharp, he will be able to pick it up automatically. All he has to find is a SHARP, SQUARE, BLACK, CLEAR FORESIGHT. When he does that, through sheer force of habit, he has gone far toward aiming perfection.

Look through it—
Not at it!

THE FRONT SIGHT

THE FRONT Sight, or Fore Sight, is the one which the marksman must clearly see. Having learned that he is to look THROUGH the back, or peep, sight he finds that the tip of the front sight is the essential point upon which he should concentrate. He now knows that it must be seen sharp, knife-edged and clear. It must be the dominant point upon which the vision is concentrated.

It would be well for the instructor, at this juncture, to impress upon the recruit that the old bogey of concentrating upon the target and to hell with the front sight is wrong and is fatal to good shooting.

When the expert golfer is about to drive the ball down the fairway, he gets his position and then concentrates his vision upon the impact side of that little white ball. He directs all his attention to the tip of the curve. He keeps his vision there so that when the club-head strikes the ball he will get a perfect shot. If he neglects to keep his eye on the ball, he will likely muff the shot and spend most of the afternoon trying to find it in the weeds or rough.

The foresight of the rifle requires similar concentration. The target is secondary. The back sight has become a means only toward seeing the front sight, sharp, clear, black and square.

The unsharpened end of a lead pencil when held up at arm's length and level with the eyes can be seen clearly. Its outline is sharp and square. But if the pencil were brought up close to the eye, its outline would be only a blur. You would know that it was there but the eye would be trying to see around it and would only pick up a hazy blob that was annoying. Similarly the finger shown in Figures 1 and 2, opposite, indicate these focus differences.

Now if the pencil were to be held at arm's length again and pointed toward a small, bright object in the distance and the eye focussed upon that object, and not upon the pencil, the latter would again have that hazy, fuzzy or indistinct outline.

The front sight is the moving part in aiming.

FIG. 1
LOOKING **AT**
THE
FINGER

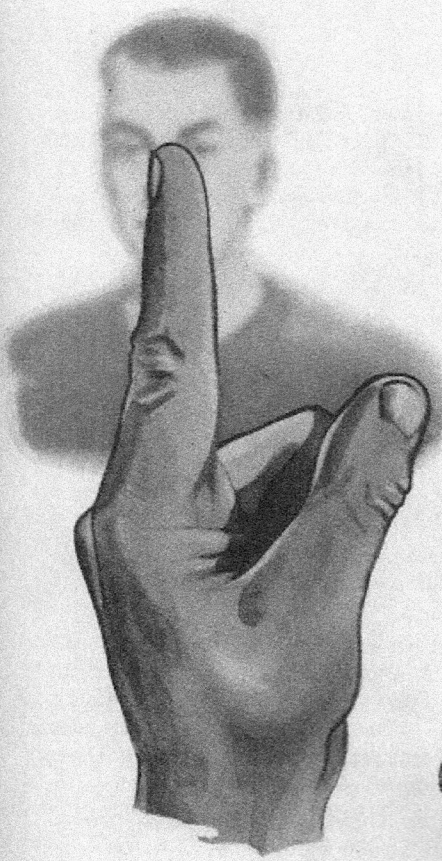

FIG. 2
LOOKING **PAST**
THE
FINGER

Just to show how the eyes play tricks, place a silver coin on the floor. While standing, bring the fingertips of your two hands together, at arm's length as in Figure 1, opposite and then look steadily at them as you lower them down to a point where the coin appears between two pairs of fingers.

Through the spaces between the joined fingers you will see the coin indistinctly. But now shift your vision to the coin and because of focussing beyond the fingers you will see the coin distinctly but the fingers will appear as sausages. See Figure 2. They aren't sausages and you know it but that is how they appear, because the eye cannot focus on distant and close objects at the same time and see both distinctly. One or the other object will be distinct — but not both.

The student marksman who looks PAST, but not AT, the front sight cannot be assured of perfect aiming. He sees the target clearly but he also sees several indistinct front sight tips so he accordingly uses different ones for successive shots. See Figure 1, below.

He gets his bullets strung out high and low on the target. His elevation has been bad. Had he looked at the sharp, square tip of the front sight (see Figure 2) and not past it, he would have grouped his shots in the centre of the target and his elevation would have been excellent.

No marksman can concentrate his vision anywhere else but on the tip of the front sight and expect the best shooting performance. The tip of the front sight must be seen as a clear, black, knife-edged and square object for every shot.

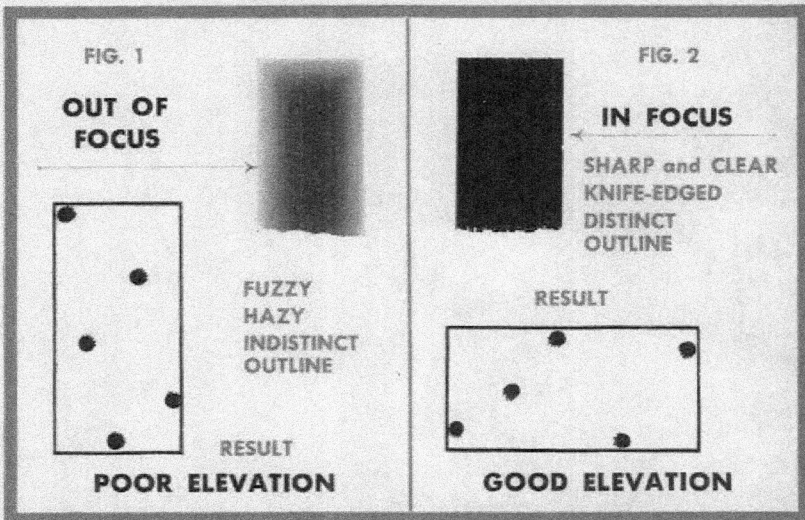

FIG. 1

OUT OF FOCUS

FUZZY
HAZY
INDISTINCT
OUTLINE

RESULT

POOR ELEVATION

FIG. 2

IN FOCUS

SHARP and CLEAR
KNIFE-EDGED
DISTINCT
OUTLINE

RESULT

GOOD ELEVATION

FIG. 1

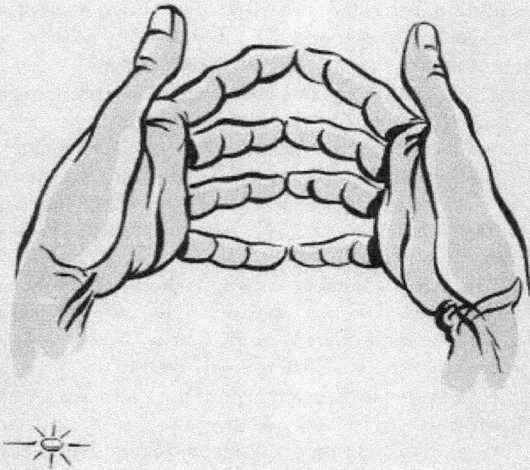

FIG. 2

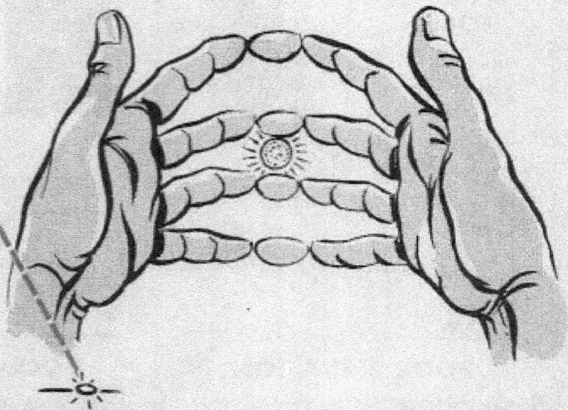

SIGHT PICTURES

THE preceding sections of this chapter have placed much stress upon the recruit looking at the front sight so that he sees it black and square. The target, so far, has been left in the background, where it rightfully belongs. The feature or centre of interest in the picture which you see is, and must always be, the front sight as seen with the aid of the optical centre of the peep.

Your recruit may say "How can I shoot accurately and not see the target clearly? If I see the front sight sharp and square the aiming mark is only a hazy blob. Maybe my eyesight isn't good enough for shooting."

His eyesight is all right. He cannot be expected to see two objects at different distances from his eye, both at the same instant and see them clearly. It only takes one-fortieth of a second to shift the focus from one focal point to another.

If you were to go to a professional photographer's studio to have your portrait made, he would place you in front of a fancy background. You would probably spend your time admiring the background while he arranged his lights and camera. As the picture was being taken you would be aware that the background was behind you, clear and defined yet when the unretouched photographic proofs were made available, you would see yourself sharp, clear and with every wrinkle, freckle and mole standing out plainly while the background of the picture was hazy and seemingly out-of-focus.

This is all because you were the centre of interest and the background was merely secondary. In shooting, the centre of interest is the front sight and the target or aiming point is the background.

Naturally your recruit will ask how he can be expected to shoot accurately if he cannot see clearly what he is aiming at.

It will be necessary for you to explain to him that if he can clearly see the aiming mark without his rifle impeding his view, he should form a mental picture of it and determine the centre of the aiming mark and just as he is about ready to shoot he should bring the front sight up in line with that mark.

The target doesn't move (and the peep sight shouldn't) so the front sight is the only part of the rifle that is the lining up factor. Therefore you must see the front sight clear, black, sharp and square as in Figure 1, opposite, not hazy or distorted as in Figure 2.

Same sight pictures insure that every
shot will count.

95

straight as the line of vision, the marksman knows that his rifle is dead upon the aiming point. However, all that he can clearly see is that front sight which he has automatically and unconsciously now chosen to focus upon. The target is still in the background.

It is not suggested that seeing the target clearly is unessential. While it is very necessary to good shooting to see the aiming point, it is nevertheless a fact that having once seen and located it perfectly in the mind's eye, it becomes secondary to the front sight, which is the moving part in aiming.

The secret, therefore, lies in the fact that you first locate your aiming mark and get it clearly established in your mind, even to picking out landmarks and shapes. When you have this perfect mental picture, then bring the front sight up, while your eye is FOCUSSED UPON THE AIMING MARK. When the front sight has come right into the centre of that mark you can momentarily shift your eye focus from that distant target to the closer front sight.

The biggest difficulty, the recruit will encounter, will be in not seeing the same sight picture for consecutive shots. He must see exact duplications, as if they were prints from the same photographic negative. Carelessness in not getting precisely the same sight pictures is what leads to serious aiming troubles.

Let us imagine that it could be possible for two cameras to be installed by painless operations, so that one was behind the Master Eye of you, the expert, and the other behind the Master Eye of your recruit. Each camera would be focussed upon the aiming point and the cameras would be loaded with numbered films. The cameras would be electrically operated and synchronised with the trigger (see Figure 1, opposite).

After you had both fired four shots, the cameras would be removed, the films developed and the prints made to correspond with the numbered negatives. You, the expert shot, would have four identical sight pictures. The recruit, who did not exercise extreme care in attaining precisely the same sight picture each time, would have four prints which resemble the selection in Figure 3. Yours looked like the four duplicate pictures in Figure 2. His sight pictures were not like yours. They were merely similar but not the same.

The Oxford Dictionary defines the adjective "same" as being "monotonous, uniform and unvarying". That is exactly what is demanded in your sight pictures when shooting. They must be monotonously uniform and unvarying.

You MUST see the SAME sight picture
for each consecutive shot!

96

straight as the line of vision, the marksman knows that his rifle is dead upon the aiming point. However, all that he can clearly see is that front sight which he has automatically and unconsciously now chosen to focus upon. The target is still in the background.

It is not suggested that seeing the target clearly is unessential. While it is very necessary to good shooting to see the aiming point, it is nevertheless a fact that having once seen and located it perfectly in the mind's eye, it becomes secondary to the front sight, which is the moving part in aiming.

The secret, therefore, lies in the fact that you first locate your aiming mark and get it clearly established in your mind, even to picking out landmarks and shapes. When you have this perfect mental picture, then bring the front sight up, while your eye is FOCUSSED UPON THE AIMING MARK. When the front sight has come right into the centre of that mark you can momentarily shift your eye focus from that distant target to the closer front sight.

The biggest difficulty, the recruit will encounter, will be in not seeing the same sight picture for consecutive shots. He must see exact duplications, as if they were prints from the same photographic negative. Carelessness in not getting precisely the same sight pictures is what leads to serious aiming troubles.

Let us imagine that it could be possible for two cameras to be installed by painless operations, so that one was behind the Master Eye of you, the expert, and the other behind the Master Eye of your recruit. Each camera would be focussed upon the aiming point and the cameras would be loaded with numbered films. The cameras would be electrically operated and synchronised with the trigger (see Figure 1, opposite).

After you had both fired four shots, the cameras would be removed, the films developed and the prints made to correspond with the numbered negatives. You, the expert shot, would have four identical sight pictures. The recruit, who did not exercise extreme care in attaining precisely the same sight picture each time, would have four prints which resemble the selection in Figure 3. Yours looked like the four duplicate pictures in Figure 2. His sight pictures were not like yours. They were merely similar but not the same.

The Oxford Dictionary defines the adjective "same" as being "monotonous, uniform and unvarying". That is exactly what is demanded in your sight pictures when shooting. They must be monotonously uniform and unvarying.

> **You MUST see the SAME sight picture for each consecutive shot!**

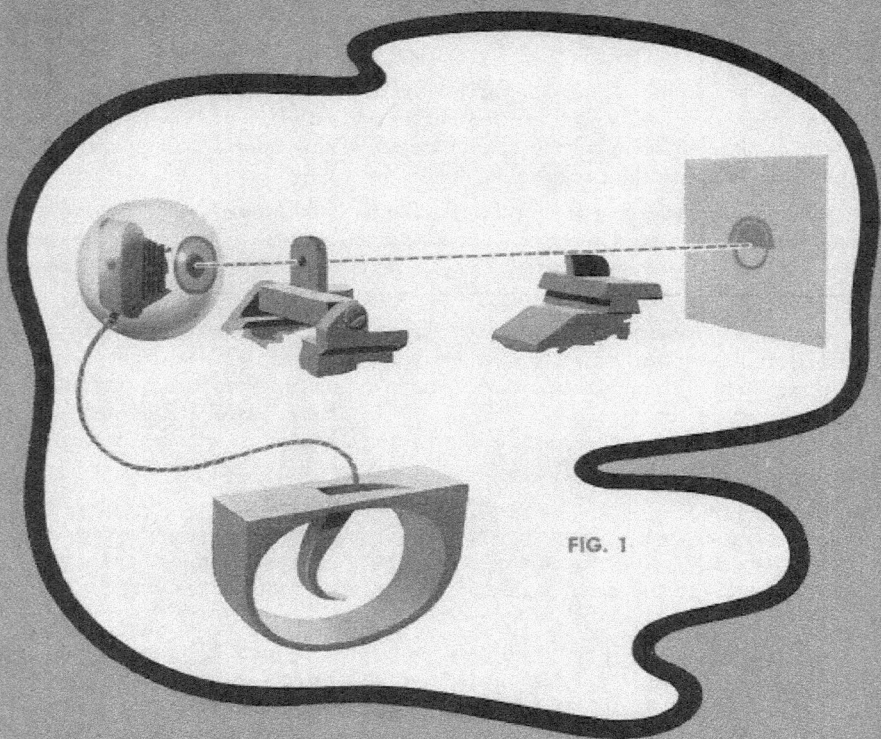

FIG. 1

FIG. 2
UNIFORMITY
OF SIGHT PICTURES

FIG. 3
LACK OF UNIFORMITY
OF SIGHT PICTURES

98

EYE DISTANCE

TO OBTAIN strictly uniform sight pictures, each time, the marksman must keep the same but safe distance between his eye and the peep sight.

He cannot be close to the peep for one shot, and far from it for the next.

He should learn to get as CLOSE to that little hole as safety from recoil will permit and ALWAYS be at that point of distance for every shot.

He must pick out the features of his target so that the circular frame which contains the optical centre, also embraces the same details of his target in exactly the same way each time. There cannot be even the slightest deviation. Any attempt to be approximately correct is all WRONG.

The wheelsman of the assault craft who doesn't keep his vessel steered toward the landmarks of an invasion coast is in deep trouble with the attack naval authorities and beachmasters. He must keep the same sight picture before him in order to perform his troop-carrying mission.

The lad who cannot get into the ball park to see the big game can usually find an unoccupied knothole. He gets his eye right up to that hole, too. In fact, if you were to look at it from the inside of the ball park, you would see a knothole filled with eye.

The same thing applies in shooting. The firer must get as close as safety will permit, to that peep hole in order to have a perfect optical centre and yet, at the same time, have a sizeable field of view which will give good sight pictures.

But some recruits will complain that they can see several targets when they look through the peep. This is natural. They should be seen but the recruit's own target, upon which his attention and sight should be concentrated, should be seen best.

The proper placing of the head against and on top of the butt, if carefully practiced so that the eye comes to the correct distance from the peep, each time, will help in maintaining uniformity of eye distance.

Above all, the recruit should practice placing his eye at the same distance so that he will automatically have this distance every time that he picks up his rifle to shoot.

> ## Get the "feel" of uniform
> ## eye distance.

99

MOVING AND SERVICE TARGETS

A COMPLAINT frequently heard is that the peep is too big. Recruits claim they are confused as to their own target. The peep has been deliberately bored its present size because in mobile warfare, with moving targets such as crawling men, lumbering tanks, speeding cars and trucks and power-diving planes, the marksman must have as wide a field as possible. Just try aiming your finger on a moving target and you will see the advantages of a sizeable field of view.

Then again, the poor light of dawn or dusk, fog, rain, smoke from shells, mines, smoke canisters and the confusion of camouflage, all demand that the soldier has the maximum of vision through his peep. He must see what is going on in order to look after himself and retard any enemy efforts.

The rifleman who is lying in a slit trench and who sees before him an enemy, whom he is about to shoot, will want to be able to see other enemy soldiers who might fire upon him.

Our soldier wants to be ready to deal with such emergencies and he can gain much confidence from the fact that a good field of view is provided by the peep sight without sacrificing precision of aim.

It may now appear to your recruit that the instruction is becoming contradictory. In one place it is recommended that the front sight is the point of visual concentration yet in another the field of view is stressed.

Your student marksman must remember that the object to be hit is determined first, and that he has a perfect sight picture of it and its surroundings.

He must not permit his attention to be distracted from that target. If a grizzly bear were coming down the trail at you and you couldn't get away, you would surely keep your eyes on the bear and not be looking around to see how the bolt of your rifle opened and closed.

When the perfect sight picture is assured, then the front sight is brought into that picture, the Master Eye focuses upon the front sight because you know the target is in the background. You then fire—and score.

Watch for the hidden sniper

alongside the decoy.

101

ON THE RANGE

Field of View

IN COMBAT

102

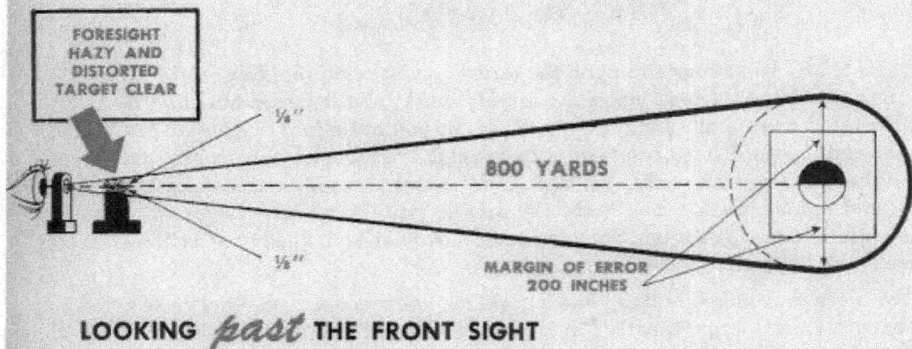

FORESIGHT HAZY AND DISTORTED TARGET CLEAR

¼″

800 YARDS

½″

MARGIN OF ERROR 200 INCHES

LOOKING *past* THE FRONT SIGHT

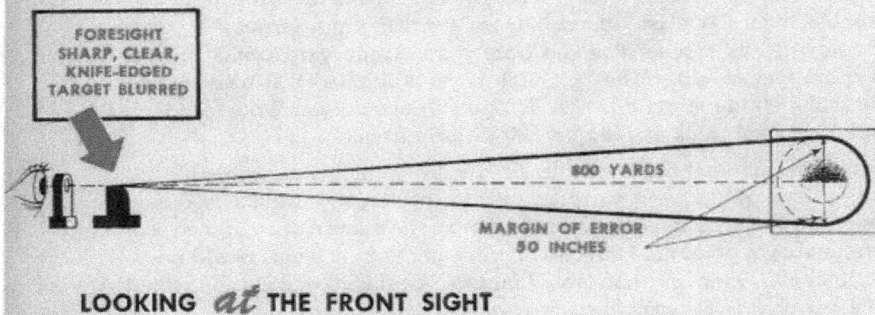

FORESIGHT SHARP, CLEAR, KNIFE-EDGED TARGET BLURRED

800 YARDS

MARGIN OF ERROR 50 INCHES

LOOKING *at* THE FRONT SIGHT

FRONT SIGHT VERSUS TARGET

Y OU MUST keep your eye upon the target as you bring that front sight up into position as it rests upon the aiming mark. Your whole attention is concentrated upon that aiming point. Then, as you are about to squeeze the trigger and the slack has been taken up, you shift the focus of your eye in that one-fortieth of a second so that you see the front sight sharp, clear and square upon that aiming mark. You know the aiming point is directly beyond the front sight and you know that your front sight is clear and steady. You then squeeze the trigger.

If we were to observe Figures 1 and 2 opposite, we would note that in Figure 1 we have seen the target clearly. It is perfectly round and sharp. The front sight is hazy, distorted and indistinct. Any aiming we do now must be by guess and a prayer.

Supposing that because of a fuzzy front sight we make an error in aiming of one-eighth inch. That isn't much but we are firing at a target 800 yards distant. Now let us assume that the front sight is one yard from the eye. (It isn't quite that much). The 1/8th-inch error multiplied 800 times would send the bullet off the target 8 feet, 4 inches. Or should you shoot 1/8th-inch low, you would likely kick up the dust 500 yards in front of you.

If it were possible that the low bullet fired with the highly questionable aid of a fuzzy front sight were to carry on toward the target it would be 8 feet, 4 inches below the aiming mark. In other words, the margin of error, because you were unable to determine the clear outline of the front sight, would be an amazing total of 200 inches or 16 feet, 8 inches. That kind of a margin would provide a fair chance for something over in the next county to be hit.

On the other hand, as in Figure 2, your front sight is sharp, black, clear and square. At 800 yards the aiming mark is a fuzzy and hazy blob of indistinct gray. It lacks definite outline. The trick is to estimate the centre of that blob and shoot with confidence because if your front sight has been clearly seen, your shot will not be more than 10 inches above or below the blob.

Extend that 10-inch margin of error until it encircles the indistinct aiming mark. The blob itself won't occupy a diameter much more than 30 inches when viewed at 800 yards and with 10 inches added above and below the blob we now have a generous area for error with a diameter of 50 inches—
JUST ONE-QUARTER AS MUCH AS WAS POSSIBLE WHEN THE TARGET WAS SHARP AND THE FRONT SIGHT INDISTINCT.

Of the two methods of aiming you will select the one where there is the least margin of error and that is the one where you see the front sight, black, distinct, sharp and square because it assures four times as much accuracy as when the target is clearly seen.

AUXILIARY AIMING MARKS

THE OLD-STYLE bull's eye was a black disc and the trick was to aim at the bottom of that disc and hope to hit the centre of it (see Figure 1A, opposite). In other words it implied that you should aim at one point and try to hit another with your bullet. Just as if you hoped to hit a nail on the head with a hammer and watched the hammer handle instead of the nail-head.

If you were following this method when shooting at the heart of an enemy you would aim at his knee.

Even if the intention had been to aim at the centre of the bull's eye and hit it there, the task was difficult because the farther the object is from the eye, the harder it is to distinguish in detail.

Later, to improve aiming, the bull's eye was horizontally halved so that it appeared to be a half disc resembling a tin hat or battle helmet, (see Figure 1B). The marksman should thus bring his front sight up to the horizontal, flat edge of the half disc and he would be perfectly on the beam. He would then have a great advantage in being able to place the TIP OF HIS FRONT SIGHT IN THE CENTRE OF THE BULL'S EYE, EXACTLY WHERE HE WANTED HIS BULLET TO STRIKE. That would be a case of aiming at what you wanted to hit and not aiming at one point which you didn't want and hoping to hit some entirely different spot.

But black sights, lined up with the middle of the black aiming marks, do not tend toward much accuracy. The blacks are inclined to blend and so precise aiming cannot be assured.

Hence, a small, white square was left in the centre of the horizontal halving line and became known as the Auxiliary Aiming Mark, a most useful consideration for recruits. See Figure 1C.

Now it is possible for the front sight to be brought up so as to have that auxiliary aiming mark sitting on top of the centre of the tip of the front sight. The marksman is now assured of the perfect placing of the front sight to exactly coincide with the spot where he wants his bullets to strike—and not somewhere else (see Figure 2).

Similarly in the hour-glass shaped targets (Figure 3) the auxiliary aiming marks have been established. Here again the front sight is brought up to the auxiliary aiming mark. When located there and horizontally centred, the aim is precise.

DEVELOPMENT
OF AUXILIARY AIMING MARKS

OLD STYLE

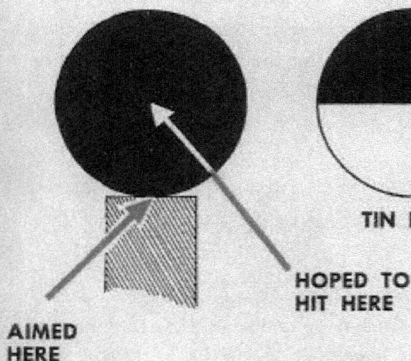

AIMED
HERE

HOPED TO
HIT HERE

FIG. 1-A

TIN HAT

FIG. 1-B

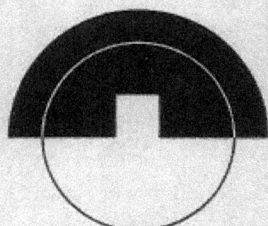

NEW STYLE

FIG. 1-C

HOW TO USE
AUXILIARY AIMING MARKS

9-C TARGET 30X

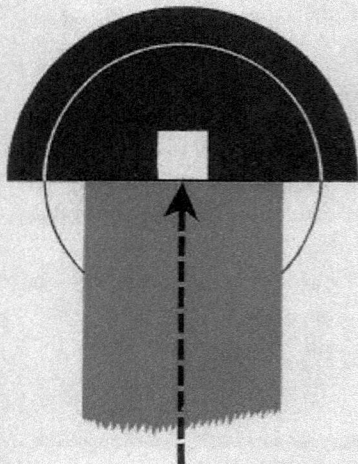

FIG. 2

4' TARGET 100X

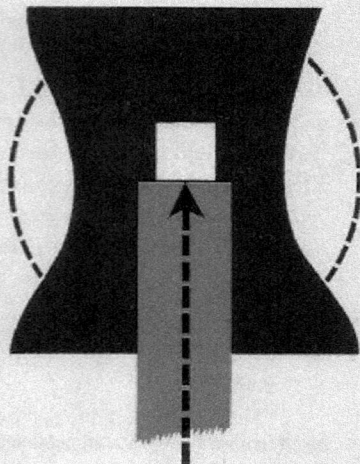

FIG. 3   113

106

SERVICE TARGETS AND POINTS OF AIM

THE prime purpose of this teaching is to develop such an expertness that when the recruits, so trained, reach the battlefields, they will possess the utmost of aiming proficiency.

For the sake of convenience, targets on the ranges have been standardized according to the range and the degree of training attained by the class. But when it comes to shooting the enemy on a tricky battlefield, where the conditions are much different than on the well-organized range, many new problems are presented.

It is maintained that if the recruit can be accurate on the range then he can be sure to plant a bullet in an enemy where it will do that enemy the most harm.

If you were to see just the head of an enemy soldier sticking out of a trench or from behind a fallen tree, there would only be the distance from the rim of his helmet to the ground to serve as an aiming mark. But you might shoot high and you most certainly do not want to miss him.

So you use common sense and all the advantages which you can muster. You will be smart, here, if you aim at the bottom of his chin or at the ground level (see Figures 1 and 1A, opposite).

If your shot has been high you will have struck him in the face. If you have shot exactly where you aimed, the bullet may hit the ground just in front of him and ricochet, with an end-over-end spiral, which will cause a far more ghastly wound. Japanese troops were deliberately taught this latter technique.

Now assuming that in addition to his head, his two shoulders are plainly in view. The same method prevails—he is a goner with this sort of aiming. See Figures 2 and 2A.

But should your enemy be standing, you now have enough target with which to become more personal. You can tie his ticket onto a bullet and aim at the centre of his body (see Figures 3 and 3A). Elevation problems will have been taken care of by the zeroing of your own rifle and the enemy will have another name on his casualty list.

If the enemy should be moving along, perfectly oblivious to your designs upon him, the trick will be to aim for the centre of his body but slightly towards the direction in which he is moving. It is just a case of pinning him down with hot lead at a point where the target is large enough to reduce to a minimum the margin of any error in aim due to movement.

ADVANTAGES

DISADVANTAGES

FIG. 1

FIG. 1A

FIG. 2

FIG. 2A

FIG. 3

FIG. 3A

115

PRECISION OF AIM

FAR too many marksmen are content to belong to the "Ancient and Honourless Order of Almost Righters". This organization is as valuable to the enemy as an elaborate espionage system. It does a terrific amount of harm because its only qualification for membership is that the rifleman must not be precise in his aim. He is permitted to come close to registering precise aim with every shot but an "Almost Righter" is not expected to insist upon his own aiming accuracy.

There are three degrees in the initiation of members. The soldier who regards his shooting as "good enough" gets his first degree with ease. Then the rifleman who is satisfied with "pretty close" aiming is a second degree member. When he can shoot "almost right" and is satisfied with that kind of work, he is a full-fledged member.

ARE YOU AN ALMOST RIGHTER?

For those exacting soldiers who are out to kill the enemy and at the same time save their own lives, there is only one kind of aiming—the precisely correct, perfect, on-the-beam, smack-in-the-centre, ideal kind. Soldiers who shoot this way never get into the "Ancient and Honourless Order of Almost Righters". They do not help the enemy—they kill him.

May we repeat—there is only one kind of aiming demanded by the Canadian Army. It is the accurate, exact, precise, perfect kind. All other kinds of aiming are *Wrong* and perfect shooting can only be attained through perfect aiming. You cannot guess at where your front sight is in relation to the aiming point. You must know where it is in order to steer your bullet right onto that aiming mark.

Precision of aim calls for accurate expression of effort. It must be definitely exact and must scrupulously observe the rules of accuracy. The watchmaker fitting a balance wheel for the sleek, ivory-tinted wrist of a movie actress knows precision because he grinds the gears down finer than a split strand of a spider's cobweb.

Just ask some of the instrument mechanics of the Royal Canadian Electrical and Mechanical Engineers about precision. They talk in terms of one ten-thousandth of an inch, as if it was a mile. They know the meaning of the word "exactness". You would surely howl "Thief!" if your garageman charged you $50 to fix your car yet left one piston sloppy in its cylinder. He only has to work within 3/1000ths of an inch.

You insist upon perfect precision in the mechanics of your watch and car yet when your own life, against that of an enemy, is at stake, you are willing to take chance? We doubt it.

Supposing you need an operation upon your eye or heart. You get a surgeon whom you know will be utterly exacting in the way he uses the knife and effects the removal of the infected parts. Your life or your eyesight will be involved so you don't fool. You are dead serious. You want precision right down to the nth degree.

That surgeon, when he first started to learn his profession, knew he had to develop precision. He practiced until he got it down perfectly. Lives would depend upon his skill and he could not afford to be careless.

Are you willing to go onto the range *without* having learned precision of aiming; *without* insisting that you will do it precisely and consistently so that when you stack up against a ruthless enemy you will know that you will get him with one accurately-fired shot?

Teaching precision of aim is a classic in the field of musketry headaches. Many recruits just hate to admit that they are not precise—exact—on the beam. They want to blame the rifle, the coach, the weather, the ammunition, the cook, their eyes and even the unit mascot. They will not tolerate for a moment that they were not precise.

Sure, they did just what the instructor ordered. But has the instructor overlooked the fact that he does not see through the eyes of his pupil? Each eye sees differently and the recruit must solve his own aiming problems by satisfying his own conscience and proving it with accurate target groups.

Possibly the most difficult marksmanship factor to get across to soldiers is this business of accurate sighting and aiming. It is difficult, not because the various steps toward good aiming are hard to explain but because the precision required for perfect results is hard to demonstrate. Only an excellent shot can appreciate the absolute precision necessary in aligning the sights, if obscure or distant targets are to be hit.

Practice, patience and determination to shoot accurately are the prime needs of the recruit. The coach can get blue in the face trying to demonstrate what is wanted but if the recruit sees an entirely different picture than the coach, how can he be expected to aim exactly as the coach?

If you will refer back to the two sets of "prints" taken on the imaginative cameras (Figures 1, 2 and 3, Page 105) you will see that the expert saw the same sight pictures for every shot. He was precise. His shooting, if consecutively aimed at the ground level of the barn door, would have placed four shots there. Just where the recruit's precisionless aim would have parked his bullets, no one can guess, but the windmill, mail box and lightning rods would doubtless have been hit.

Don't be an almost righter—Be a PRECISER.

110

BLACKENING SIGHTS

YOUR attention is drawn to Figures 1A, 1B and 1C below. Figure 1A shows a front sight that is dirty. It is smudged with lint, grease and Heaven knows what else. It cannot perform its functions in giving accurate aim if its outline cannot be seen clearly, sharply and squarely.

On the other hand, a polished front sight as in Figure 1B, so clean that it shines like a prim spinster's nose, cannot be clearly distinguished either. Your eye cannot cope with the glare.

The ideal sight is one that is clean, dull, jet black as in Figure 1C. It must give a clear, sharp outline and yet carry neither dirt nor glare.

To attain this kind of sight condition, wipe all grease and dirt from the sight (see Figure 1, opposite); place the butt on the floor with the muzzle pointing upwards at approximately an angle of 65 degrees with the sight on the under side of the barrel. Hold a match or cigarette lighter (as in Figures 2 and 3), so that the tip of the flame will play upon the sight. It will soon be covered with a clean, even, sooty coat of dull lampblack, provided of course you were careful to first remove all oil or grease.

Similar treatment of the back sight is of equal assistance in aiming accuracy.

FIG. 1 A

FIG. 1 B

FIG. 1 C

FIG. 1

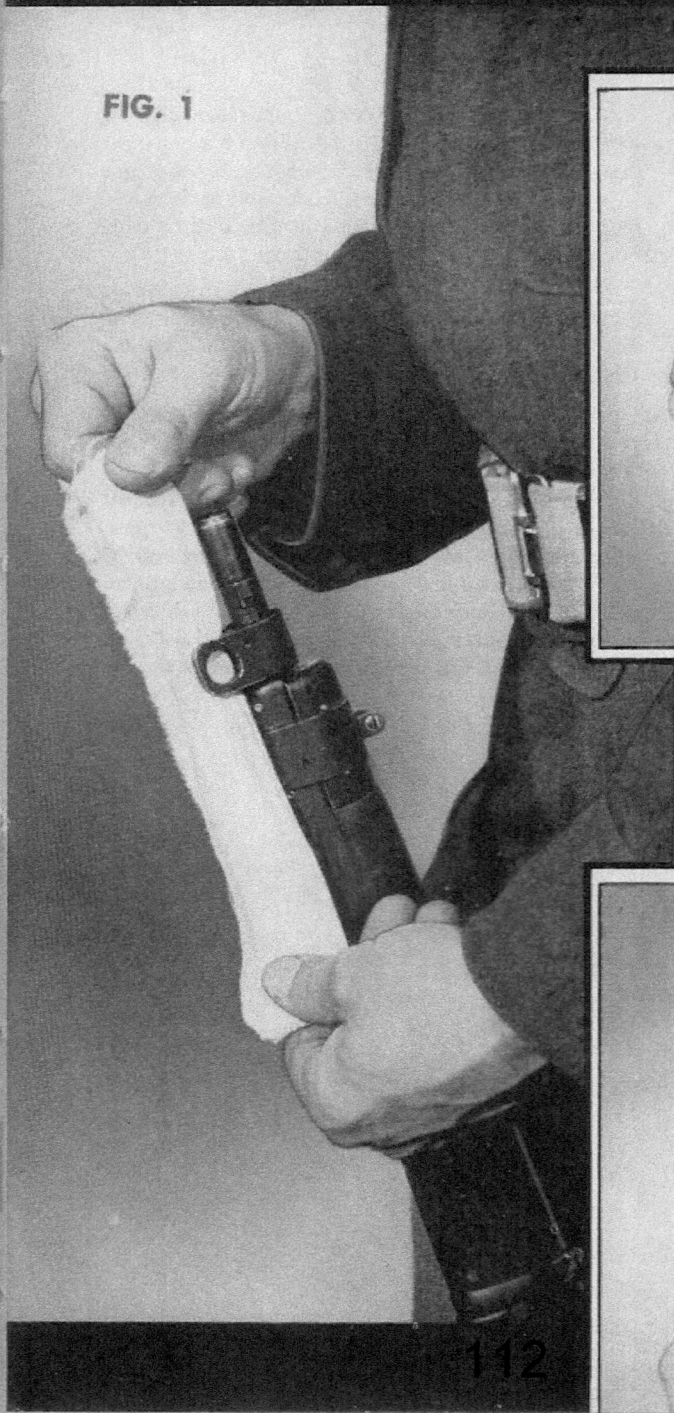

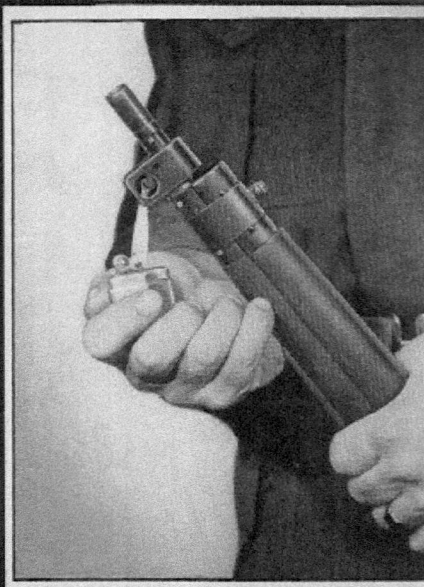

FIG. 2

FIG. 3

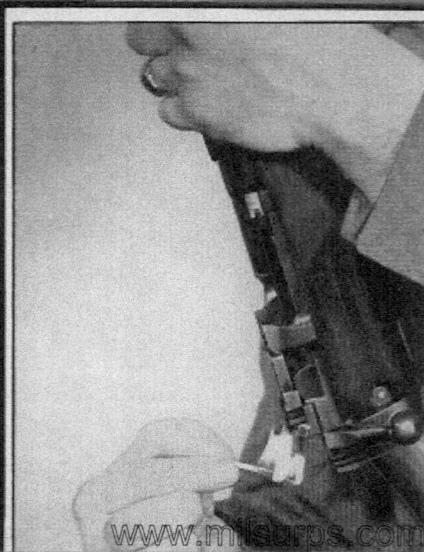

112

"WHY SERGEANTS GET GRAY"

BY
Little Chief Wildshot

THE EQUIPMENT OF AIMING

YOU have impressed your recruits that eyes are different; that no two people can see exactly the same things under the same conditions. You have also impressed upon each recruit that precision of aim has a top priority.

But soldiers will argue strongly, their aiming is perfect. If their shots go wrong, their rifle is to blame, it hasn't correct sights, the barrel is rusty or one of a score of other mechanical defects prevail. No sir, the recruit never makes mistakes. He is just like the typist who blames the typewriter for spelling errors. His pride, his ego, or whatever you want to call that human defensive trait, just won't let him admit a mistake.

You, the instructor, have the responsibility of sending those soldiers out to look after themselves on the battlefield. You are therefore going to make certain that every lad in your class does aim accurately. You are not going to take his excuses, his bluff nor his alibis. You are going to check his accuracy. And if he finds that he cannot get away with claims of accuracy which are not well founded, he will know that he is open to ridicule. He may know that you won't be too severe about it but his classmates will be able to flatten his boasts of perfect marksmanship.

In order that the coach may check upon the recruit's aiming accuracy, several sighting devices have been designed. They are somewhat different in construction, one from the other but they all perform the same job. Moreover they are foolproof and will impress upon the recruit the precision of aim required, so that when he gets onto the ranges he will know exactly what to look for.

> *Aiming Equipment,*
>
> *if used,*
>
> *produces marksmen.*

THE AMERICAN SIGHTING BAR

THE American Sighting Bar, specifications for the construction of which are shown in the accompanying sketches (opposite), is valuable in teaching aiming to recruits. It consists of a strip of wood, one inch wide, two inches in depth and fifty-four inches long, on one end of which a black piece of sheet metal has been solidly and squarely fixed. This is called the eyepiece. A small hole has been drilled in this metal, one half-inch from the top. This hole should be centred in the metal strip.

Twenty-eight inches beyond the eye-piece a slot is cut and into it a metal plate, similar to a backsight, can be inserted. This sheet of metal should have a hole the size of a 25-cent coin centred in its upper half. This is known as the aperture.

Continuing 20 inches farther, a right-angled piece of metal is placed so that a short, upright end will approximate, or resemble, a rifle's front sight. One half-inch beyond, a slot should be cut into which a "tin hat" aiming mark or half-disc black target card can be inserted.

The idea is for the hole in the eyepiece, the aperture, the upright "sight" and the centre of the aiming mark to be brought into strict alignment. The precision this requires should impress itself upon the recruit.

As the recruit looks through that little hole, which is the eyepiece, he should see the two-bit sized hole (the aperture in the upright metal plate). Next he should see the sharp, clear, square outline of the front sight (see Figures 1 and 2, respectively). Then as the target is inserted in its slot he should be able, by adjustment of the target card, to bring the tin hat aiming mark directly into line with the front sight so that the flat side of the target's shape appears to sit on top of the tip of the sight and dead in the middle of the vertical centre of the aperture (Figure 3).

This exercise can best be worked out by the recruit looking through the eyepiece while the coach has most of the bar resting upon his shoulder. The coach's back should be toward the recruit so that he may adjust the target card in response to the directions of the aimer. The coach can thus watch the preliminary approach of the recruit toward precision of aim.

ACCURATE AIMING IS
UNQUALIFIED.

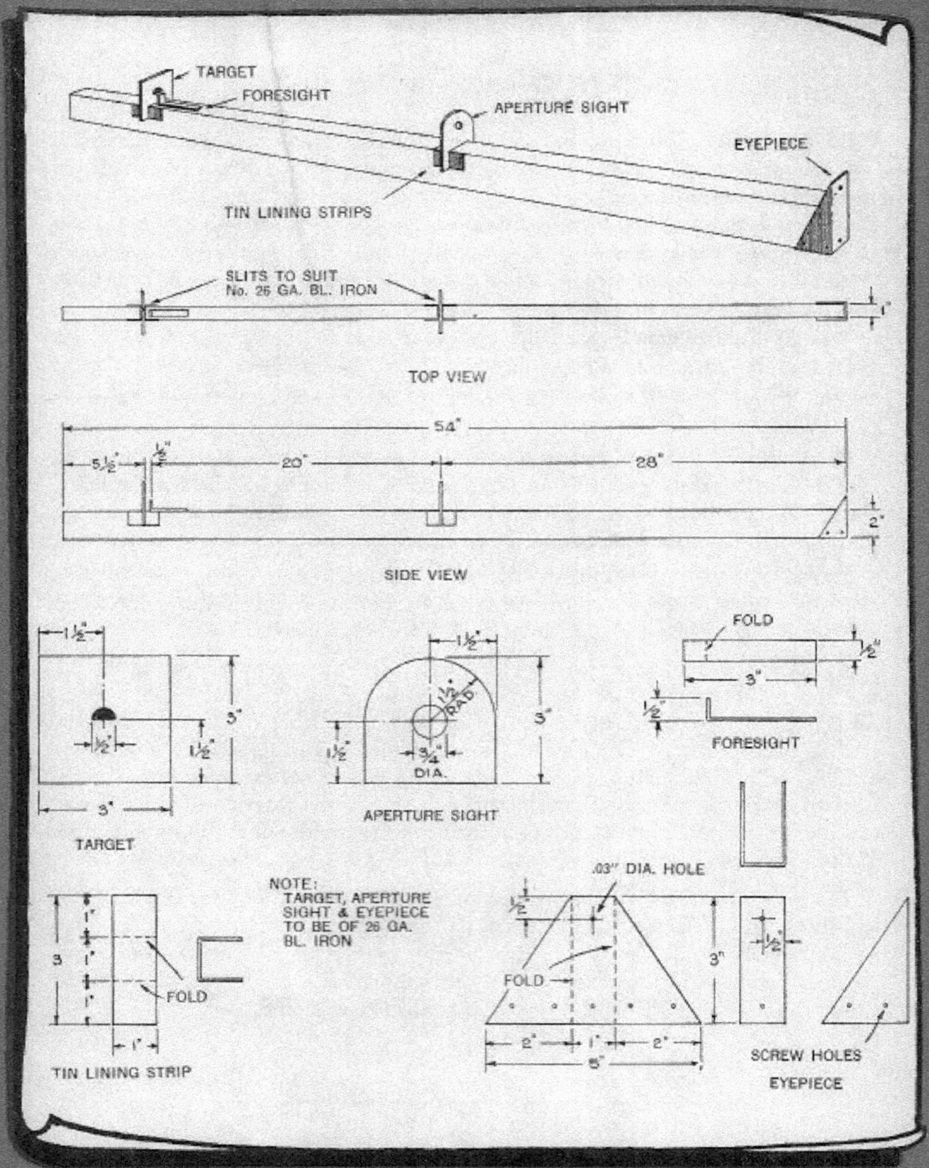

TARGET
FORESIGHT
APERTURE SIGHT
EYEPIECE
TIN LINING STRIPS

SLITS TO SUIT
No. 26 GA. BL. IRON
1"

TOP VIEW

54"
5,1/2" · 1/2" · 20" · 28"
2"

SIDE VIEW

1/2"
3"
1/2"
1/2"
5"
1/2"

TARGET

1 1/2"
1/2 RAD
3/4 DIA.
1 1/2"
5"

APERTURE SIGHT

FOLD
1/2"
3"
1/2"

FORESIGHT

NOTE:
TARGET, APERTURE
SIGHT & EYEPIECE
TO BE OF 26 GA.
BL. IRON

.03" DIA. HOLE
FOLD
1/2"
3"
1/2"
2" · 1" · 2"
5"

SCREW HOLES
EYEPIECE

3
1"
1"
1"
1"
FOLD

TIN LINING STRIP

FIG. 1    FIG. 2    FIG. 3

116

THE AUSTRALIAN SIGHT BAR

THE Australian Sight Bar provides a means of measuring precision of aim. It is a similar strip of wood to that of the American Bar, but this time only 39 inches long with a similar eyepiece of metal at one end but with a sliding aperture sight, the hole of which is only one half-inch in diameter. A wooden block, which resembles in outline, the front sight of a rifle, is beyond and is also moveable. At the other end of the board, a target is inserted in upright guides so that the target card may be raised or lowered.

The recruit, this time, should be permitted to first look through the eyepiece and thence through the aperture sight. See Figure 1, opposite. Then he should be permitted to bring the front sight into the dead centre of that aperture (Figure 2). This is done by movement of the two sliding devices. Now the target is inserted and he should bring the tip of the knife-edged, clear, square front sight up so that it fits right under the auxiliary aiming mark of the target (Figure 3).

The instructor now checks the accuracy of his recruit's aim by marking the point at which the front sight rested on the wooden bar. This is done without the knowledge of the recruit, who is then given another chance to aim. He should be able to demonstrate his aiming precision three consecutive times.

If he is exacting, the three pencil marks will be on top of each other. But if he only guesses at the precision of his aim, then you can easily alter the height of the target and keep exercising him until he becomes consistently accurate at any target height.

The recruit will find that if the aperture is always at the same eye distance his sight pictures will improve and he will see the value of precise aim.

Note the specifications and operation plans shown on the opposite page.

117

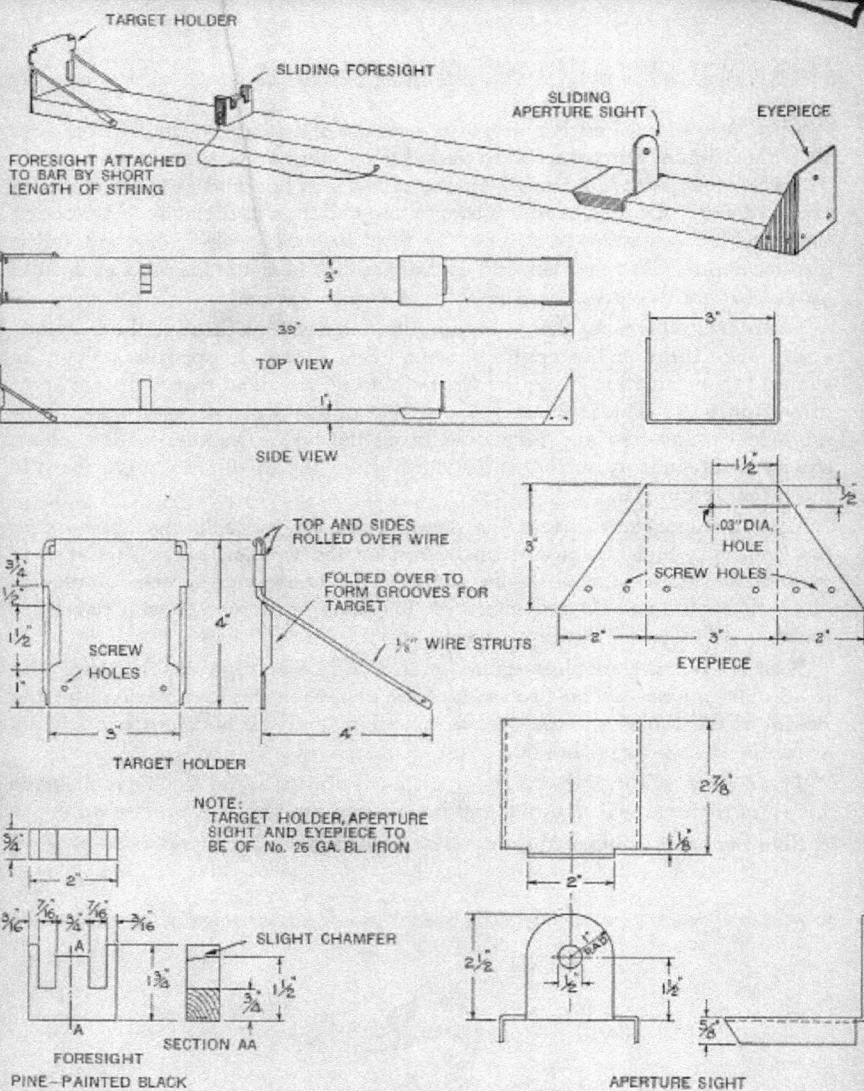

TARGET HOLDER

SLIDING FORESIGHT

SLIDING APERTURE SIGHT

EYEPIECE

FORESIGHT ATTACHED TO BAR BY SHORT LENGTH OF STRING

3"

39"

TOP VIEW

SIDE VIEW

3"

TOP AND SIDES ROLLED OVER WIRE

FOLDED OVER TO FORM GROOVES FOR TARGET

1/8" WIRE STRUTS

3/4

1/2

1 1/2

1"

SCREW HOLES

4"

3"

4"

TARGET HOLDER

1 1/2"

.03" DIA. HOLE

SCREW HOLES

3"

2"

3"

2"

EYEPIECE

NOTE:
TARGET HOLDER, APERTURE SIGHT AND EYEPIECE TO BE OF No. 26 GA. BL. IRON

3/4

2"

2 7/8"

1/8"

2"

3/16 7/16 3/8 7/16 3/16

A

1 3/8"

SLIGHT CHAMFER

3/4

1 1/2

A

FORESIGHT
PINE—PAINTED BLACK

SECTION AA

2 1/2

1/2

1/2

1 1/2

5/8

APERTURE SIGHT

FIG. 1

FIG. 2

FIG. 3

118

THE JOHNSON SIGHTING BAR

THE Johnson Sighting Bar provides a further check upon the recruit's aiming accuracy.

This bar consists of another 39-inch long, 2 by 2-inch piece of wood, similar in design to the Australian bar but with graduated slots for an off-centre aperture sight, so that it may take a variety of positions, heights and eye distances (see Figure 1, opposite). There is also a front sight which is moveable upon a scaled elevation slope and a graduated series of target slots in which the target card may be moved sideways in each slot. Note the steps in sighting as shown in Figures 2 and 3.

Specifications for the construction of this bar are shown in the drawing on the opposite page.

With this bar, the instructor can check the accuracy of the recruit for three consecutive aims by means of a scale on the side of the elevation slope. The position of the front sight is indicated on the scale. By moving the aperture sight, the front sight or the target for additional tests, the consistency of the recruit's aim will be proven by his accuracy as recorded on the scale.

This bar provides an ideal means for Tests Of Elementary Training of aiming.

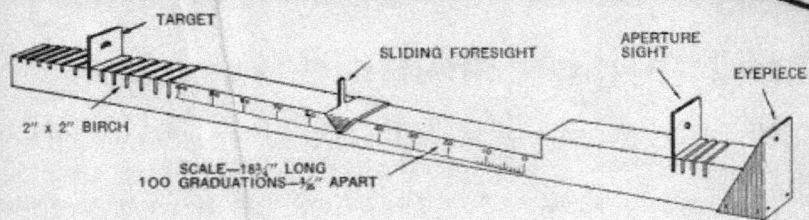

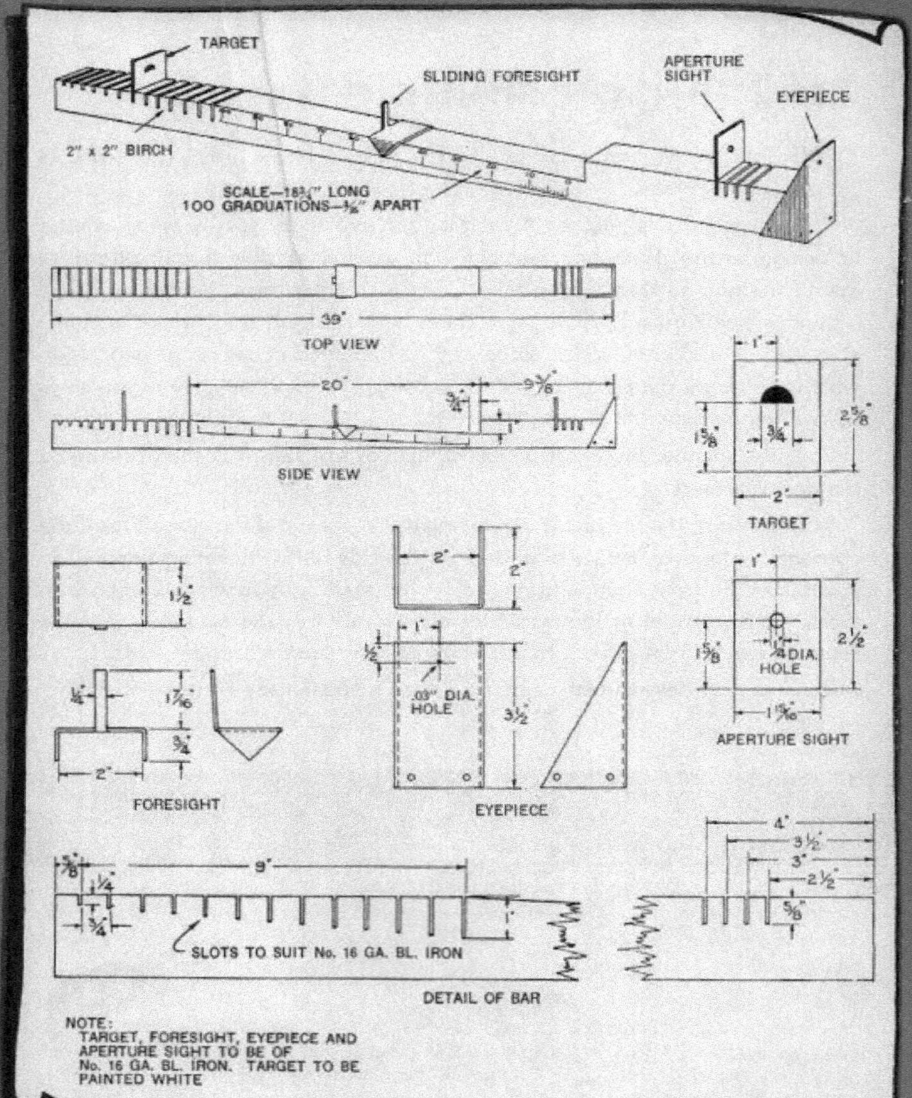

TARGET

SLIDING FORESIGHT

APERTURE SIGHT

EYEPIECE

2" x 2" BIRCH

SCALE—18¾" LONG
100 GRADUATIONS—⅛" APART

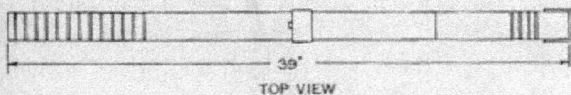

39"

TOP VIEW

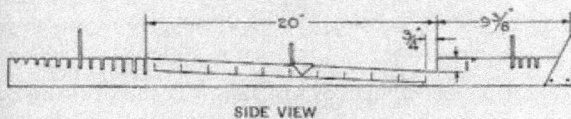

20"   ¾"   9⅞"

SIDE VIEW

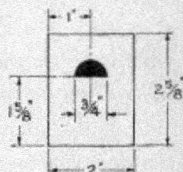

1"

1⅝"   ¾"   2⅝"

2"

TARGET

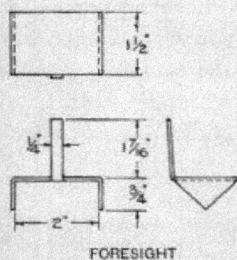

1½

¼   1⁷⁄₁₆   ¾

2"

FORESIGHT

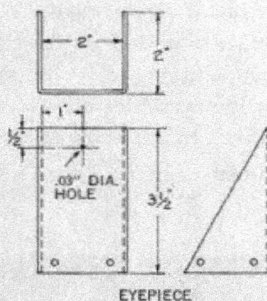

2"   2"

1"   ½"   .03" DIA. HOLE   3½"

EYEPIECE

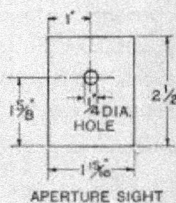

1"

1⅝"   ¼ DIA. HOLE   2½"

1⁵⁄₁₆"

APERTURE SIGHT

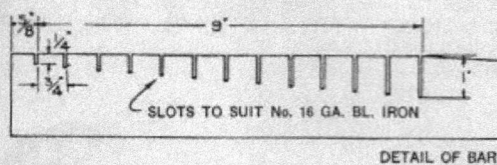

⅝"   ¼

¾   9"   1"

SLOTS TO SUIT No. 16 GA. BL. IRON

DETAIL OF BAR

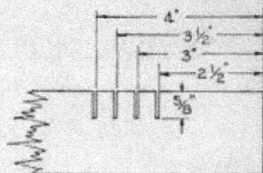

4"

3½"

3"

2½"

⅝"

NOTE:
TARGET, FORESIGHT, EYEPIECE AND
APERTURE SIGHT TO BE OF
No. 16 GA. BL. IRON. TARGET TO BE
PAINTED WHITE

FIG. 1

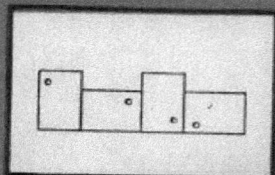

FIG. 2

FIG. 3

WINTER'S SIGHTING DEVICE

THE various aiming and sighting bars provide the ground work for the recruit in determining his degree of accuracy which precise marksmanship demands. But to tie the rifle into the picture the Winter's Sighting Device is recommended.

This can be constructed at a cash outlay of a 75-cent bevelled mirror of good quality, a few pieces of lumber and some nails. A carpenter, or anyone who can saw straight and hammer a nail, can quickly make the device. The specifications are shown on Page 133 and the operation shown on pages 130 and 131.

The Winter's Sighting Device is NO triangulation gadget. If precision is to be attained in marksmanship there isn't room enough for even triangles. The points of correct aim must be piled right on top of each other. Hence the Winter's Sighting Device provides ACCURACY DOTTING exercises.

Its use permits the rifle which has been firmly attached to the device to be naturally gripped by the right hand while the cheek and head have properly fallen into correct position over and upon the butt and the heel of the butt is against the recruit's muscle pad where it belongs.

An adjustable eyepiece must be attached to the rifle so that the eye will come right up to it, always in exactly the same position when looking through the sights. Thus the vision is directed through the optical centre of the back sight to the sharp, square, clear front sight—all in perfect alignment.

The mirror, however, reflects an image of the aiming mark of any target that is desired. This aiming mark is placed on one leg of a giant-sized clothespin or yoke which straddles the recording board. The recruit is able to manipulate the target which he can see only through the mirror. This is done by the left hand and the target can be moved around so that its reflection in the mirror comes to rest squarely upon the tip of the front sight for a perfect sight picture.

When this accuracy is attained, a pencil is inserted into a hole. This hole will only accommodate a pencil which is finely pointed. It is in the leg of the yoke that is used for moving the target leg into position. The point of accuracy is marked with a fine dot (all that is possible because of the finely-tapered pencil hole) upon a paper which has been attached to the recruit's side of the recording board.

The yoke is then moved aside and the recruit is ready to repeat the test. He should practice this accuracy until he can place three consecutive dots upon each other.

The student using this device is able to prove that he can aim consistently with accuracy and that he cannot bluff his way out of this test. He knows that he can now master accuracy with his own rifle and even before he reaches the ranges he has the necessary confidence that there is nothing wrong with his aiming ability. He and his classmates should be encouraged to practice on this device and, if they wish, engage, in a bit of friendly competition with it. As a game it beats snooker pool.

The device is virtually fool-proof, can be made for either the prone, sitting or standing positions and is easily adopted for checking Bren gun or pistol sighting.

It will work as well indoors as out and will accept miniatures of every target type and size. The mirror's slope can be altered in two different ways by manipulation of the wing nuts behind the springs which hold it in place. This permits an average-sized class to use one score card on the recording board

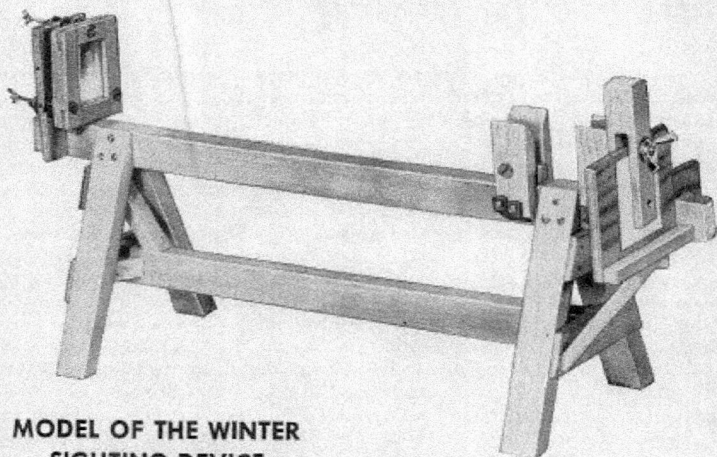

MODEL OF THE WINTER SIGHTING DEVICE

as the mirror can be shifted each time a new recruit commences a test and thus no two recruits will work on exactly the same spot.

Three separate exercises may be performed on the Winter Sighting Device. The instructor can explain and demonstrate each exercise and then have the men perform each of them. Instructors should closely supervise the exercises on the first go-around. After that they should leave it up to the men.

EXERCISE No. 1—CORRECT SIGHTING AND ADJUSTMENT OF EYEPIECE.

The instructor shows the assembled students a series of prepared cards which illustrate correct sight alignment. These should be drawn by the instructor to show first a picture of the peep sight; secondly the peep and front sights properly aligned; thirdly the peep, front sight and aiming mark all correctly in line.

He then demonstrates how to mount the rifle on the Winter Sighting Device and cautions the men that the clamps must be set up tight so the rifle will not shift its position when the shoulder is placed against the butt. The recruit must see the same sight picture each time he looks through the rear sights. This is the time of stressing the necessity of holding the eye exactly the same distance from the rear sight for successive shots when firing on the range.

The instructor explains next that the rifle is pointing into the mirror at the end of the bar and that the mirror will reveal the sight picture through the eyepiece. He indicates how the sights appear in correct alignment by moving the adjustable arm of the eyepiece. The instructor should then have each

122

pupil in turn, at this point, set up his rifle in the device, attach the eyepiece and adjust it for alignment.

EXERCISE No. 2—AIMING EXERCISE AND DOTTING PRACTICE.

The instructor next introduces the target into the sight picture by moving the yoke which controls the target. It is so moved that the target is brought into the mirror's field of view. He should draw attention, verbally, to the fact that he keeps adjusting the yoke until he can place the target so that its reflection rests upon the front sight, as seen through the optical centre of the peep sight.

At first use a tin hat or half-disc type of target of sufficient size to give the appearance of being actually 200 yards distant when viewed through the mirror and rear sight.

When correctly aligned the instructor demonstrates the Dotting Exercises. The recording board is prepared for this exercise by mounting a piece of paper or light card upon the side of the board nearest the operator. Thumb tacks will do the trick but Scotch or adhesive tape is much better in attaching the paper to the board.

The instructor now inserts the point of a finely sharpened pencil into the tapered hole in the near leg of the yoke. This causes a dot to be made upon the paper thus registering the correct alignment of sights and target reflection.

He then swings the yoke out of position thus moving the aiming mark out of

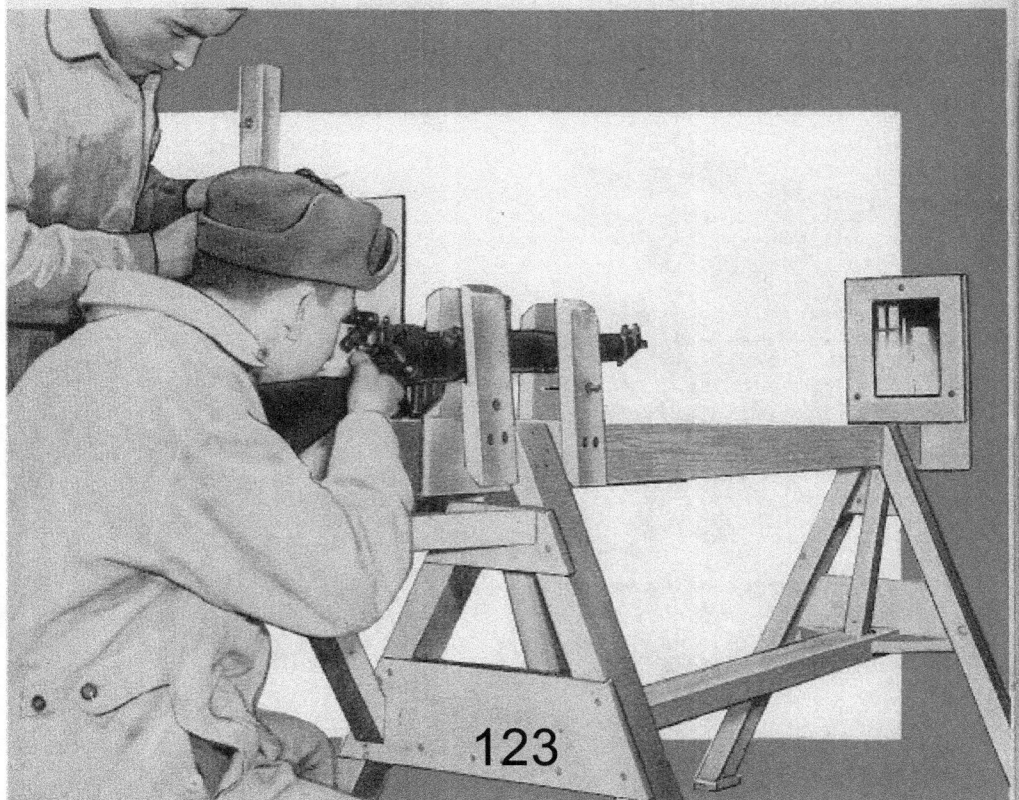

123

alignment with the front sight. Now he brings it back again, into perfect alignment with the front sight and makes a second dot. Before making that second dot, however, the instructor should stress the necessity of aligning the sights to the target IN EXACTLY THE SAME MANNER EVERY TIME A SHOT IS FIRED.

He then states that the second and each successive dot will demonstrate whether or not the recruit is attaining precision of sight pictures because if he aligns his sights upon the aiming mark in exactly the same way each consecutive time, the dots will be superimposed upon each other.

Five tries should result in some superimposed dots.

The exercise should be repeated until there are five consecutive dots superimposed upon the recording board. NO ERRORS will be permitted.

The pupils then carry on the exercise, the size of the cluster of each man's work giving a picture of his aiming ability.

EXERCISE No. 3—BATTLE PRACTICE.

Using the No. 4 rifle with the eyepiece and the battle-peep sight, have the recruit practice under the instructor's supervision correct sighting and aiming at suitable combat targets fitted to the device to simulate combat targets up to a range of 300 yards; a man crouching behind a bush at 200 yards or a kneeling man at 300 yards.

The instructor will be satisfied the recruit knows correct aim when his dotting cluster is made up of superimposed dots.

RECORDING BOARD

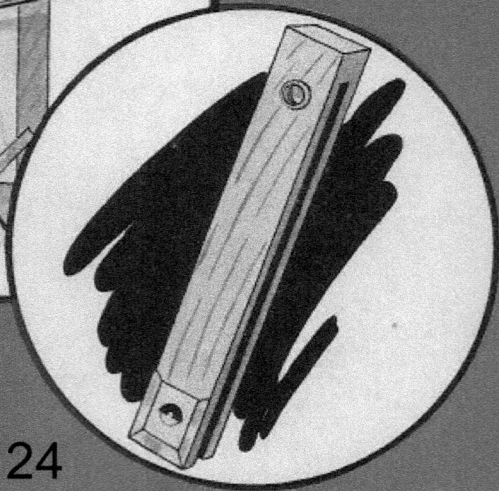

THE YOKE

124

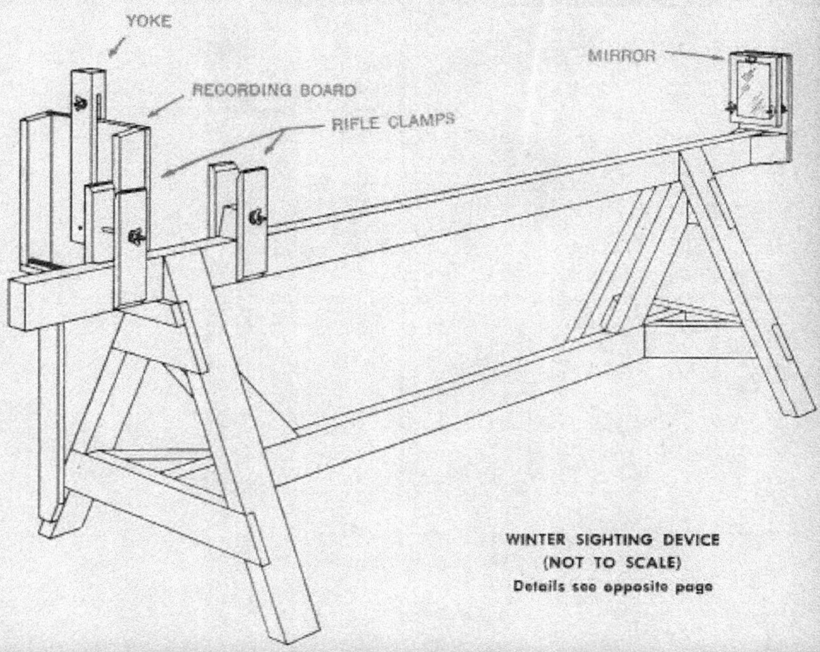
YOKE
RECORDING BOARD
RIFLE CLAMPS
MIRROR

WINTER SIGHTING DEVICE
(NOT TO SCALE)
Details see opposite page

MacLEAN EYEPIECE

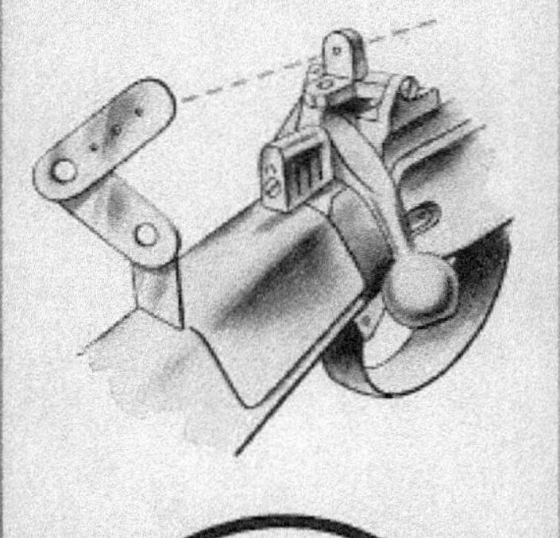

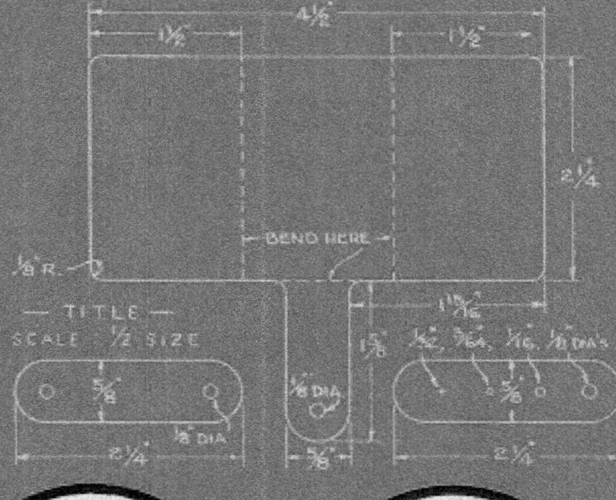
4½"
1½"
1½"
2¼"
BEND HERE
⅛ R.
1 15/16"
— TITLE —
SCALE ½ SIZE
5/8
1/8 DIA
2¼"
1/8 DIA.
1 5/8"
5/8"
1/32, 3/64, 1/16, 1/8 DIA'S
5/8
2¼"

APPLEYARD EYEPIECE

SPRING CLIP EYEPIECE

WARREN EYEPIECE

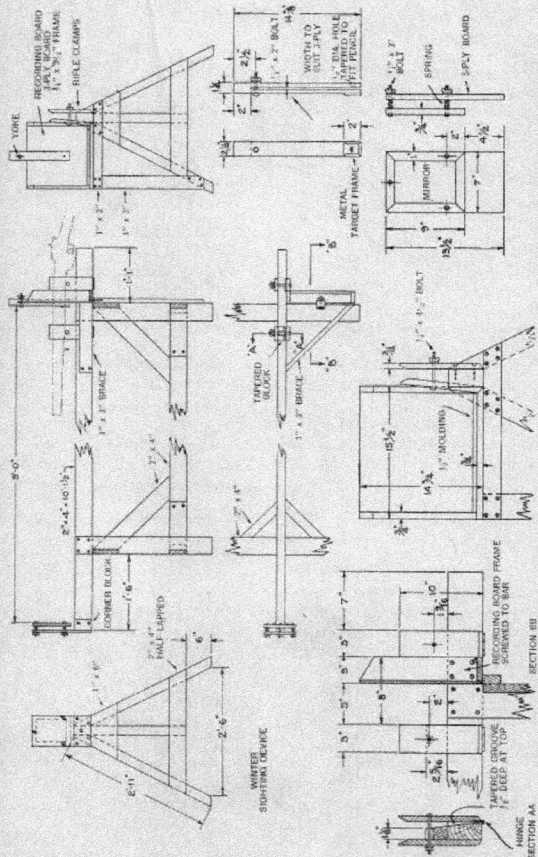

NEW RULES OF AIMING

AIMING a rifle has been a phase of good shooting that has been over-emphasized and kicked around a great deal, in the past. The arguments that have raged over the merits of various methods will not be dusted off for review here. The methods which have been outlined in this chapter will produce Aiming PRECISION providing the following rules are followed religiously:—

FORESIGHT—The tip of the front sight must be placed upon the point which the recruit wants his bullet to strike.

SIGHT PICTURE—The marksman must ALWAYS see the SAME sight picture.

OPTICAL CENTRE—The eye must automatically find the Optical Centre of the back sight and then focus its vision upon the knife-edged, square, clear tip of the foresight.

APERTURE—The marksman must look THROUGH the aperture of the back sight and NOT AT it.

PRECISION and PRACTICE—The recruit must understand precision of Aim and then practice it religiously.

Mr. Instructor you have a grave responsibility resting upon you. You must teach every member, of every class you are called upon to train, that thoroughness of aim and drive toward even more precise shooting is paramount just as even an ace golfer dreams of the day when he will be so expert he can tour an 18-hole course with 18 holes-in-one.

CHAPTER SIX

Trigger Control

TRIGGER Control is the top priority item in teaching expert shooting. There is nothing in this whole course that will reflect itself so much upon the expertness of the shooting, by your class, as will a thorough understanding of what Trigger Control is and the value of its constant use and practice.

Trigger Control is the manipulation of the trigger with such unqualified skill that you will not disturb, or impart any motion into, your rifle's front sight.

Too many recruits believe that the only way in which to fire a rifle is to grit the teeth, shut the eyes and jerk the trigger, letting the bullets fly where they may. This is a musketry crime. It can have no place in the minds of soldiers. There is only one way in which to release a rifle bolt properly and that is with a firm, controlled, slow, steady, deliberate and cumulative squeeze of the forefinger upon the trigger. All other methods are all wrong.

The soldier who lacks this kind of trigger control is hopelessly without the ability to steer bullets straight to the aiming point.

You have doubtless seen an unfortunate lad who hopefully jerked his trigger while the muzzle of his rifle vibrated. He was probably afraid of recoil and with muscular exertion gripped his rifle in the anticipation it would stay still. His only hope of registering a good shot—the kind all marksmen want—was to yank the trigger as the front sight went merrily dancing past the aiming mark.

The boy with this combination of problems needs your patient attention. He has not grasped the elements of the preceding principles of expert marksmanship and must be brought up-to-date with the rest of his class so that he is fully receptive to the fundamentals of Trigger Control. If, then, he learns what is wanted in the proper trigger squeeze, he will practice it diligently because he will feel that he is now on the right track.

The accepted considerations of the world's leading rifle shots have placed the importance of Trigger Control at almost twice the combined importance of all the other Basic Principles of shooting.

This may jar the pet theories of those who have accepted the older methods of teaching marksmanship BUT just as warfare has been modernized, so has been the business of using weapons. Just as the clumsy old tanks of 1914-18 have given away to the modern, fire-spitting behemoths of battle, so has old musketry style been superseded by up-to-date procedures.

The ace marksmen have determined that in the scale of relative importance Aiming only embraces five percent. Position, Holding and Breathing each demand but ten percent, or twice as much consideration, each, as Aiming. Hence, four of the five Basic Principles have only taken up 35 percent of the importance scale.

The balance of 65 percent has been given to Trigger Control. This is 13 times the amount awarded to Aiming and six and one-half times as much as to each of the other Basic Principles. Why is this?

No matter how expert one may be in the preliminary phases of good marksmanship, all this effort can be easily lost if faulty operation of the trigger causes aiming precision to be disturbed even the slightest.

The world's crack shots can be graded by means of their Trigger Control. The difference between poor and fair; fair and good; good and excellent; excellent and expert can all be judged by the skill which one class has over the others in keeping the rifle steady during Trigger Control.

No matter how well a recruit may be in position, may hold his rifle, may breathe properly, may aim with precision, he will not be able to shoot accurately every time unless and until he masters the steady, correct, deliberate squeeze of the trigger so that no motion registers upon the front sight as the bullet is sent speeding on its way.

How, then, can Trigger Control be mastered? The answer is: A thorough understanding of what trigger squeeze means and then practice, PRACTICE, *and more PRACTICE*

You don't learn to play the piano with five easy lessons. You learn it through constant practice. You wouldn't expect to take a mail order course in drafting and after reading the books set out to be a top-notcher in the field without practice.

When you left civilian life and entered the Army the squad drills were confusing and so, maybe, were some of the commands, too. But drill, which is practice by another name, gave you perfection.

If the world's champion riflemen, pistol shots and trap shooters regard practice as a daily requisite, the Canadian soldier must consider it is the solution to his eventual expertness on the battlefield. It is demanded and the recruit who does not practice it, is selling his life cheaply to the enemy through sheer, unadulterated carelessness and apathy.

But practice is never effective if it is boring. A recruit can only take so much of it. He can get mighty tired if it is imposed upon him for long periods. He will respond to two or three, five-minute practices of trigger squeeze a day but anything longer than that length, per period, will become tiresome to him and will implant a fast-growing germ of thought that trigger control is too monotonous and hard to learn.

The old adage "Practice Makes Perfect" never had a better application than in Trigger Control.

"HE KNEW HIS TRIGGER SQUEEZE!"

130

THE SQUEEZE

THE instructor must be patient with his class when teaching Trigger Control. It is not to be picked up by a recruit without much painstaking effort and practice. You can probably get across to him the general idea of what the trigger squeeze really is but you will be an extreme optimist if you believe that with just one or two demonstrations the recruit will be able to perfect it.

You cannot speed merrily past each phase of this basic principle of good shooting. You must take plenty of time and allow for much practice of each step as it is taught.

The erroneous impression which is entertained by many recruits that the trigger must be jerked, is an out-cropping of the silent movies, or the pupil's cap pistol days. When he takes his rifle into his hands he steels himself for an ordeal which he fears as much as an anti-typhus injection.

Again, the squeeze must be gentle, steady, cumulative and a building-up of pressure by the forefinger upon the trigger.

When you are giving your molars their morning maul and are squeezing the dentifrice out of its tube, you squeeze it and control it between your thumb and forefinger. You are gentle about it so that just the right amount for your needs will curl out onto your toothbrush. If you gripped it and gave an uncontrolled squeeze, big gobs of the stuff would squirt out to spatter you and your surroundings.

When you were a youngster you used to take a ripe cherry and gently squeeze it so that the pit would suddenly spurt out. You did not just know when that cherry stone would part company with the flesh. So it is when squeezing a trigger. You gently build up pressure not knowing when the striker will be released.

But the finger, by itself, cannot be expected to be steady unless it has a counter-pressure. The forefinger is one lever against another (the trigger) but in order to function properly it must work in counter direction to something else. Thus the thumb serves the latter purpose well, just as in squeezing toothpaste tubes and cherries.

How do the forefinger and thumb work together to produce the gentle squeeze that imparts no motion to the front sight before the bullet is fired?

Supposing you could affix a clamp so that one jaw was upon your forefinger as it rested in proper position upon the trigger and the upper jaw was on the thumb as it clasped the small of the butt. See the illustration, opposite. Should the thumb screw of the clamp be tightened slowly and with steady, continuous motion, the two jaws would move toward each other with equal, steadily-increasing pressure bringing with them the forefinger, trigger and thumb.

As this was done you would not know at what precise moment the clamp would be tightened to the point where the trigger was back far enough to release the bolt. It is that kind of steady pressure which is demanded of expert control.

The soldier who is trying to win the favour of his pet blonde doesn't slip his arm around her waist and give her a rib-cracking hug. She may like a "he man" but there are some limitations. He is, instead, gentle with her

131

and as his ardor is kindled he slowly increases the pressure until she asks whether they will have a military wedding or does he mind if she can't cook.

Taking up the slack of the trigger is an important factor in shooting. It is the safety or "get set" play which is as vital to rifle operation as the slack in your automobile's clutch or brake. If there wasn't slack in your clutch you would not be able to shift the gears of your car with the smoothness which you have mastered. If there was no slack in the brake pedal, a mere touch would give you no warning and you would be banged up against the windshield.

The slack is the means by which you prepare for the actual firing. It is the safety allowance. There isn't much slack to be taken up but there is just enough that if you were to continue to draw the trigger back, the firing pin would be released and the rifle would fire. When the race starter shouts to sprinters "On your mark! Get Set! GO!" the "get set" is the taking up of slack muscles. The trigger slack should always be taken up at the same time as the pre-firing sigh is given. It must be practiced diligently so that it is fully understood and mastered.

After the instructor has explained to his class the kind of squeeze that is demanded, he should have his recruit assume a prone firing position (which by now should be perfect) and close his eyes. Then the recruit should take up the slack as he gives his sigh. The closed eyes will permit the recruit to concentrate upon the squeeze without distraction and enable him to understand the type of squeeze that is wanted.

A false notion of rifle shooting is that a marksman must anticipate the precise moment that the bullet is discharged from the rifle. This is unnecessary and very wrong. If you try to break a glass rod by slowly increasing pressure of your fingers, you cannot judge the exact moment in which it will snap in two.

The belief that you must determine the instant when the bullet will be discharged is born out of faulty position, holding, breathing and aiming. The recruit whose front sight is cutting fancy capers endeavors to figure out when the front sight will be going past the aiming point. Thus he tries to calculate his fire for that precise moment. The recruit who does this is an almost hopeless failure and will require a great deal of attention from the instructor. Note the three steps of squeezing a trigger and the action of the mechanism, in Figures 1, 2 and 3, opposite.

But let us analyze the way in which the expert marksman performs. His position, holding, breathing and aiming are ideal. He knows that he doesn't have to estimate just when the bullet will be discharged. He is concerned with steadying the rifle so that it is dead upon the aiming point as he builds up the squeezing pressure on the trigger. He is aware of the fact that if he concentrates upon his front sight, the bullet will land upon the aiming mark if he doesn't jar the rifle in releasing the firing pin.

He is determined that he is going to hit the aiming point and if he doesn't get the steadiness he desires, starts over again with a fresh sigh. When his rifle stays dead upon the aiming point and the pressure is slowly building up he knows that the rifle will do the rest.

Figure 1 shows the trigger mechanism when cocked. Figure 2 shows it after the slack has been taken up and in Figure 3 the bolt has been released.

133

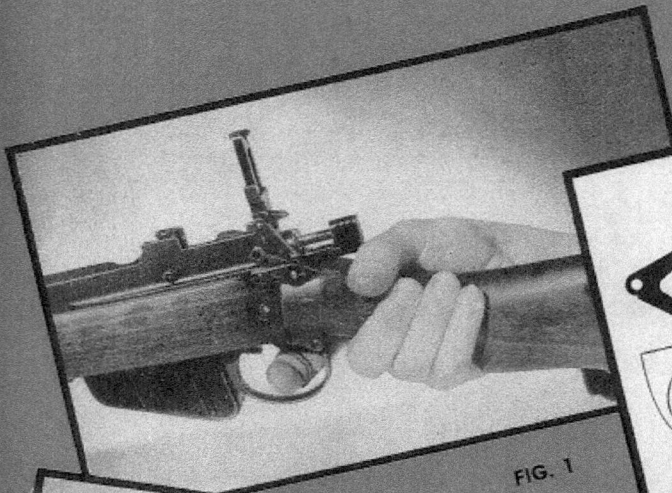
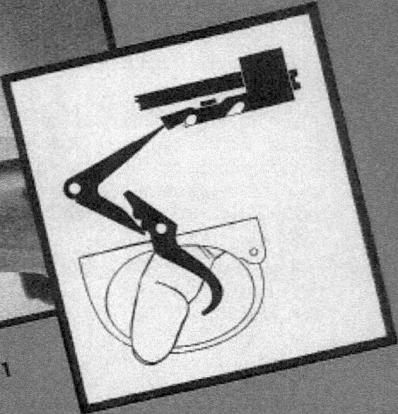

FIG. 1

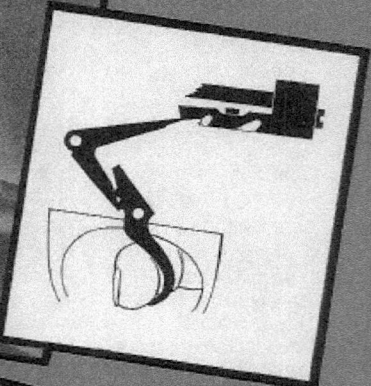

FIG. 2

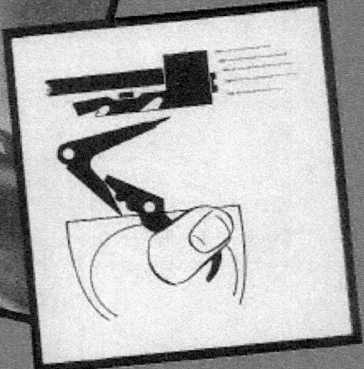

FIG. 3

FIG. 1

135

There is not too much space with which to play, between each phase, so that the few seconds that are involved in perfect trigger squeeze bring scoring dividends.

The squeeze of the trigger is so important that the coach must demonstrate and check—check and demonstrate and then insist upon practice so that there will never be a question that the lesson has not been well and truly learned.

While the pupil is in the firing position with his eyes closed, the coach should place his hand over the shooting hand of the pupil with his forefinger upon the trigger finger of the recruit (see Figure 1, opposite). The slack should then be taken up and the instructor should then apply the correct squeezing pressure upon the thumb and forefinger. This MUST be painstakingly done a minimum of five times until the recruit knows the kind of action you want.

If there are other members of the class they should observe the pressure marks upon the top of the recruit's thumb and the top of the trigger finger as the coach's hand is removed. These will be marked by white spots with forced-out blood rushing back into the cells under the skin.

The recruit should now practice so that as the rifle is steadied by the sigh, the thumb and forefinger are contracted toward each other slowly, steadily and with determination. This effort must not be erratic nor jerky and without any stuttering pressure which would impart unwanted tremble to the rifle's front sight. The increase of pressure must be as smooth and as steady as the well-oiled, finely-threaded thumbscrew of a clamp that is slowly and continuously tightened.

Now you should let your class practice in pairs. They will fight it out among themselves and you can go from pair to pair, carefully checking their drill.

CHECKING RECRUITS' TRIGGER CONTROL

THE coach cannot exercise too much care in making certain that every pupil he teaches understands and practices Trigger Control. The reliable method of gaining assurance that the recruit does know what is meant by the proper squeeze is in the instructor taking the prone firing position and having the recruit apply the squeeze.

This is actually a reversal of the demonstration (Figure 2) in which the recruit was in the firing position.

Have the recruit place his hand over yours and then apply the proper trigger squeeze (see Figure 2, opposite). When he can do it correctly five consecutive times, he is on the road toward learning Trigger Control.

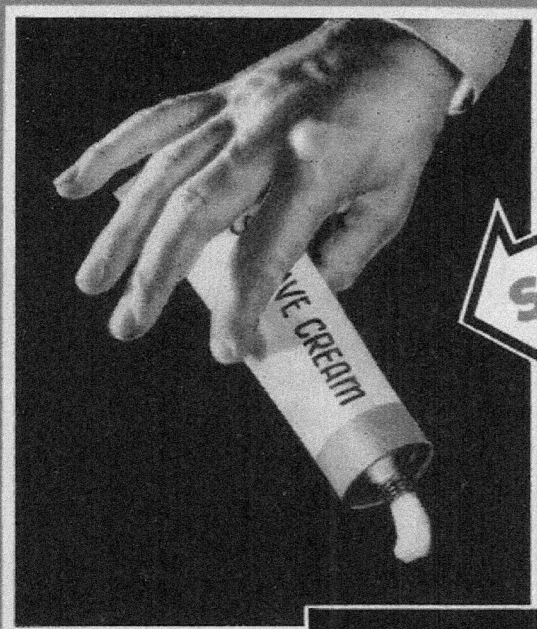

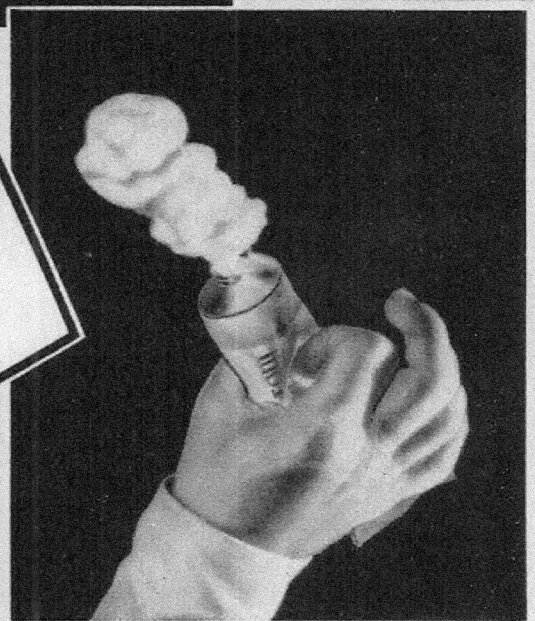

137

"SQUEEZING? HECK HONEY, I'M ONLY TAKING UP THE SLACK!"

DIRECTION OF TRIGGER MOVEMENT

THE trigger must be drawn backward and upward at an angle of 45 degrees. It is the natural way for the trigger to move because of the manner in which the hand has gripped the small of the butt with the forefinger around the trigger.

If a heavy weight were to be lifted vertically and also drawn backward by equal pressure, the weight would move upward and backward together, at an angle of 45 degrees to the ground level. The same angle prevails in the drawing, in a combined upward and backward movement, of the trigger.

The recruit should practice this movement at least ten times, at this juncture in the course.

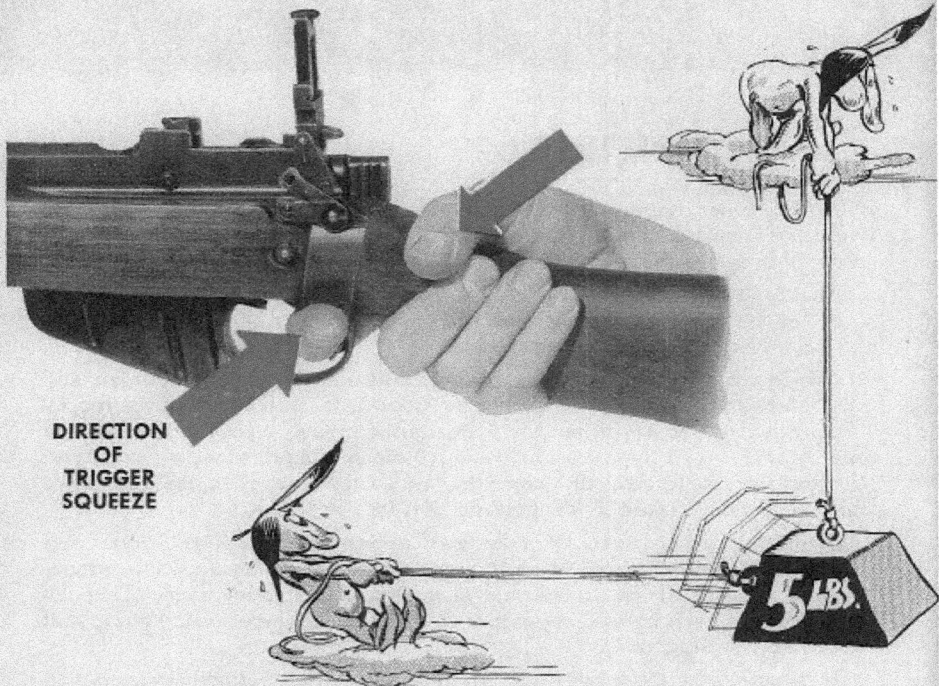

DIRECTION
OF
TRIGGER
SQUEEZE

139

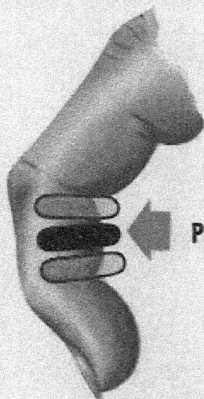

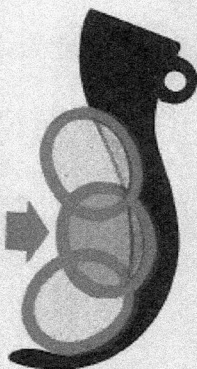

POSITION CORRECT ➤

POSITION OF FINGER
ON TRIGGER

FIG. 1   FIG. 2

FINGER ON TRIGGER

AS THE index finger must pass at right angles over the curved trigger, the position of the finger must be such that the marksman will get the maximum of pressure and control with it.

The tip of the forefinger has little muscular control and is unsteady. Similarly the section of the finger closest to the body of the hand is limited in its movement so it cannot be used because of lack of flexibility.

The logical position would be halfway between the tip of the finger and the hand or upon the middle section or link. It is not meant that the recruit should deliberately try to put the finger in the creases between the first and second sections, or the crease between the second and third sections. Rather, the trigger should naturally come to rest somewhere upon the second or middle section. There it will perform best (see Figure 1, above).

Similarly the finger should be midway between the top of the trigger and the tip. If it were at the top of the trigger there would be insufficient leverage, while if it rested at the tip it would have uncontrollable leverage. Thus the midway position is best. Note Figure 2, showing the finger in the curve that has been provided for it.

In other words, the trigger and the finger should be perfectly crossed.

APPLICATION OF TRIGGER CONTROL

WHEN the principles of Trigger Control have been taught and practiced in small doses at frequent intervals, the instructor should encourage his class to determine the degree of control by the fact that during the squeeze, the less movement there is apparent in the front sight, the closer the recruits are to having perfect trigger control.

This calls for careful treatment by the instructor because he must get his men to focus their Master Eyes upon the front sights. The instructor should know that frequent practice of this focus upon the front sight while the trigger is being squeezed lays the foundation for "Calling Your Shots". It makes the recruit keep his aiming eye open not only while aiming but also when the rifle is being discharged. It defeats flinching.

Practice of this exercise should be done at least ten times and you can explain merely that the purpose of the drill is in being able to discharge the rifle so that no movement is imparted into the front sight. Good shooting demands this kind of control.

It seems to be a habit of front sights to want to wander. They can be placed directly under the auxiliary aiming mark, yet just when you would like to squeeze the trigger a little more, they shift off to one side or to the other. This is invariably caused by improper, jerky, stuttering, unsteady trigger squeeze. Note Figure 1, opposite, which shows a wandering front sight while Figure 2 is the result of such wandering when registered upon the target.

The good shot who encounters this bit of difficulty will know from experience that if his position and automatic alignment are both correct and if his elevation is correct due to the application of major and minor adjustments, the sight which wandered off the aiming mark will, if given time, wander right back to where it naturally should come to rest.

The expert who has taken up the trigger slack and is slowly and steadily applying the trigger squeeze does not relax his finger and start over again. He knows that if he did this on the battlefield he would waste much time— time that might provide the difference to him between life and death.

Thus the expert, not knowing the precise moment at which the rifle is to be discharged, pauses. He doesn't increase the pressure and he doesn't relax it. He just exerts complete control of his finger so that he can wait for the sight to wander right back to where it naturally should come to rest. Then he commences to increase the clamp-like pressure on the trigger, steadily again. In other words he only builds up the finger pressure upon the trigger when the front sight is at rest and points exactly to the spot he wants his bullet to hit.

141

FIG. 1

WANDERING FRONT SIGHT

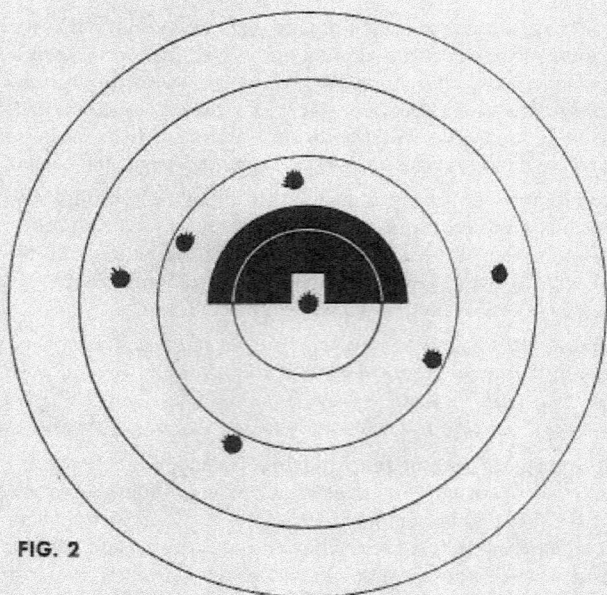

FIG. 2

ITS RESULT

149

142

FOLLOW THROUGH FOILS GREMLINS

143

FOLLOW THROUGH

THE baseball player whamming out a home run whips the bat around and after it collides with the ball it continues its swing. This is known as "Follow Through" and helps to steer the ball directly over the left field fence. The golfer, the bowler, the hockey player, the curler and the tennis star all practice Follow Through because it is the steadying, steering influence.

So there is Follow Through in shooting, too. It consists of keeping the front sight upon the aiming mark during the trigger squeeze and after the firing pin has been released. The tendency of many recruits is to let all their effort to achieve perfect aim be relaxed. They seem to say to themselves, "Well, I got that one away, so why worry?"

The marksman does not know the precise moment that his trigger squeeze is going to cause the firing pin to be released. So he cannot judge the precise moment when he should relax. Then, too, it takes but a fraction of a second for that firing pin to whip up to the cartridge, ignite the priming charge and start the bullet on its way. It takes another fraction of a second for the priming charge to ignite the cordite and still another fraction of a second for the bullet to leave from a standing start and yet another fraction of a second for it to move from its chamber up the length of the muzzle.

Therefore, it is cold logic that if the rifle must have perfect control before the firing pin is released then there should be the same, co-ordinated control during the accumulated fractions of a second when the mechanics of the rifle and bullet do their part.

Hence the Follow Through provides that steadying influence which good shooting demands. It is the maintenance of the rifle upon the aiming mark prior to the rifle's discharge and continuing through and after the mechanics of the discharge.

Experts constantly practice

their follow through.

144

CHECKING FOLLOW THROUGH

AN EXCELLENT exercise has been developed for checking Follow Through and it has been found that two-man teams are best when it is used. It pays big dividends. Instructors should study the illustration at Figure 1, before proceeding.

Have one man of the team get into the firing position. Then offer the second man of the team a thin sheet of foolscap-sized paper on which pencil lines have been vertically and horizontally drawn through the centre of the sheet to form a cross. See Figure 2, opposite.

At the top the word "Up" is marked, at the bottom is marked "Down" and at the right and left sides "Right" and "Left" are shown respectively from the firer's point of view. It would be well for the feet of the firer to point toward the light, as the movement of the silhouette or shadow of the muzzle upon the paper will be used for checking.

Before going any further with the exercise, this is an ideal place for a brief lecture on Safety First. Have the second man of each team insist upon seeing to his complete satisfaction that the rifle is not loaded. He is going to be sitting or lying right opposite the business end of that muzzle and he is entitled to know that there is NO AMMUNITION in the rifle. The firer should check and so should his helper. This will be a perfect opportunity for them to realize the importance of careful measures in avoiding accidents.

With the helper directly in front of the muzzle, he holds the paper so that the tip of the foresight is directly lined up with the centre of the crossed lines, which serve as a guide for the firer in detecting any movement of the front sight upon the release of the firing pin of the unloaded rifle. See Figure 3.

The muzzle of the rifle will now appear to the helper as a round disc, on the reverse, and unmarked side of the paper. As the pre-firing sigh is taken, the muzzle's silhouette will be shown moving upon the paper. See Figure 4.

The firer now takes his careful aim and his steadying breath and as he commences the slow, steady squeeze the firing pin will be suddenly released. If there is any visible movement it will be quickly apparent to the helper but it should also have been seen by the firer.

The helper must NOT call the shots. The firer MUST call his own and the helper should either confirm or reject the call. The firer should practice this until he can call nine out of ten consecutive shots correctly. The team should then reverse positions and repeat so that all the class will get the benefit of the exercise. If the instructor wishes he may select a recruit and give a demonstration of this test of Follow Through before assigning the exercise to the class.

FIG. 1

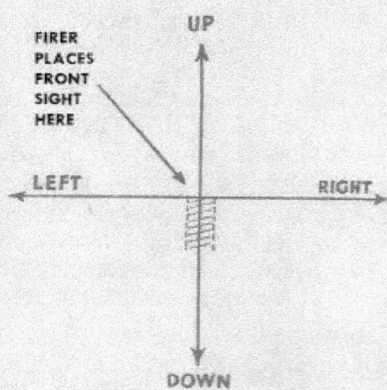

FIRER PLACES FRONT SIGHT HERE

UP

LEFT

RIGHT

DOWN

SHOT Nº	CENTRE	L	R	D	U
1			✓		
2		✓			
3		✓			
4	✓				
5					✓
6				✓	
7		✓			
8					✓
9			✓		
10		✓			
SCORE	1	4	2	1	2

FIG. 2

FIG. 3
FIRER'S VIEW

146

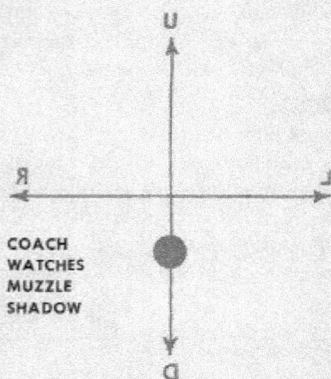

U

Я

L

COACH WATCHES MUZZLE SHADOW

D

FIG. 4
COACHES' VIEW

CALLING THE SHOTS

CALLING the shots as indicated in the Method of Checking Follow Through is the standard by which you indicate your expertness. It is the proot by which the recruit can attain the "professional" touch to his shooting.

If you fire a shot and don't know what happened then how can you correct any mistakes you may have made? Supposing you aim at the auxiliary aiming mark of a target and plant your bullet at 10 o'clock, how will you ever be able to correct your error if you don't know what you did wrong?

The expert marksman always knows where his bullets are going to land because he knows whether the foresight of his rifle moved or not. If it didn't move, then the bullet will be right on the aiming point. If it moved, he will be able to correct his faulty trigger control for the next shot. He is able to do this because he has focussed his whole attention upon the front sight and has kept it there all during the firing process.

If you cannot call your shots correctly it means you did not know where the sights were pointing when the rifle was fired. In other words you closed your eyes and fired afterwards.

The illustrations opposite show what happens when you squeeze and call your shots correctly.

Squeezing the trigger correctly and the ability to call your shots properly are two extremely important rules of good shooting.

147

FLINCHED

GUESSED

SQUEEZED

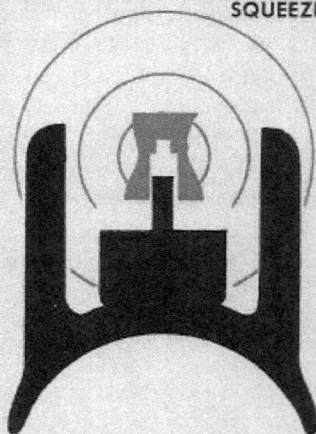

CALLED

MISSED

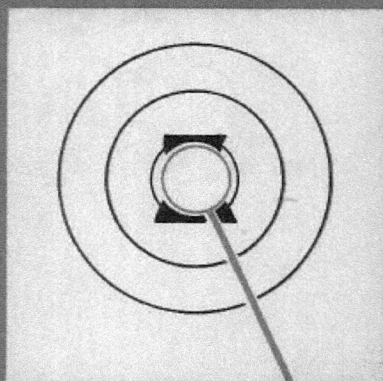

BULL'S EYE

TRIGGER SOLITAIRE

ONE of the best practice methods is called Trigger Solitaire. This little game calls for the honesty of the pupils just as playing solitaire with cards demands no cheating. It can be played in off-duty hours with the butt of the rifle resting upon the lap and the muzzle pointing upwards. Note the illustration of Trigger Solitaire, opposite.

The squeezing of the trigger *after the slack has been taken up* constitutes the game. By watching the tip of the finger to see any movement of it during the build-up of pressure you can determine whether you have scored or not.

If you cannot see any movement of the finger tip between the slack and the release of the striker, you have won a goal. If you do see movement you have lost a goal.

A game consists of five squeezes and at first you should get at least three out of five. With practice this should come up to perfect scoring every time.

CHECKING FRONT SIGHT

JUST as in Trigger Solitaire there is a valuable practice trick for all riflemen, whether they be recruits or experts. It consists of getting down into a prone position and practicing the release of the firing pin five consecutive times without the front sight moving even the slightest.

It may seem like a silly routine to the "know-it-all" but to the recruit who is anxious to succeed and become a crack shot there need not be much coaxing. The piano player or the opera singer spends many hours practicing the diatonic and chromatic scales. If a musical virtuoso needs such routine practice then the rifle virtuoso must similarly practice.

Twice a day—during off-duty periods—will go far toward producing that expertness of Trigger Control which will bring dividends in confident shooting. Keep the practice periods down to ten consecutive shots, each time.

149

THIS IS
"TRIGGER
SOLITAIRE"

How to Fire Bullets and Influence the Enemy

As your Mother bakes delicious pies,
And the growing baby louder cries,
And your best girl rolls her big, blue eyes—
It's practice, Brothers, *PRACTICE!*

As the golfer breaks more tricky pars,
And the salesman sells more shiny cars,
And the drunkard darkens all-night bars—
It's practice, Brothers, *PRACTICE!*

As the MP growls "Show me yer pass!"
And the brindle cow seeks greener grass,
And admiring ankles you shout "Some class!"
It's practice, Brothers, *PRACTICE!*

So here we've given the basic rules
Of using the marksmen's battle tools.
Follow them well and don't be fools.
Just practice, Brothers, *PRACTICE!*

COIN GAMES

PERFECT Trigger Control can be approached by placing coins and an empty .22 calibre shell upon the foresight posts. The coins should be of 50, 25, 5 and 10 cent denominations.

Placing the coins, one at a time upon the two posts protecting the front sight, have each recruit squeeze the trigger to release the firing pin five consecutive times without the coin falling. A miss means that the recruit must start over again.

It is best to work these tests in pairs. As one man engages in the test the other should place the coin in position, removing it only to permit the firer to cock the weapon and then replacing it.

As the 50-cent piece is mastered the recruit should rest and allow his associate to try it. Then the first firer should try the 25-cent coin while the helper rests and so on until the five-cent piece and the dime have stayed in place for five consecutive shots each. Note Figures 1A, 1B, 1C and 1D, opposite.

IT IS ESSENTIAL THAT THE RECRUIT REST BETWEEN COIN TESTS.

Now to make it especially certain that the firer can hold his rifle steady and exert the correct pressure upon the trigger, place an empty .22 shell upon the top of the muzzle as in Figure 2. Make certain that it will remain there for five consecutive shots.

If he wants to vary the location of the shell he can select sites as indicated in Figure 3. These are somewhat more difficult.

TRIGGER CONTROL GAMES

FIG. 1-A

FIG. 1-B

FIG. 1-C

FIG. 1-D

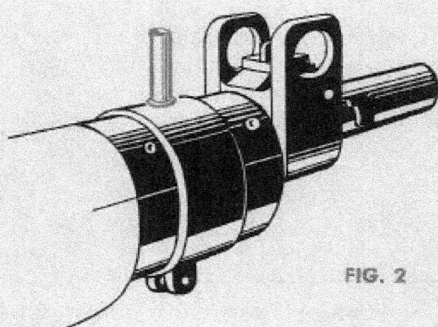

FIG. 2

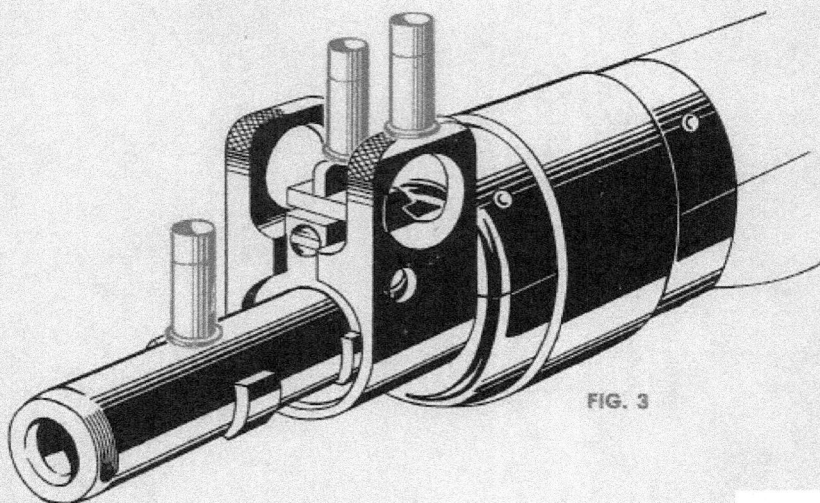

FIG. 3

RECAPITULATION

SUMMING up Trigger Control, the points to stress and practice, practice and stress and then practice again, are:—

1.—Trigger Control occupies 65 percent of the importance scale of Good Marksmanship and is thirteen times as important as Aiming.

2.—Practice of Trigger Control is a first, last and always requisite but it must be taken in easy and frequent doses.

3.—The trigger slack must be taken up first.

4.—The trigger squeeze must be slow, steady and cumulative like a thumb-screw. It must not be jerky, stuttering or unsteady.

5.—Don't try to anticipate when the firing pin will be released.

6.—The middle of the forefinger should rest upon the middle of trigger so that both will operate to the best leverage advantage.

7.—The trigger should be drawn backward and upward at a 45 degree angle to the axis of the rifle.

8.—The trigger squeeze should be so steady that it will not jar the front sight, the slightest. If the front sight does wander, the forefinger should pause before continuing to increase the squeeze.

9.—Understand and practice Follow Through and learn to accurately call your shots,

and

Practice Every Day!—

—Several Times a Day!

CHAPTER SEVEN

Co-ordination

THE hockey team that plays with complete teamwork wins the championship. There must be complete harmony among the members of the organization, each being thoroughly trained by an expert coach to do the specific job to which he is assigned.

The goal tender must know precisely how to stop all the opponent's shots. The two defence men must know when and how to body check or to seize the puck for glorious, thrill-inspiring rushes down the ice. The centre must be the rover who is all over the skating surface and the two wing men must know how to share the puck with others who are on the team and be able to make passes within their on-side lines. They must all be precise and on-the-button with every play.

Let us pretend that you and your rifle constitute a hockey team which we will call the "Basic Principle All-Stars". The rifle can be the goal tender because it is the means by which goals should not be scored against you. We will put Correct Position and Good Holding at the two defence positions because they are the solid types. Then we will put Trigger Control at centre ice because he is the key man of the whole team. The two P-Boys, Precise Aim and Proper Breathing, will be on the wings. "Sarj." Instructor will be the manager-coach. And let us further pretend that we are playing the "Enemy Six". The championship is at stake, and this is the last period of the series' last game and the score stands at "0-0".

Will your team work as such or will there be a weak member? Will every player do his own job, perfectly and precisely? Will they work smoothly, together?

They will act as a CO-ORDINATED whole. They won't be individualists, each trying to do a job in his own way. They will make every play precisely the same way each time. They will come down the ice, always in the same correct spot to give and receive passes. They will work together with the mechanical exactness of finely-tooled gears.

In shooting, the five Basic Principles must all function together, in exactly the same way for each shot, in order to produce perfect teamwork. This is easier to say than to do but every little trick about perfect position must be done automatically. Everything about perfect holding must be done just right. The proper sigh must be correctly taken as if it were the most natural thing to do. You must aim with precision and then you must squeeze the trigger gently, steadily and deliberately when your front sight is perfectly directed to the point where you want your bullets to hit.

If you can do all these, in the same way for each of five consecutive shots, your five bullets will make clustered holes upon the target so close together they can be covered by the unpointed end of an average lead pencil.

BUT just let down a little bit on one of these Basic Principles. Get careless with the position of the elbows (like the hockey wing man who is not in position to take a pass). Or fail to place the butt of your rifle against the shoulder muscle pad. Forget to properly place your head upon and against the butt. Pass up the backward pressure of your two hands. Miss the steadying sigh. Fail to focus your Master Eye through the aperture of the back sight to the tip of the front sight (just like the centre player who after a brilliant rush down the ice shoots the puck wide of the goal). Or neglect any one of the many of things you have been taught to do and your shots will go wild. You may be perfect on three or four shots but if you missed one little item, no matter how seemingly insignificant or unimportant it appears, then you can expect an Orphan Annie on your target card.

> YOU MUST DO EVERYTHING YOU HAVE BEEN TAUGHT TO DO AND NOTHING MORE NOR LESS. YOU MUST DO IT IN THE SEQUENCE IN WHICH IT WAS TAUGHT TO YOU AND IN EXACTLY THE SAME WAY EACH TIME, SO THAT IT WILL BE PERFECTLY PUT TOGETHER INTO ONE, COMPLETE SERIES OF MACHINE-LIKE, PRECISIONED OPERATIONS, BLENDING TOGETHER TO BECOME ONE WHOLE.

Miss one and you have missed them ALL.

CORRECT USE OF SANDBAGS

SAND BAGS are provided for recruits in their preliminary learning of good shooting and in their range work. They serve to steady the lower half of the left forearm, only. The fact that an embryo marksman spends tedious periods in the prone firing position necessitates this consideration of his comfort and welfare.

As his ability to shoot properly is slowly acquired, the need for the sandbag will diminish. He won't have a caddie or a busboy running around after him with a sandbag when he gets onto the battlefield although he may find support for his left forearm in the natural characteristics of his slit trench.

In the heat of battle he won't take time to seek some object to rest his elbow against because the muscles of his arms will be so sufficiently well conditioned that he can fire accurately with or without such assistance.

The sandbag should contain from one-half to three-quarters of its capacity of earth. The bag should be tied tightly at the top of the sack so as to provide a looseness to the shape which the bag will take.

If you will note Figure 1, below, the bag has to be placed to FIT THE MAN — NOT the man's whole position altered to fit the bag. The forearm and elbow should be partly surrounded by the bag which should be shaped like an over fat letter "U". In fact it should look somewhat like a pair of inflated water wings.

The wrist and hand *MUST NOT TOUCH* the sandbag or rest upon it. Anyone who pulls that bogey on you is a gremlin. Don't fall for it. The bag only steadies the LOWER part of the left forearm.

FIG. 1

157

THE SANDBAG
SHOULD BE "U"
SHAPED, AND

NOT TOO
FULL!

THE SANDBAG IS USED TO
SUPPORT THE FOREARM—
NOT TO CARRY
YOUR RIFLE!

165

158

THE TWO-FOOT CIRCLE

THERE is only one place where the coach can do his job efficiently when his pupil is on the range and that is to be as close as possible to the pupil without interfering with his shooting.

The correct place is down beside your recruit so that his head and shoulders are enclosed within an imaginary circle, two feet in diameter and centered approximately at the firer's right hand.

Note Figures 1 and 2 opposite to see the application of this circle to good coaching. Figure 1 portrays the location of the circle while Figure 2 shows the coach's position with respect to the circle.

In this way you are close enough to the recruit to *lightly* place your hand upon his shoulder and check for body tensions, position and breathing rhythm.

You are close enough to him to permit you to check his pre-firing sigh, his trigger squeeze and the performance of his eyes during the sighting and firing process.

You will be able, also, to observe whether he flinched or blinked. You will be able to check his backward pressure, his head and chin pressure and most of the vital phases of the preliminary training which you have given him.

Moreover you are near enough to give him words of advice and encouragement which will put him on the proper track toward becoming a good marksman. Remember, this recruit is now trying to put into effect all you have taught him and he will need your quiet, patient help.

The two-foot circle also permits you to keep a check and call card, a most valuable aid to good coaching but which will be explained in the chapter "Target Analysis".

> *The two-foot circle is the*
>
> *proving ground.*

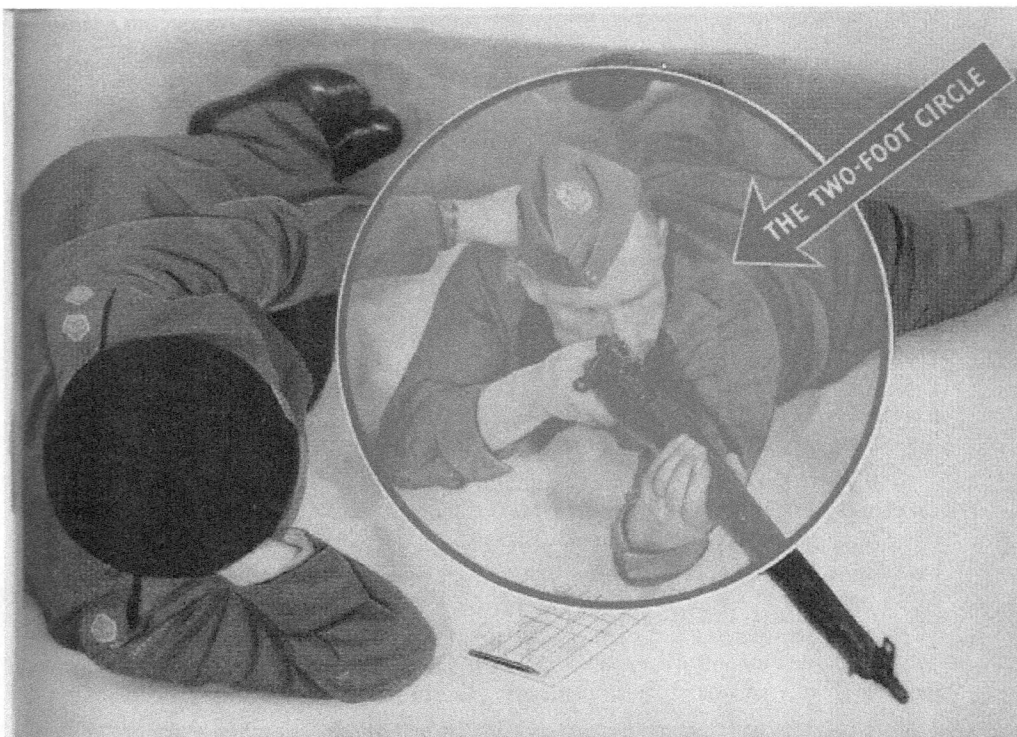

THE TWO-FOOT CIRCLE

FIG. 1

160

FIG. 2 — POSITION OF COACH AND PUPIL

To Instructors!

The preceding chapters have dwelt solely with the teaching of perfect Marksmanship. They have contained the material which should be taught to the classes of recruits.

All the phases as outlined in the chapters dealing with Basic Musketry Principles have been carefully presented in text and illustrated material.

The following chapters are given solely for your benefit. They will provide you with the information which, with serious application, will give you that expertness all keen instructors continually seek.

The material which follows is for YOU only and is NOT to be taught to your classes. The only exception to this is in the teaching of Rapid Fire and Snap-Shooting which is an advanced phase of musketry.

The following chapters give the methods by which your course can be successfully presented and then accurately appraised.

—THE AUTHOR.

CHAPTER EIGHT

The Range

BY NOW you have skilled your recruit in the essential training of good shooting, as developed through the five basic principles. You have taught him just the same as an athletic coach skills his team in the fundamentals of a game. You, as the musketry coach, are now prepared to put your men to the test of a practice game. Their abilities in this test will indicate their relative abilities for that bigger contest, which is in coming face to face with a ruthless enemy.

Probably your class of recruits won't show it, but they will be extremely keen to get onto the range, whether it be miniature or .303. It is their big moment and deep down inside each one of them there is that sporting instinct which urges them to show you, and the rest of the class, what expert shooting looks like.

R·I·P

"HE DIDN'T KNOW IT WAS LOADED"

162

There will be a few skeptics in the class, who may not be too sure of the results as shown on the targets. They will probably be the members of the class who have had to alter a variety of misapprehensions about their shooting. They have had to learn the hard way to get rid of bad shooting habits.

Just as the baseball or football coach tells his men to "Get out there and play ball", a word of encouragement to your men to "Get out there and shoot top scores", will give them added incentive to produce well drilled bull's eyes. Let them all feel that you are keenly interested in how they perform. Be sincerely their coach.

Your actual teaching of marksmanship has ended but your COACHING has just begun. If you are coaching a boy on the range, do it whole-heartedly. Make sure that you put all your knowledge of good shooting into the job. Later on, instruction will be given as to the correct methods of scoring targets, analyzing them and passing on to the recruits the advice and recommendations which will further improve their musketry skill.

SAFETY FIRST

PROBABLY the most pathetic words ever spoken are those much-too-often used "I didn't know it was loaded." This feeble excuse, after someone has been killed through ignorance or carelessness in the operation of firearms, is on a par with the smart Aleck who rocks the boat, speeds his car recklessly through crowded streets or fools with a light switch while taking a bath.

An Army rifle is no toy. It is a wartime comrade to be respected. No matter how much you care for it, that weapon still deserves the respect you would give to a gallon of nitro-glycerine or a sleeping rattlesnake.

Impress upon your recruit before he goes to the range that accidents are CAUSED. They don't just HAPPEN. Range training will overcome the ignorance that causes accidents and range discipline will deal with the carelessness. The coach must exercise extreme caution at all times by teaching his men the right way of using firearms and then insisting that his lessons are strictly followed. Courts of inquiry are sticky affairs when the rifle coach cannot explain away the fact that he was careless himself by permitting carelessness by his men.

When on the .22 range, no one should be down or near the rifles while targets are being placed or adjusted. Instead, rifles should be left lying upon sandbags and pointing down the range with the bolts OPEN. This is an extra safety measure and should be followed up by prohibiting anyone from touching a rifle while anyone else is in front of the muzzle. Neither should the coach, himself, get in front of the muzzle while adjusting a sandbag. When the CEASE FIRE order is given, all firers must open the bolts of their rifles and remove their hands from the weapons.

When using the .303 range, the coach should insist upon the use of the "pull through" in all rifles to clear out grease and obstructions. Sights should then be carefully cleaned and blackened. The rifle should then be left, with bolts open, upon the sandbags. They should point down the range.

Leave the bolt open until the order has been given to fire. However, if there is a sandstorm at the time of the shoot, common sense should dictate as to the advisability of keeping the bolt open, having in mind, of course, serious consideration of complete and unqualified safety measures.

CHAPTER NINE

Target Analysis

ONE of the most interesting phases of musketry coaching is the ability to accurately read, understand and speak the Language of Bullet Holes. Having taught your recruit the fundamentals of shooting you must be prepared to determine, accurately, the progress which your recruit makes from his targets. Of course, it is the measuring stick upon which you can establish your own ability as a coach.

The Language of Bullet Holes is to good shooting what half-time is to football. The gridiron coach who has sweated it out all week teaching the plays for the big game, uses the rest period midway in the game as the opportunity for a general review of his team's playing style.

While the players suck on oranges and have their damp, grimy faces wiped by the trainers the coach paces up and down the dressing room, praising the good points of the play and correcting the faults he has noted. He wants his team to win during the last half and his knowledge of the game assists him in telling his gridders how to effectively play the last half.

The same applies in shooting. You, the coach, must be able to study the cause for each shot but you must also be able to study the effect. This calls for analysis of your recruit's shooting style as you watch him within the two-foot circle. It also calls upon you to analyze the bullet holes upon the target to determine what steps are necessary for improvement.

This is known as Target Analysis. It is the study of the effect of your recruit's shooting done under your coaching. It provides you with that half-time opportunity to encourage, correct and improve the shooting of your men. It is the time when progress can become startlingly apparent.

All bullets should be clustered in the same small area. Any other kind of shooting is not good enough for the Canadian Army.

The super sleuth of the Metropolitan police department is called to the scene of what appears to be an obvious suicide. The shapely, beautiful blonde body lies on the floor with a Colt automatic in one hand, a suicide note in the other and powder burns on her temple. An odor of alcohol and some cigar ashes on the inner side of a highball glass suggest that she had been given a Mickey Finn. But the whole picture doesn't point to suicide. Expert observation of the clues is needed.

The crime expert checks up on cigarette butts in an ash tray near the glass. Close to the body are more cigarette butts with a slightly different shade of lipstick apparent than was shown upon those in the ash tray. A flustered smoothy and a hard-faced brunette, whose tears do not seem too real, bemoan the suicide. The detective has quickly observed the peculiar red of the brunette's lipstick. It is different than what is to be seen on the dead girl's lips. And there are cigar ashes on the blue serge vest of the droopy male. So the sleuth blasts the alibis of the pair who had claimed they came into the the room to find the blonde dead. He arrested them both because he was able to quickly sum up the evidence before him.

You as the coach of musketry must be the detective of bullet-hole clues. Expert study of a target will provide the opportunity to tell your recruit exactly and scientifically what is wrong with his shooting. You are the crime expert who arrests faulty firing habits. Like a good policeman you are interested in preventing crime and in the Canadian Army poor rifle shooting IS A CRIME.

Go to your family doctor with an illness and he will test your pulse and then ask you to open your mouth and say "Ah!" While he is peering into your mouth he is checking the clues to ascertain your illness whether it be measles, tonsilitis, vitamin deficiency, lead poisoning, scarlet fever or one of a hundred other ailments.

When the doctor has diagnosed your case he starts to prescribe a cure. Mr. Instructor, you are not only a detective but also a doctor of shooting ills. By curing your recruit's musketry ailments you are going a long way towards saving his life. You will show him how to shoot more accurately and confidently and his morale will be good because he will learn that he can outshoot and whip any enemy he encounters.

Thus the stress upon detecting and curing shooting ills in the early stages of training becomes a matter of major importance. If your recruit can leave your course as a crack shot because you were able to correct his mistakes, you have done a good coaching job.

Note the targets reproduced, opposite. You will see that in the upper target five bullets are in a scattered area. Yet the coaching given the soldier on this course was responsible for a great decrease in the group area on his second target.

The coach showed progress, too, because he got what he was after from his pupil—tangible decrease of the area of bullet hole groups. But his efforts would have been wasted if he did not point out this startling progress to the pupil. If the pupil can see his own progress toward perfect marksmanship by means of coaching, then he is inspired.

The psychological value of showing your recruit this tangible progress can never be over-stressed. Don't overlook, either, that these decreasing groups show the degree of your coaching ability and progress, too.

Note:

For future reference, all the bullet groups reproduced on the following pages, were selected at random from fired official 9-c targets.

TANGIBLE PROGRESS

166

SHAPES OF BULLET HOLE GROUPS

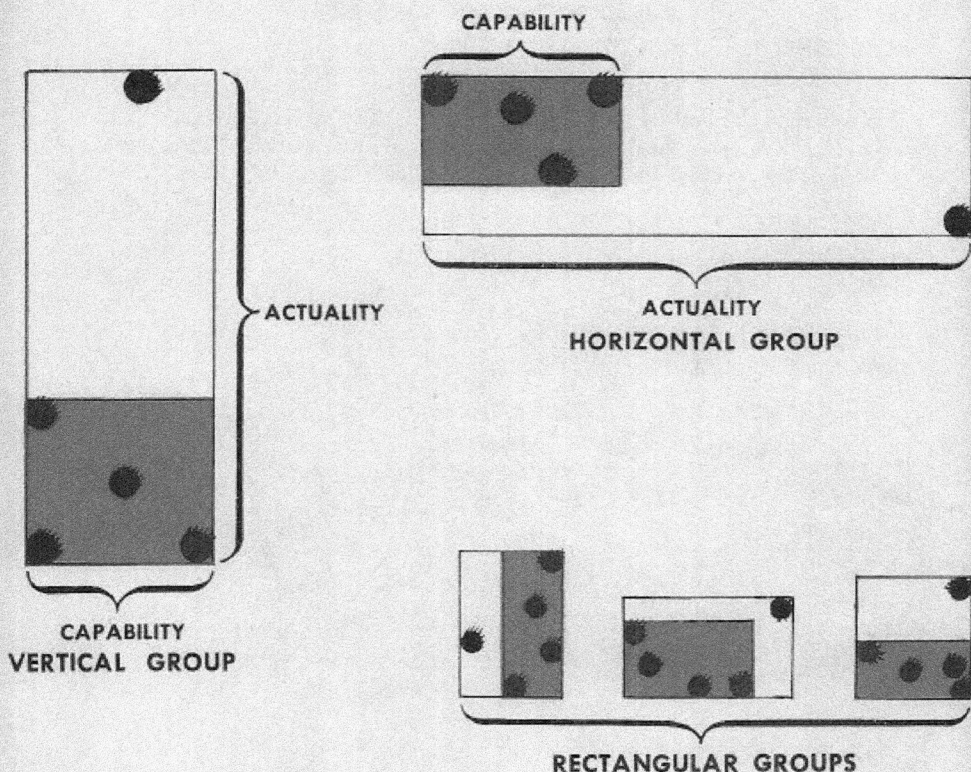

CAPABILITY

ACTUALITY

ACTUALITY
HORIZONTAL GROUP

CAPABILITY
VERTICAL GROUP

RECTANGULAR GROUPS

TO DIAGNOSE the shooting ills of your recruit the clues must be taken in logical order. Let us assume that you have your recruit's target before you. Place the cluster of five shots (it is to be hoped he got all five shots on the target) within a pencilled enclosure. Taking the outer edges of the outer bullet holes as guides, draw a square or rectangle so that its top and bottom are parallel with the top and bottom of the target card and the sides parallel with the sides of the card. Triangles or other irregular shapes will not suffice. You will have noted how this was accomplished on the two targets shown on page 173. The rectangle or square should enclose the five shots.

If the bullet holes are in a vertical line, the group will be vertical. If they are in a horizontal line, the group will be horizontal. If scattered around horizontally and vertically the group should be close to square. It may be perfectly square or it may be slightly higher than wide or wider than high.

VERTICAL GROUP SHOWS } GOOD TRIGGER SQUEEZE POOR ELEVATION

The rectangle formed by your lines now represents the actual shooting of the recruit. It is his first or ACTUALITY group. Let us assume that he had a vertical group of actuality shots. (Figure 1, below). What happened?

One or several of the following faults prevailed:—

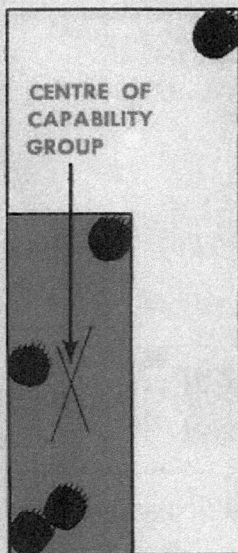

CENTRE OF
CAPABILITY
GROUP

1. *Varying position of butt upon the shoulder.*
2. *A low vertical triangle.*
3. *Failure to focus upon the front sight.*
4. *Incorrect eye distance to the back sight.*
5. *Lack of aiming precision.*
6. *Sight picture varied.*
7. *Faulty pre-firing breathing.*
8. *Position of left elbow wrong*
9. *Varied backward pressure.*
10. *Varied head pressure.*
11. *Poor follow through.*

FIG. 1

WAS THIS THE BOY YOU TAUGHT?

Did he have all or any one of these faults?

Whatever he has done wrong enough to give him this score can be blamed upon YOU, Mr. Instructor. You did not discharge your responsibility to him. That rosy-cheeked kid is going out to fight an enemy and you haven't told him how to do it. You can't bawl him out nor get angry with him. The recruit cannot be blamed if he has trouble in learning.

Take that boy out, alone, and try to find his mistakes and then correct them. Make sure that the next time he fires at a target he will bunch his shots in an area the size of a dime.

Supposing, that instead of the vertical group shown on Page 175, your recruit shot a horizontal one as shown below. What happened there? You, as the coach, will immediately be able to judge that he had a good elevation (lacking in the vertical group) but that his Trigger Control was faulty. One, or several of the eleven most common errors in red, below, were to blame.

HORIZONTAL GROUP SHOWS | GOOD ELEVATION POOR TRIGGER SQUEEZE

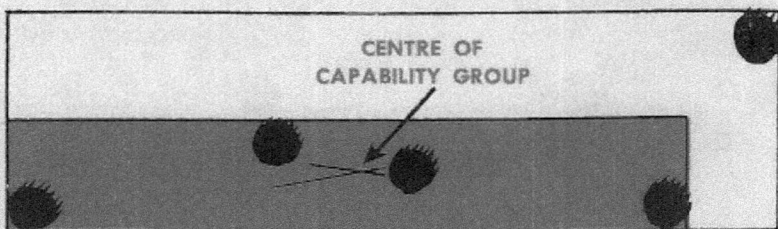

CENTRE OF
CAPABILITY GROUP

1. High vertical triangle.
2. High right shoulder.
3. Wandering front sight.
4. Holding the rifle with muscular effort instead of resting it upon the bones.
5. Jerking the trigger.

6. Hurried trigger squeeze.
7. Movement of the right elbow.
8. Varying chin pressure.
9. Lack of aiming precision.
10. Faulty automatic alignment.
11. No stability of position.

It is possible that your recruit, however, shot a group that is rectangularly close to being enclosed within a square. This shows a co-ordination which combined the five basic principles of good shooting in approximately the same manner for five successive shots. See the groups shown on the opposite page.

IF GROUP CAN BE COVERED WITH . . .	THE CO-ORDINATION IS . . .
1. A DIME	EXCELLENT
2. A POSTAGE STAMP	GOOD
3. SMALLER THAN ONE HALF A PLAYING CARD	FAIR

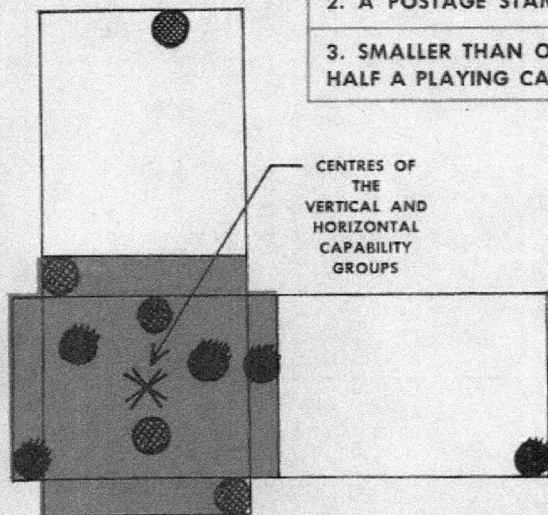

CENTRES OF
THE
VERTICAL AND
HORIZONTAL
CAPABILITY
GROUPS

RECTANGULAR
GROUP SHOWS
THE DEGREES OR
LACK OF DEGREES
OF
CO-ORDINATION

FIG. 1

SHAPES OF BULLET HOLE GROUPS—Continued

The size of that rectangle or square (see Figure 1, above) shows the extent to which the co-ordination has prevailed. For instance, if the cluster of five bullet holes can be covered by a dime your recruit has excellent co-ordination. If a postage stamp (not air mail) will cover all five holes, the co-ordination is then good but could be improved. If the cluster requires half a playing card or better in order to be covered then the recruit has shown NO CO-ORDINATION.

By now you have considered the actual shooting performance of your recruit and have selected and narrowed down the clues or shapes of three groups of actualities. Now draw another box within the first one with its sides parallel to the sides of the first enclosure. This new box will enclose the four most closely-clustered shots, within the smallest possible area. (See Figure 1, again).

This enclosure will show the kind of shooting of which your recruit is capable and is known as the second or CAPABILITY group. You cannot complain, too much, if he got four shots away and only one went astray.

The detail of this most important Group is contained in the subsequent sub-topics of this chapter. Samples of these groups have been shown in all the targets heretofore portrayed in Target Analysis.

170

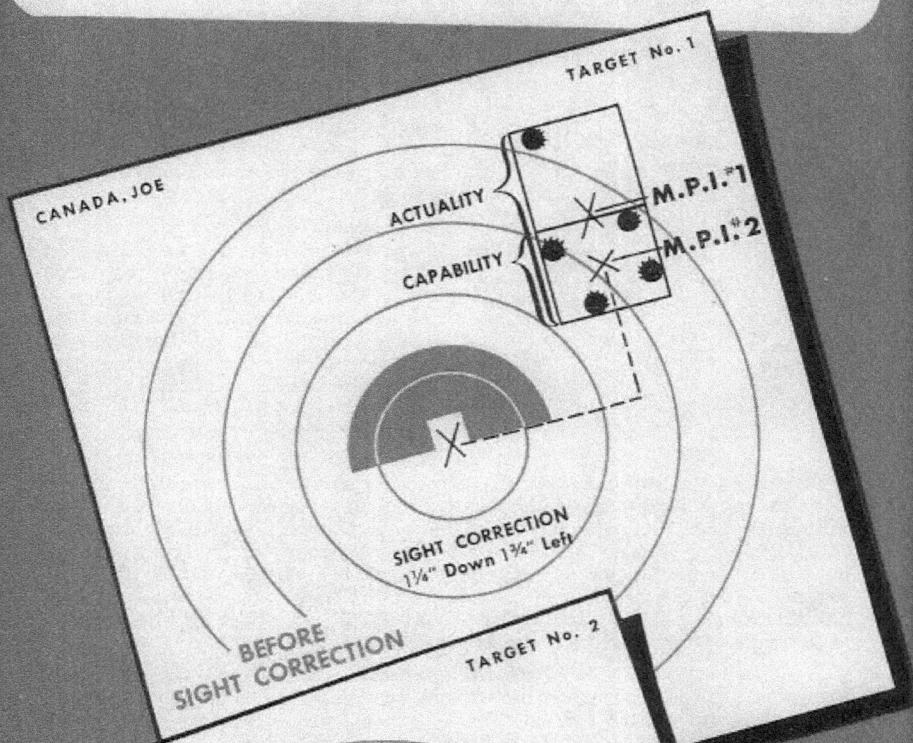

CANADA, JOE

TARGET No. 1

ACTUALITY

CAPABILITY

M.P.I. #1

M.P.I. #2

SIGHT CORRECTION
1¼" Down 1¾" Left

BEFORE
SIGHT CORRECTION

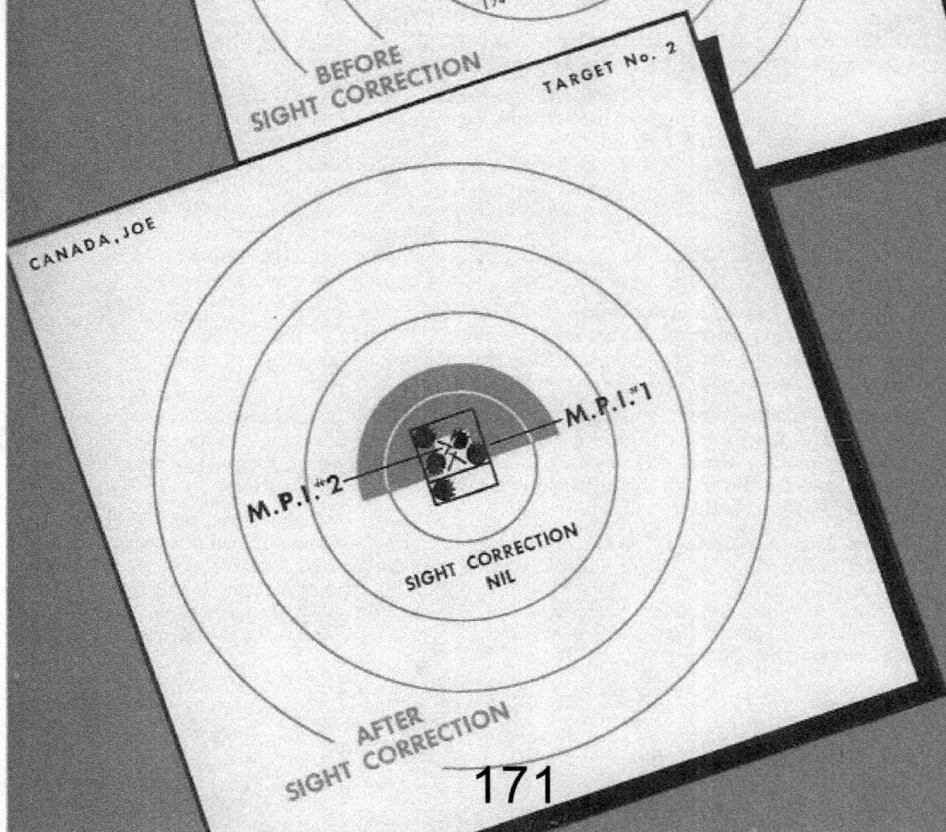

CANADA, JOE

TARGET No. 2

M.P.I. #2

M.P.I. #1

SIGHT CORRECTION
NIL

AFTER
SIGHT CORRECTION

SIGHT CORRECTION

YOU now see, on target No. 1, opposite, that the cluster of four capability shots is above and to the right of the centre of the target, where the recruit aimed. What caused this?

It is probable that the sights of your pupil's rifle have not been adjusted to fit him. You will recall that under "Eyes and Aiming" it was stressed that no two people see precisely the same. The armourer may be satisfied that the rifle will fire perfectly true yet neither you nor your recruit can get the precise results you both want from it because it has not been fitted to either of you. In other words, the recruit's shots are not striking the bull's eye.

To correct the sights so that the Capability Group (and we hope all five shots) on his second target will come directly upon the aiming mark, it is well to find the Mean Points of Impact of the bullet clusters in both the Actuality and Capability Groups. This is done by drawing diagonal lines from opposite corners of the rectangles or squares so that they just meet and cross in the centre. Thus you are able to determine the EXACT centre of each group and this is called the MEAN POINT OF IMPACT. This point will be referred to hereafter in text and drawings as the MPI.

If you will refer to Target 1, you will see that the MPI of the Actuality Group, shown as MPI No. 1, has been determined as well as the MPI of the Capability Group, shown as MPI No. 2. The latter one shows the more accurately determined shooting ability of the recruit, thus a dotted line is placed so that it will show the direction and extent of the required correction of the sights. On Target No. 1 you will see that it extends downward to a point opposite the object of aim and then at right angles to the left until it reaches the centre of the aiming mark. Target No. 2 shows how the sight adjustment has brought the group downward and over onto the aiming mark, with a corrected rifle.

This dotted line known as the Sight Correction Line is of much value to the armourer or instructor in adjusting the sights of a firer's rifle so that it will shoot accurately. In other words, the sights have been adjusted to fit the eyesight of the recruit.

It is discouraging for the recruit to find that no matter how closely clustered his shots are, they are far from the object which he wants to hit. He naturally feels that he has not made the progress he wanted because every recruit wants to put the bullets dead in the centre of the target. He never loses his desire to register right on the bull's eye.

If his shots are not in the bull's eye he will believe that his rifle is not shooting accurately and thus he will endeavour to compensate for this difference by guessing at an imaginary aiming point, in the hope that the bullets will land on the bull's eye. He will not develop this off-aiming bad habit if he can be assured that correct adjustment of his rifle's sights is the cure for a wayward bullet cluster.

CALL AND CHECK CARD

THE box score of your recruit's shooting is all shown on his target and on his Check and Call Card which is kept by the coach. Note the illustration of the card at the bottom of the opposite page.

This card is used by the coach as he lies in proper position alongside his pupil so he can view the recruit's shooting within the two-foot circle. It assists appreciably in reading the story each bullet hole tells. The card shown here deals with an actual target which will be analyzed as an illustration.

Under the column headed "No." list the number of shots as 1, 2, 3, 4 and 5. Under the heading "Call" the coach will show, for each shot, in the circle under "Diagram" the location of the bullet hole on the target as called by the firer. If the firer is observant of the performance of his front sight as taught in "Calling the Shots" he will be able to fairly accurately tell where each shot landed on the target. Under the sub-heading "Letters" the coach will correspondingly duplicate each "Call" by the firer. He will do this by using the abbreviations "Lo" for low, "C" for centre, "Le" for left, "H" for high, "R" for right and a question mark "?" for instances in which the firer has not known where his shot went. This is usually a fair indication that the firer flinched or blinked and hence guessed as to where his shot went.

The column headed "Check" is used by the coach to insert the usual "V-shaped check-marks of agreement when the call and the coach's diagnosis as well as the target result, all agree. An "X" under this column would indicate a disagreement between what the firer thought happened and what actually occured.

In meeting this condition, it is usually best to deal with the positive clues first and then by continuing the elimination, deal with the questionable ones.

It is recommended that the check column be at the extreme right end of the card in order to facilitate checking but, of course, if the diagram shown in the accompanying sketch and also shown on distributed musketry training charts is preferred, it can be used.

The column "Observations" provides the space for the coach to write a cryptic but running commentary of notes on the recruit's performance as viewed in his proper position alongside him. It is what the coach can report as having seen within the two-foot circle. These observations are the play-by-play notes which acccompany the box score and describe what happened and gives your own expert opinions and clues of why each shot went where it did. This card is a most valuable aid when analysing targets.

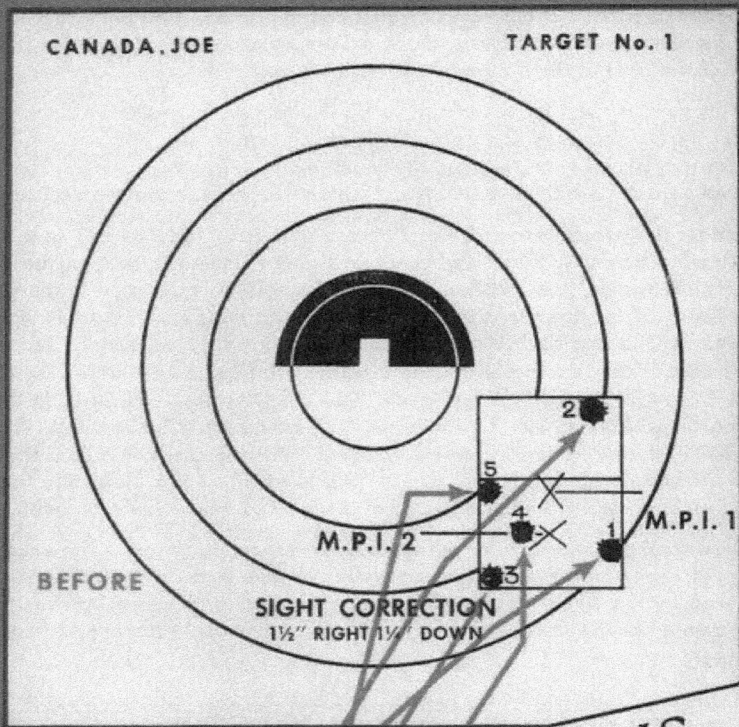

CANADA. JOE   TARGET No. 1

M.P.I. 2   M.P.I. 1

BEFORE

SIGHT CORRECTION
1½" RIGHT 1½" DOWN

OBSERVATIONS

FORGOT CHIN PRESSURE—
TRIGGER CONTROL FAST, JERKY
VERY LOW VERTICAL TRIANGLE—STRAINED—
HOLDING WITH MUSCLES

QUESTION CALL—BREATHING FAULTY

GOOD BREATHING AND TRIGGER SQUEEZE—
CO-ORDINATION FINE

COMPLAINED OF FORE SIGHT MOVEMENT—
TIRED—TRIGGER SQUEEZE HURRIED

N°	CALL		CHECK
	DIAGRAM	LETTERS	
1	⊙	C	X
2	◯	H	✓
3	◯	L°	✓
4	⊙	C	✓
5	◯	Lᴱ	✓

* It is recommended that the
check column be at the extreme right end of the card in
order to facilitate checking,
but if the diagram shown on
distributed musketry charts
is preferred, it may be used.

174

MEASURING BULLET HOLES

THERE are four classes into which a bullet hole may be graded. The coach who is analyzing a target must be able to appraise the value of each bullet hole quickly, because it is vital in showing the progress of the recruit.

In measuring or grading bullet holes, the Actuality and the Capability Groups must be outlined and their MPI's determined. Then an average-sized lead pencil can be horizontally laid upon the target so that it covers the MPI No. 2. It should be so placed that it rests parallel with the top and bottom of the group outline. This horizontal pencil provides for the measurement of the shots for Elevation. The bullet holes which are now beneath the pencil, either wholly or partially, or those which touch the pencil, can be graded as having EXCELLENT elevation. Note Figure 1, opposite.

Those holes which are the width of one bullet hole away from the pencil are rated as having GOOD elevation. Those two or three bullet holes from the pencil have FAIR elevation and all others have POOR elevation.

Checking for Trigger Control you merely place your pencil vertically upon the MPI No. 2 so that it is parallel with the sides of the Capability Group outline. The value of the shots from the standpoint of Trigger Control can now be measured in the same manner as was done for Elevation.

Figure 2 is the same target as in Figure 1, and an examination of the bullet holes shows Shot 1 as being partially beneath the vertical pencil establishing it as EXCELLENT for Trigger Control but as it is the width of one bullet hole away from the horizontal pencil (Figure 1) its elevation can only be graded as GOOD.

Shot 2 touches the horizontal pencil and thus has EXCELLENT elevation but as it is the width of one bullet hole to the right of the vertical pencil its Trigger Control is rated as GOOD.

Shot 3 is two bullet holes below the horizontal pencil and two bullet holes to the right of the vertical pencil thus it is classed as FAIR for both Trigger Control and Elevation.

Shot 4 is similar because it is in the opposite corner of the Capability Group having three bullet holes between it and the horizontal pencil thus placing it in the FAIR category for both Trigger Control and Elevation.

Shot 5 is definitely the "Orphan Annie" of the group. It is a stray which is more than three bullet holes from either pencil position and thus grades POOR for both Trigger Control and Elevation.

M.P.I.2

175

MEASURING BULLET HOLES

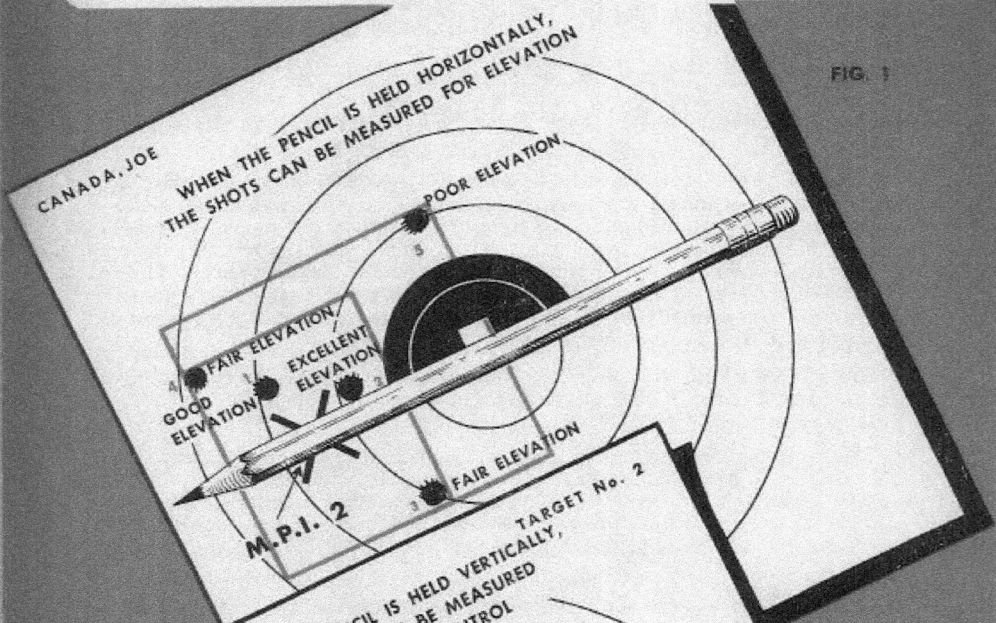

FIG. 1

CANADA, JOE

WHEN THE PENCIL IS HELD HORIZONTALLY, THE SHOTS CAN BE MEASURED FOR ELEVATION

POOR ELEVATION

FAIR ELEVATION

GOOD ELEVATION

EXCELLENT ELEVATION

FAIR ELEVATION

M.P.I. 2

TARGET No. 2

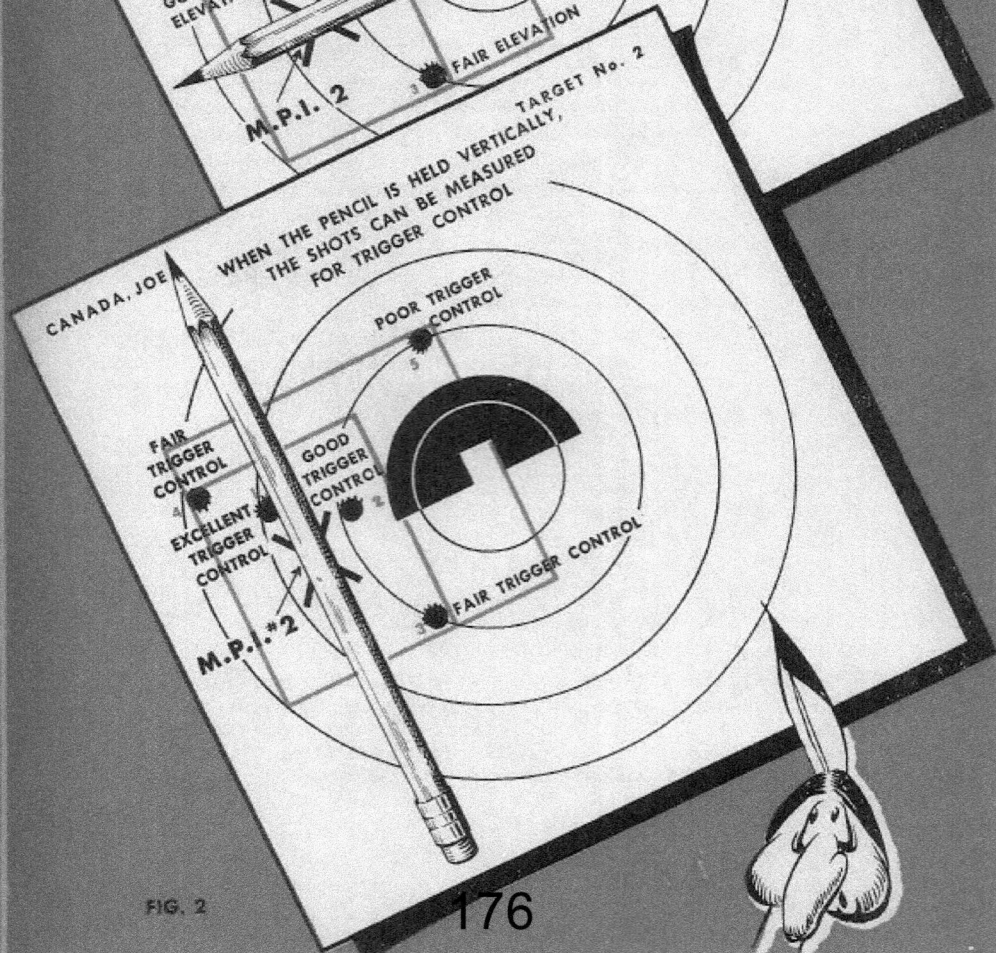

CANADA, JOE

WHEN THE PENCIL IS HELD VERTICALLY, THE SHOTS CAN BE MEASURED FOR TRIGGER CONTROL

POOR TRIGGER CONTROL

FAIR TRIGGER CONTROL

GOOD TRIGGER CONTROL

EXCELLENT TRIGGER CONTROL

FAIR TRIGGER CONTROL

M.P.I. *2

FIG. 2

176

NUMBERING THE SHOTS

EACH bullet hole tells its own story. It is the chapter which, when joined with the stories of the other bullet holes individually and collectively, provides the entire book of clues to the recruit's shooting performance.

You have shown the tangible progress of decreasing areas of groups. You have determined the general faults from the group shapes. In other words you have shown whether faulty elevation or trigger control were the predominant difficulties encountered by the recruit. You have taken care of the sight correction of the rifle and you have kept your Call and Check Card.

If you will refer to the illustration on the opposite page, you will note a target with five bullet holes. The first step to take after the Actuality and Capability Groups with MPI's have been shown and the sight correction line drawn, is to determine which bullet hole represents the first shot fired, which hole represents the second shot and so on.

This is done with the invaluable assistance of your Call and Check Card and of your grading of the bullet hole as "Excellent", "Good", "Fair" or "Poor".

Now let us find the first shot. The Call and Check Card shows that the firer only called one shot "High" and that was his second where there was faulty holding and a low, unsteady vertical triangle. Accordingly the high, right bullet hole outside of the Capability Group is the likely No. 2, and for want of positive clues the No. 1 shot has been temporarily passed by.

The firer called his third shot "Low" and the coach noticed faulty breathing which might cause it to be low, hence the shot shown in the lower left corner of the Capability Group is obviously Shot No. 3.

One shot was called to the left and the coach observed a hurried squeeze of the trigger while the firer complained of foresight movement. The only remaining shot which answers all of these clues is the one at the upper left corner of the Capability Group and the matching call and observations list it as Shot No. 5.

The two remaining bullet holes must be the first and the fourth. Both were called as "Centre" but the first shot was questionable because of faulty chin pressure and trigger control while the coach noted that the firer performed well nigh perfectly on his fourth shot. Hence his clues are reasonable enough to mark Shot No. 4 as the one which was closest to both the horizontal and vertical pencils. It was the best shot.

Only one shot now remains and it must be Shot No. 1, and to prove it, the observations listed when it was fired recorded faulty trigger control and chin pressure which could reasonably place it well to the right.

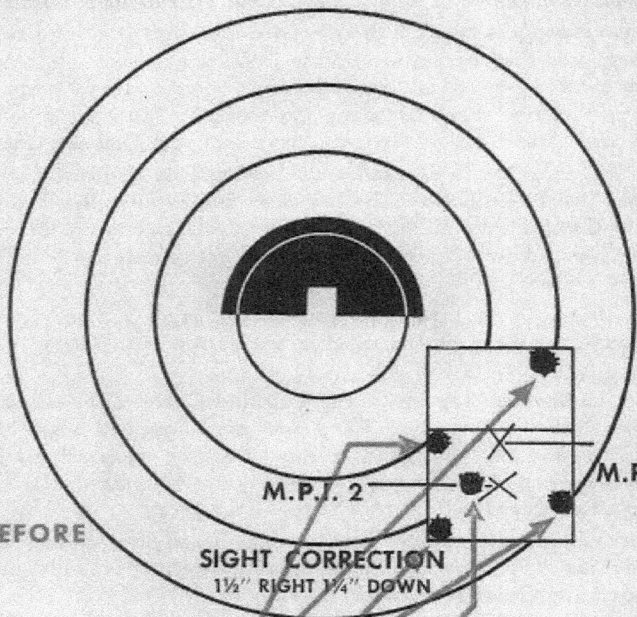

CANADA, JOE   TARGET No. 1

BEFORE

M.P.I. 2   M.P.I. 1

SIGHT CORRECTION
1½" RIGHT ¼" DOWN

OBSERVATIONS

No	CALL		CHECK	
	DIAGRAM	LETTERS		
1	●	C	X	FORGOT CHIN PRESSURE— TRIGGER CONTROL FAST, JERKY
2	◑	H	✓	VERY LOW VERTICAL TRIANGLE-STRAINED— HOLDING WITH MUSCLES
3	◐	Lᴼ	✓	QUESTION CALL—BREATHING FAULTY
4	●	C	✓	GOOD BREATHING AND TRIGGER SQUEEZE— CO-ORDINATION FINE
5	◑	Lᴱ	✓	COMPLAINED OF FORE SIGHT MOVEMENT— TIRED—TRIGGER SQUEEZE HURRIED

* It is recommended that the check column be at the extreme right end of the card in order to facilitate checking, but if the diagram shown on distributed musketry charts is preferred, it may be used.

178

THE LANGUAGE OF BULLET HOLES

WITH the bullet holes numbered and matched with the Call and Check Card clues, it is now your duty to diagnose your recruit's shooting difficulties and show him the steps that are necessary to bring his shots closer as possible to the MPI No. 2.

You do not have to worry about the fact that these shots are not on the bull's eye, because sight adjustment will take care of that. It is more important now to get all the shots clustered together in the smallest possible area around the MPI No. 2.

You can do this effectively by marking the criticism and advice for each individual shot alongside each bullet hole. This advice is determined from your observations of the recruit as he fired his group and as you recorded them upon the Call and Check Card under the column marked "Observations". His call of the shots will further assist you.

Make this criticism and advice with fairness, so that you can encourage your recruit to eliminate the faults that are apparent. Be absolutely certain that you have diagnosed his faults correctly and that you have prescribed the correct medicine.

Don't guess at your analysis of each shot. You are not a crystal gazer. You must rely SOLELY upon FACTS and FUNDAMENTALS. You cannot shoot by guesswork and neither can you analyze targets and shooting with anything other than cold, sound, logical, scientific, reasoning.

ENCOURAGEMENT AND ADVICE

THERE would be little value to analysing targets unless the results of the analysis could be passed along in some form to the recruit whose target is under review. Thus, there are two phases in which the analysis can effectively be presented to the firer. One is Encouragement and the other is Advice. Both must be fair, sincere and merited.

The recruit who looks at a target similar to that shown in the target opposite is apt to be very disappointed. He is of the opinion that his No. 4 shot was the only one that was close enough to the aiming mark and that the others were all the result of very bad shooting.

Your analysis of his group should reverse this viewpoint and as his surprise gives way to an appreciation of the logic of your analysis, he sees that his shooting was not so bad after all; that with sight adjustment he can get his five bullet holes closer to the aiming point; that if he follows the five basic principles, which you so carefully taught him, he can put all five shots in the centre of that aiming mark. You have captured not only his determination to shoot better, but you have shown him that he is capable of better shooting than he at first believed.

179

ENCOURAGEMENT AND ADVICE—Continued

But you have to go further. The way you have marked up his target gives him a small ray of hope that you are trying to help him. Words of Encouragement at the TOP of his target will condition his viewpoint so that he will be more receptive to the advice which you will offer later.

Note the Encouragement which was placed upon this target (below) and remember that this was an actual target picked at random from those turned in by a musketry class, and copied for reproduction here with only the name changed.

Note too, the approach in the Advice given at the BOTTOM of the target. You will see that the Sight Correction instruction to the armourer has come first.

Secondly the coach has told what is generally wrong with the recruit's shooting style and in pointing out errors has not belabored them but has dealt directly, adding sensible recommendations as to how the faults may be corrected.

The soldier given this kind of personalized treatment will accept such advice as helpful, and will, in 999 out of 1000 cases apply himself to correct what was wrong. He will not have to be "pressured" in order to improve his shooting skill. He will do it on his own accord. You have given him the bottle of medicine to cure his shooting ills.

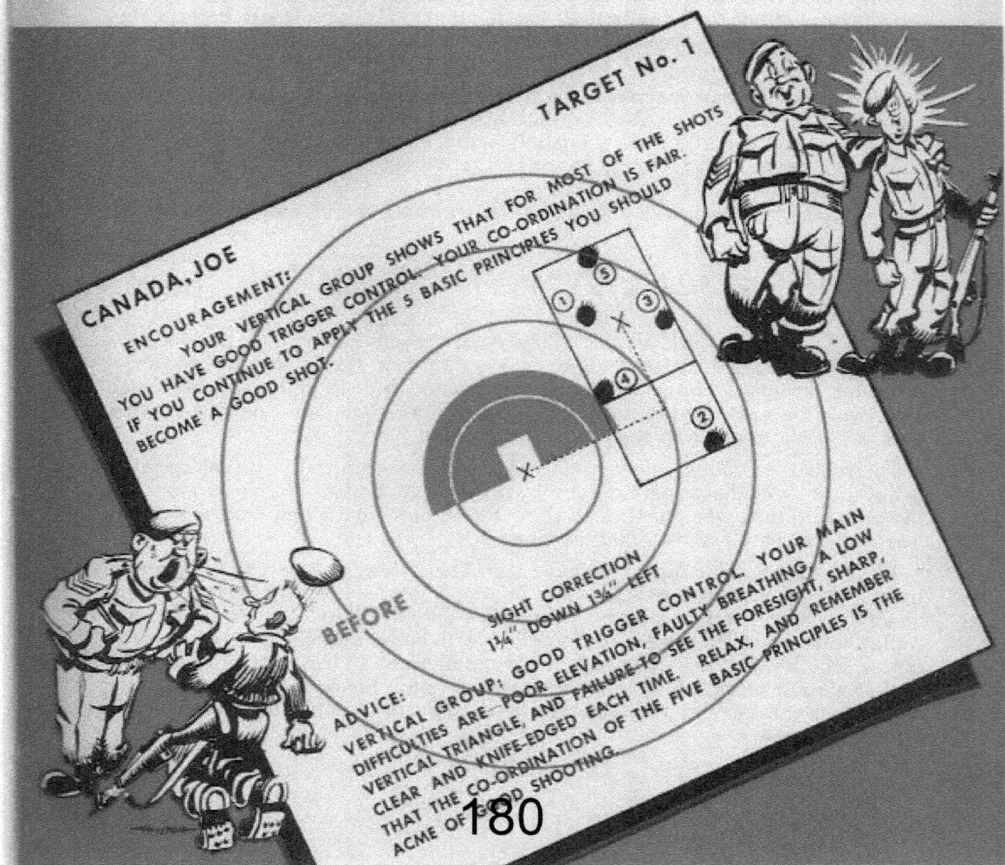

TARGET No. 1

CANADA, JOE

ENCOURAGEMENT:
YOUR VERTICAL GROUP SHOWS THAT FOR MOST OF THE SHOTS YOU HAVE GOOD TRIGGER CONTROL. YOUR CO-ORDINATION IS FAIR. IF YOU CONTINUE TO APPLY THE 5 BASIC PRINCIPLES YOU SHOULD BECOME A GOOD SHOT.

BEFORE

SIGHT CORRECTION
1¼" DOWN 1¼" LEFT

ADVICE: VERTICAL GROUP; GOOD TRIGGER CONTROL. YOUR MAIN DIFFICULTIES ARE POOR ELEVATION, FAULTY BREATHING, A LOW VERTICAL TRIANGLE, AND FAILURE TO SEE THE FORESIGHT, SHARP, CLEAR AND KNIFE-EDGED EACH TIME. RELAX, AND REMEMBER THAT THE CO-ORDINATION OF THE FIVE BASIC PRINCIPLES IS THE ACME OF GOOD SHOOTING.

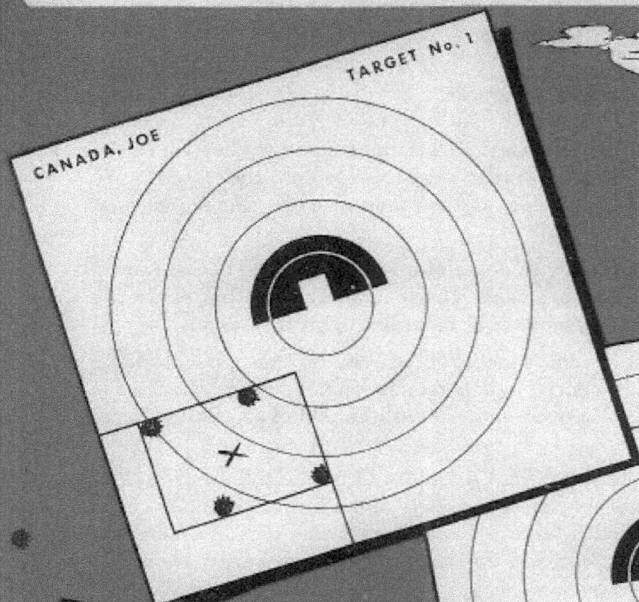

TARGET No. 1

CANADA, JOE

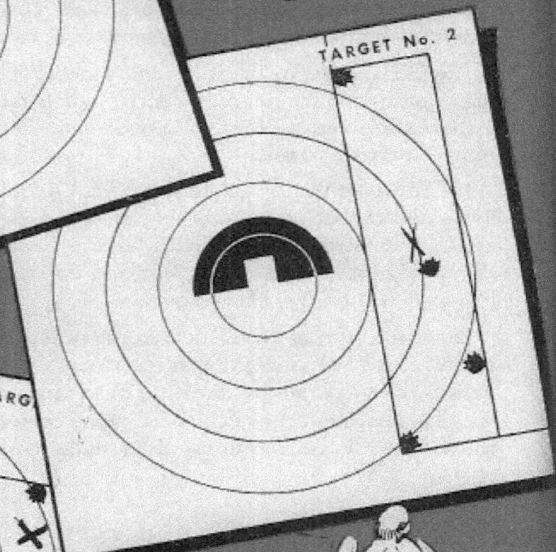

TARGET No. 2

CANADA, JOE

TARG

NADA, JOE

HOW TO DEAL WITH
FOUR-SHOT TARGETS

ONE of the saddest men on any range is the unfortunate soldier who fired five bullets but only four of them registered upon the target. He is apt to take a joshing from his friends, just at a time when he was hoping that he had fired a good group.

The smart coach will act quickly in cases of four-shot targets, to insure that a maximum of encouragement is given. This is usually done by taking the utmost advantage of all the known factors revealed upon the target.

It will be noted in the four-shot targets reproduced on the opposite page, that the direction taken by the stray bullets cannot be determined, hence the analyst has given the recruit, in each case, the full benefit of as small a Capability Group as possible.

He has done this by establishing the Capability Group and then extending two edges of that group until they meet the edge of the target to thus form the smallest determinable Actuality area. In this way, the recruit's actuality group is kept at a minimum size and the capability group is still workable, just as it was on five-shot targets.

However, it must be remembered that this method will *not* be sufficient for targets that have anything less than four shots, because three or less bullet holes will not permit the drawing of square-sided groups which are essential for the determining of MPI's for sight correction and to illustrate to your recruit the diminishing areas of his bullet-hole groups.

182

THE COMPLETED STORY

CANADA, JOE   TARGET No. 1

ENCOURAGEMENT:
    YOUR CO-ORDINATION IS   WORST SHOT
    FAIR, AND THE RECTANGULAR   GOOD TRIGGER CONTROL
    GROUP SHOWS THAT YOU HAVE   POOR ELEVATION
    MASTERED BOTH ELEVATION AND   LOW VERTICAL TRIANGLE
    TRIGGER CONTROL TO A CERTAIN
    DEGREE. YOUR CAPABILITY   GOOD ELEVATION
    IS ONLY HALF THE SIZE OF YOUR   GOOD TRIGGER CONTROL
    ACTUALITY NOW, AND IF   WANDERING FORESIGHT
    YOU CAREFULLY FOLLOW THE   HURRIED TRIGGER SQUEEZE
    ADVICE GIVEN BELOW
    YOU SHOULD SHOOT A
    POSSIBLE NEXT TIME   BEST SHOT
                                    EXCELLENT TRIGGER CONTROL
                                      EXCELLENT ELEVATION
                                     CO-ORDINATION PERFECT

BEFORE   SIGHT CORRECTION   ACTUALITY
                          2¼" UP 1¾" LEFT   M.P.I. 1

                          M.P.I. 2   CAPABILITY

ADVICE:
WATCH YOUR VERTICAL TRIANGLE, YOU
HAVE A HABIT OF LETTING YOUR LEFT
ELBOW SLIP OUT FROM UNDER THE RIFLE   GOOD ELEVATION
TAKE GREATER CARE WITH YOUR FOLLOW   FAIR TRIGGER CONTROL
THROUGH, AND WATCH THE FORESIGHT   NO CHIN PRESSURE
RELAX, CO-ORDINATE ALL 5 BASIC
PRINCIPLES.   GOOD ELEVATION
                                     FAIR TRIGGER CONTROL
                                     BREATHING, LACK OF AIMING PRECISION

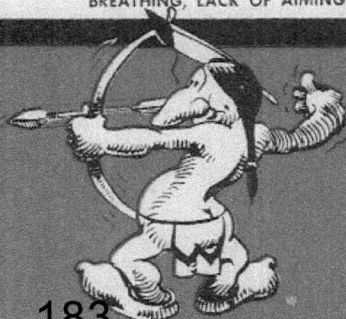

183

THE COMPLETED STORY

PLEASE observe the illustration on the opposite page. It is the target as analyzed and the Encouragement and Advice have been given. It has been pretty badly marked up but it is the completed work. Probably nothing in the term of service of the recruit has surprised him more. It has awakened latent determination to go out and do a better shooting job next time.

If you have analysed the target properly you have placed a boy on the right track toward expert marksmanship. From here on it is pretty much up to him to succeed or fail. He won't do the latter if your course has given that steady, interesting, encouraging build-up for this moment.

Your treatment of his first target will convince him that you have an interest in him. The adjustment of his rifle's sights assured that.

When he comes to his second target he will find that he is putting the bullets right around the Point of Aim and if, as in the case of the soldier who shot this target, he squeezed the trigger the same, slow, steady way for each shot; kept his position and used bones instead of muscles to support his rifle; kept the same backward and chin pressures; breathed the same for each shot; kept the same eye distance from the back sight; focussed upon the front sight and did not blink nor flinch and at the same time exercised follow through, his second target will look like the target shown on page 192.

That is exactly the kind of shooting the Canadian Army must have. Accurate shooting infantrymen are still the boys who win the battles. The artillery, the tanks and the planes may do the softening up of an enemy but it is the keen-sniping riflemen who clean up the resistance pockets.

A noted war correspondent describing the siege of the City of Cherbourg, France, in the late summer of 1944, said the attacking forces paid little attention to the earth-shaking hell of the artillery, naval and aerial bombardment of the vital supply port but when the "ping" of the sniper's bullet was heard, everyone in the area "ducked". The reason for this is that the sniper's bullet is so personal. It is meant to kill YOU.

The only way in which to counteract enemy sniping is by more and better rifle performance on the part of Canadian soldiers, and that can only be developed by the careful training of our men in the five basic principles of musketry; then, through the medium of target analysis, prove to the soldier himself, that it can be further improved.

Mr. Instructor, your responsibility is clear-cut and seriously important. It is a challenge you must meet and execute well.

THE COMPLETED STORY (AFTER)

TARGET No. 2

CANADA, JOE
ENCOURAGEMENT:
YOUR CO-ORDINATION IS EXCELLENT, AND ALL FIVE SHOTS CAN BE COVERED
WITH A DIME, A GREAT IMPROVEMENT OVER YOUR LAST TARGET!

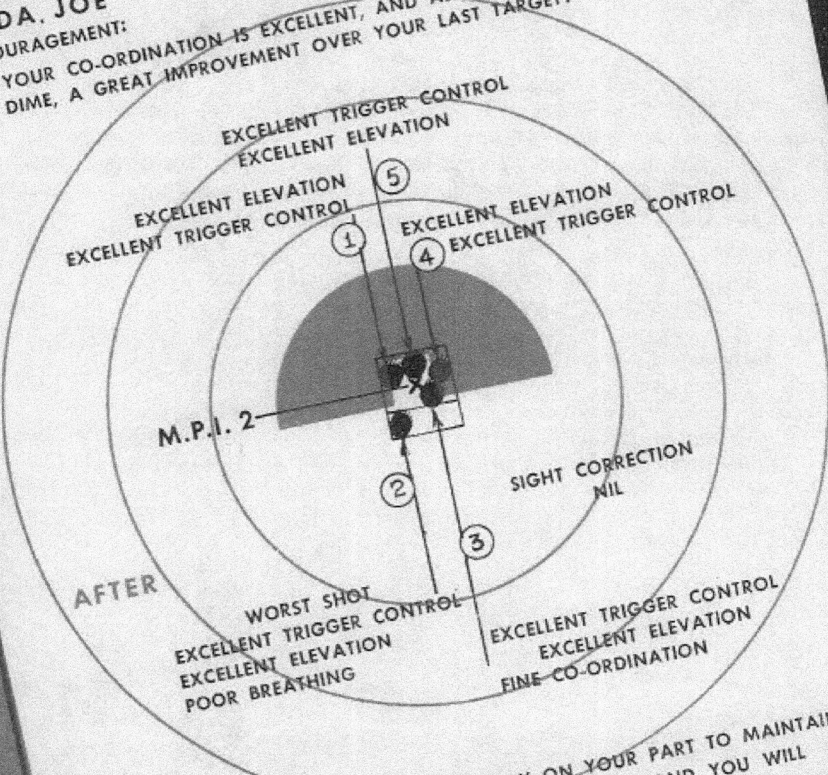

EXCELLENT TRIGGER CONTROL
EXCELLENT ELEVATION

EXCELLENT ELEVATION
EXCELLENT TRIGGER CONTROL

EXCELLENT ELEVATION
EXCELLENT TRIGGER CONTROL

M.P.I. 2

SIGHT CORRECTION
NIL

AFTER

WORST SHOT
EXCELLENT TRIGGER CONTROL
EXCELLENT ELEVATION
POOR BREATHING

EXCELLENT TRIGGER CONTROL
EXCELLENT ELEVATION
FINE CO-ORDINATION

ADVICE:
CONSTANT PRACTICE WILL BE NECESSARY ON YOUR PART TO MAINTAIN THIS
HIGH STANDARD OF CO-ORDINATION. KEEP AT IT AND YOU WILL
... CONSISTENT.

185

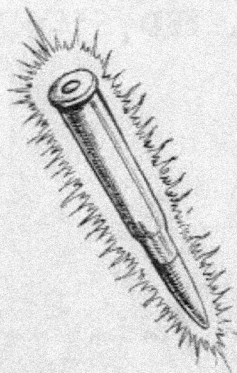

ON THE .303 RANGE

WHEN it comes to analysing the targets on the .303 range, the situation is somewhat different. You are not able to take the targets down from their frames and mark them as you have done for the .22 range which have been the basis of the discussions on Target Analysis up to this point.

Your analysis of the shooting by your recruit must be done verbally. You must do it while he is watching you and you must be quick enough to determine his Capability Group and its MPI accurately and analyze his target from that MPI. That means you must get the best of cluster shots together in determining the Capability Group.

The shots on the .303 range target will be numbered for you by the men of the butt party. So with your Call and Check Card you can quickly show how your analysis of his actual shooting is reflected in the target result.

Give him his Encouragement first or as you score his shots. Make certain that you have given him the best possible aggregate of points by placing the centre of the scoring ring to coincide with the MPI No. 2. Be fair with the firer.

Having encouraged him you now give him the Advice. You indicate to the armourer the sight adjustment. Then you show by each shot as described by the Call and Check Card, how with more correct firing habits he could have brought all his shots into one small cluster dead upon MPI No. 2.

His second target will prove that he is out for better .303 shooting. He sees much tangible progress and he is well on the road to shooting perfection.

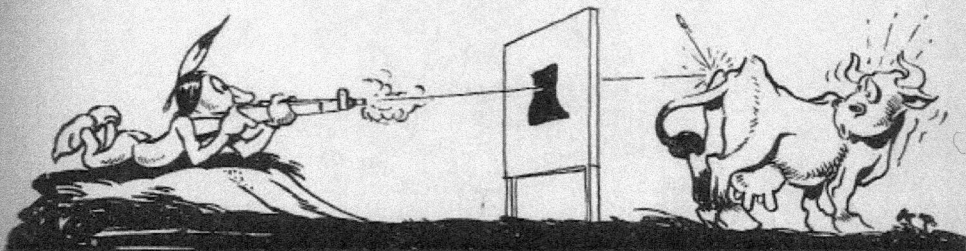

CHAPTER TEN

Zeroing

FITTING the rifle to the soldier is as important to him as issuing his correctly-sized boots. If your recruit needs glasses or false teeth, they are fitted very precisely to him. He could probably get by without the glasses and he could live on a soft food diet because he had no teeth. However, his usefulness will be totally lost, if his rifle is not adjusted so that it will strike the point upon which he has directed his front sight.

No matter how much shooting precision a soldier may have, he soon loses it if his rifle will not plant the bullets right where he wants them and he always wants them precisely upon the object of his aim.

You will recall that during the analysis of the .22 targets, it was pointed out on page 179, the value of adjusting the indoor range rifles so as to encourage the kind of shooting you wanted the recruit to produce. It was stressed there that unless the sights of the rifle were fitted to the eyesight of the individual soldier he would endeavour to aim at non-existent points of aim in an effort to affect his own sight correction and thus defeat all of the training which you had given him about bringing the knife-edged, black, square, clear fore sight up to and in the centre of the aiming mark.

The same condition prevails in the case of the .303 rifle which has been issued to him and which he will carry with him through all his service. It therefore must be fitted to him. It is his weapon. It must be fitted as to butt length and now it must be fitted as to the sights.

There are many models of the same type of aperture or back sights on the Canadian Army rifle. In any event the sight adjustment does not concern the back sights as only the front sights affect the changes which may be required. But remember! ALL ZEROING MUST BE DONE WITH THE BAYONET FIXED AND WITH THE BATTLE SIGHT OF WHATEVER MODEL OF BACK SIGHT IS IN COMMON USE OR AFFIXED TO THE RIFLE.

The term "Zeroing" is applied to sight adjustment because it represents the steps taken by the firer, the coach and the armourer, to bring the rifle sights into position so that when accurately fired by the soldier for whom it has been adjusted, it will send the bullets to the centre of the aiming mark at 300 yards. Therefore, the aiming mark is the starting point in the measurement of the soldier's shooting skill. Zero is the starting point from which positive and negative quantity is reckoned, hence its application to sight adjustment, just as in a thermometer, temperature is registered above and below a measuring point known as Zero.

In zeroing, the first step is for the coach to find the Capability Group and its MPI. By measuring the distances vertically and horizontally, between the auxiliary aiming mark's lower side and the MPI No. 2, the required sight adjustment is determined.

But there are differences in range facilities so the points of impact have to be altered according to the length of the range and the target used, in order that when more distant targets are involved, the trajectory of the bullet may be compensated for, so that it will land where you want it to hit.

This may appear, at first, to be very involved but you are well aware that if you were playing centre field of the town baseball team and were pegging the ball to second base to halt the base runner, you would throw the ball not in a perfectly straight line, but rather give it an upward curve so that it would travel in an arc.

Artillerymen firing their big guns at distant targets aim the muzzles up in the air so that the shells will travel in an arc. If their computations are correct, the shells will land exactly where they want to strike. Howitzers and mortars are good examples of this type of trajectory consideration.

Your rifle builds up terrific muzzle velocity for the size and weight of the bullet it fires, hence the factor of trajectory is not quite so pronounced as in many other weapons.

You may see your point of aim at 300 yards but in seeing it your line of vision is one perfectly straight line. But if your bullet were to travel along that line the resistance of the air against the bullet and the downward pull of gravity would cause it to land below the Point of Aim.

In other words, if you were firing at a standing enemy soldier, 300 yards away, and aimed at his heart the bullet would probably strike somewhere around his left knee. That is not very satisfactory in war because your job is to kill him.

Thus it becomes most essential that rifles be zeroed or adjusted so that they will compensate for the factors of gravity, decreasing velocity, etc., and plant the bullets right where you want them to strike. When your rifle is zeroed, you are able to select your aiming point as the mark you want to hit and the corrected sights will take care of the bullet's flight so that you aim at the heart and register the shot there.

Observing Figure 1 you will note that the rifle has been sighted so that if a soldier was firing it he would be able to look through the back sight to the front sight correctly directed toward the aiming marks, first of a target 30 yards beyond, a second target 100 yards away and a third target 300 yards in the distance. The 300-yard target approximates the average distance of battle targets hence it must be the one for which the sight adjustment is made.

The trajectory which the bullet will take in striking all three targets so that the one 300 yards away may be accurately struck is also shown. In order that the bullet will take this arc-like course it becomes necessary for the rifle's sights to be so adjusted that while the sights are dead upon the aiming point the muzzle will steer the bullet along the line of the arc.

Because all training centres have not the complete facilities for zeroing rifles at 100 yards, the methods of zeroing have been made available for both the 30-yard and 100-yard targets, although the latter is better. In either one if you aim precisely at the point of aim, the sights should cause the bullets to strike the 30-yard target 2.25 inches above the auxiliary aiming mark's base and if it were to continue to the 100-yard target it would strike 8.5 inches above the auxiliary aiming mark's base.

Should it continue on to the 300-yard target in the distance, it should fall directly upon the aiming point. Again, note the illustration, Figure 1, opposite.

Before dealing with the specific details, it is stressed here that rifle sights CAN ONLY BE FITTED FOR THE SOLDIER WHO POSSESSES THE RIFLE. Neither the coach nor the armourer can see precisely the same as the soldier when using his rifle. Therefore they cannot adjust the sights to suit themselves and expect the recruit to shoot accurately with it. After all, the soldier is the one who will be using that rifle on the battlefields and not the coach nor the armourer. The coach will therefore confine himself to determining the amount of sight correction required and of so instructing the armourer who will then make the adjustments. The coach will also see to it that the sight corrections have been made by checking subsequent targets.

Your attention is drawn to Figure 2 which shows what happened when more than one person using the same rifle on the same target attempted to get the same results. The soldier for whom the rifle had been zeroed was the only one who had his group upon the point of aim.

189

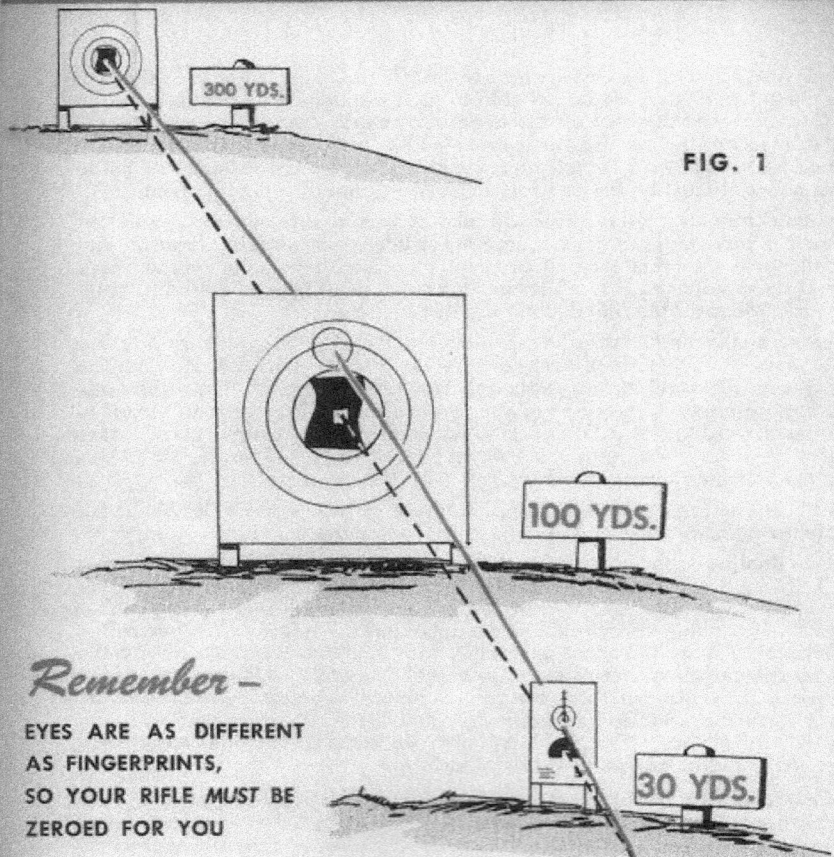

300 YDS.

FIG. 1

100 YDS.

30 YDS.

FIRING POINT

Remember –

EYES ARE AS DIFFERENT
AS FINGERPRINTS,
SO YOUR RIFLE *MUST* BE
ZEROED FOR YOU

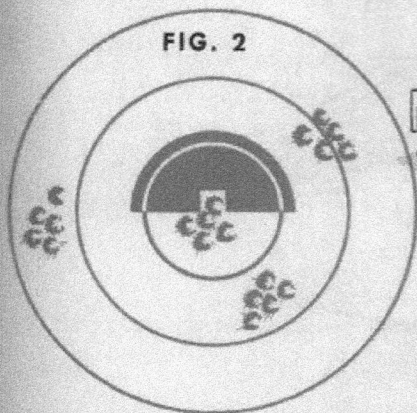

FIG. 2

190

ROUGH ZEROING

THE soldier gets his first familiarization with the shooting performance of his rifle when he is at his Basic Training Centre. If he has been taught the five prime principles of musketry he should be in a position to register fairly compact bullet hole groups upon his first .303 target. His rifle can then be roughly zeroed. It should be remembered that he fired his first target with BAYONET FIXED.

This first test is usually done with the 9C target placed 30 yards from the firing point. The front sight must be brought up to the flat side of the black half-disc which is the aiming mark and the white, square auxiliary aiming mark should be sitting on the centre of the front sight.

If the rifle is to be zeroed for service conditions, the bullets must land at a point two-decimal-two-five (2.25) inches above the point of aim. You will note that in Target 1, the coach has determined the Actuality and Capability Groups, has found the MPI of the latter and has marked in the sight correction line for the armourer.

As you follow this procedure, you will send the soldier with his rifle and target to the armourer who will then make the necessary adjustments to the sights. When the second target is shot, it will be seen that the armourer has installed a sight which brought the Capability MPI not quite high enough but took it too far to the right. Another sight adjustment line is then drawn (this time on his new target) and the soldier is sent with his rifle to the armourer again. The third target should show the capability cluster of the firer to be right where it was required. (Note the MPI in Target 3).

The illustration marked Target 4 shows a correctly zeroed target.

It must be remembered that the recruit who has had his rifle zeroed at his basic training centre has only a roughly corrected weapon. It has been given its first correction so that it may help in his musketry instruction later. The accurate zeroing, which will be discussed next, will be the sight adjustment which should remain with the rifle all through the soldier's service.

ROUGH ZEROING
FIRST STEP

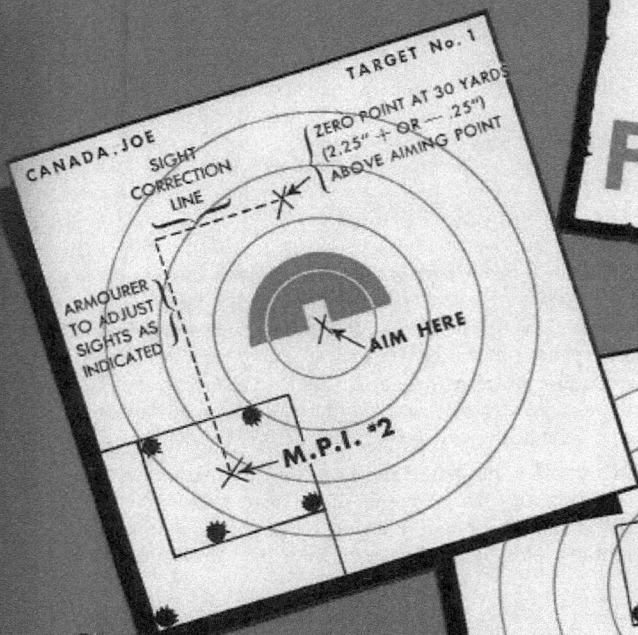

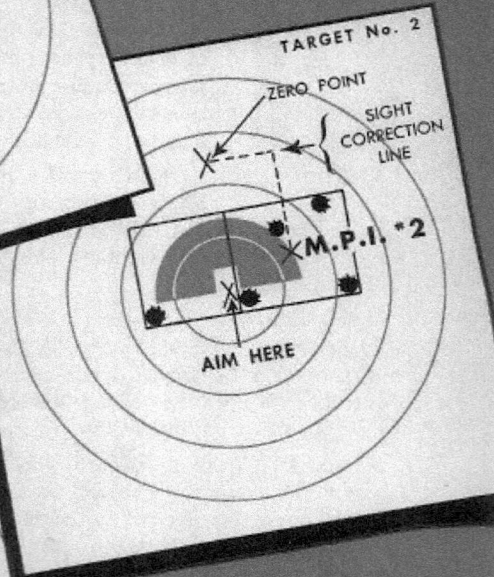

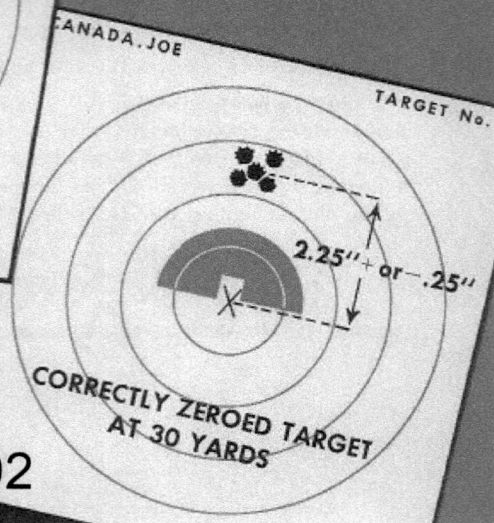

TARGET No. 1

CANADA, JOE

SIGHT CORRECTION LINE

ZERO POINT AT 30 YARDS
(2.25" + OR - .25")
ABOVE AIMING POINT

ARMOURER TO ADJUST SIGHTS AS INDICATED

AIM HERE

M.P.I. #2

TARGET No. 2

ZERO POINT

SIGHT CORRECTION LINE

M.P.I. #2

AIM HERE

CANADA, JOE

TARG

NO SIGHT ADJUSTMENT NEEDED

ZERO POINT

M.P.I. #2

AIM HERE

CANADA, JOE

TARGET No.

2.25" + or - .25"

CORRECTLY ZEROED TARGET AT 30 YARDS

192

ACCURATE ZEROING AT 30 YARDS

THERE are two methods of accurately zeroing a .303 rifle, either one of which should prove suitable. In fact if both were used it would provide a double check upon the accuracy and be more convincing to the recruit. Accurate zeroing is usually done during Advanced Training.

The first method applies to a 30-yard range, where a Standard Zeroing Target (see Figure 1) is used. There were many variations of this target but this one has been found most suitable for the purposes of accuracy.

The aiming mark is similar to that of the 9C target and 2.25 inches above that aiming mark is the centre of a circle one-half ($\frac{1}{2}$) inch in diameter. This half-inch circle must enclose the MPI. It forms the centre for another circle, two inches in diameter in which the Capability Group must (and the Actuality Group should) be clustered when the rifle is properly zeroed.

The graduations on the vertical line represent one size each of foresight adjustment. These changes are made in conjunction with the size-stampings on the base of the fore sight. They are marked +.090, +.075, +.060, +.045, +.030, +.015, +.000, —.015, —.030, —.045.

To determine the correct sights in relation to the markings on the Standard Zeroing Target of the soldier whose rifle is being adjusted, and in relation to the sizes of the front sights, it must be remembered that IF A RIFLE SHOOTS LOW, IT WILL NEED A LOWER-SIZED FRONT SIGHT TO BRING IT HIGHER. IF IT SHOOTS HIGH, IT WILL NEED A HIGHER FRONT SIGHT FOR THE SHOTS TO LAND LOWER UPON THE TARGET.

On this Standard Zeroing Target, a horizontal line extends from either side of the auxiliary aiming mark and is graduated in inches to further facilitate sight adjustment to the right or left as required.

Instructions to the armourer should be legibly contained in the space required, with vertical adjustments listed first and lateral adjustments listed second.

There should be space for the Regimental Number, Rank, Name and Platoon of the soldier whose rifle is being zeroed as well as space for the Armourer's initials which will indicate that he has made the corrections as reckoned.

Stress must be laid on the fact that the FIRER MUST TAKE HIS OWN TARGET RIFLE TO THE ARMOURER. Note the target on Page 202, then compare it with the second target on Page 203 which shows the result of the zeroing.

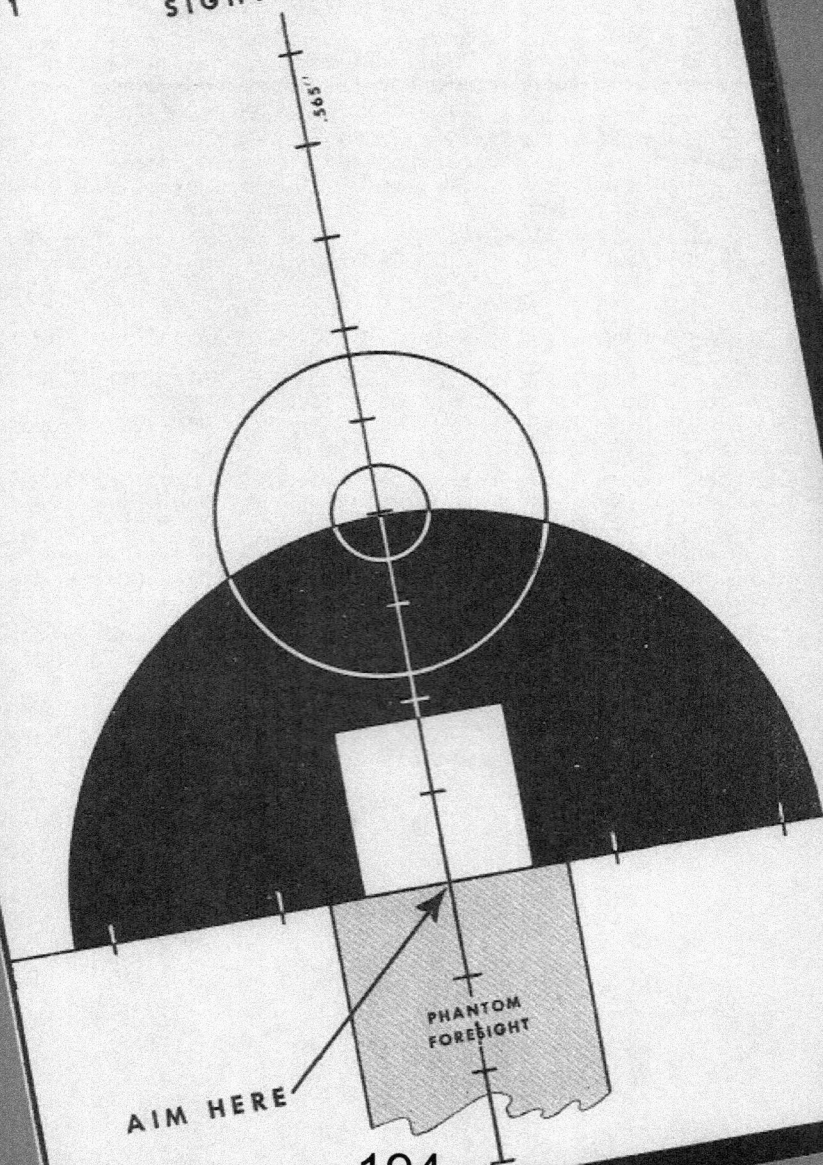

STANDARD 30 x ZERO TARGET

FIG. 1

VERTICAL
ADJUSTMENTS
SIGHT SCALE

.565"

PHANTOM
FORESIGHT

AIM HERE

194

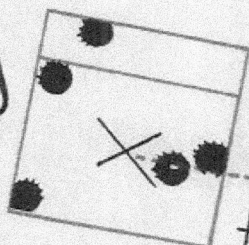

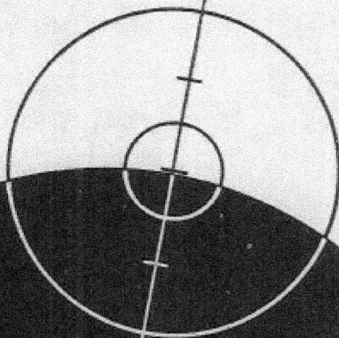

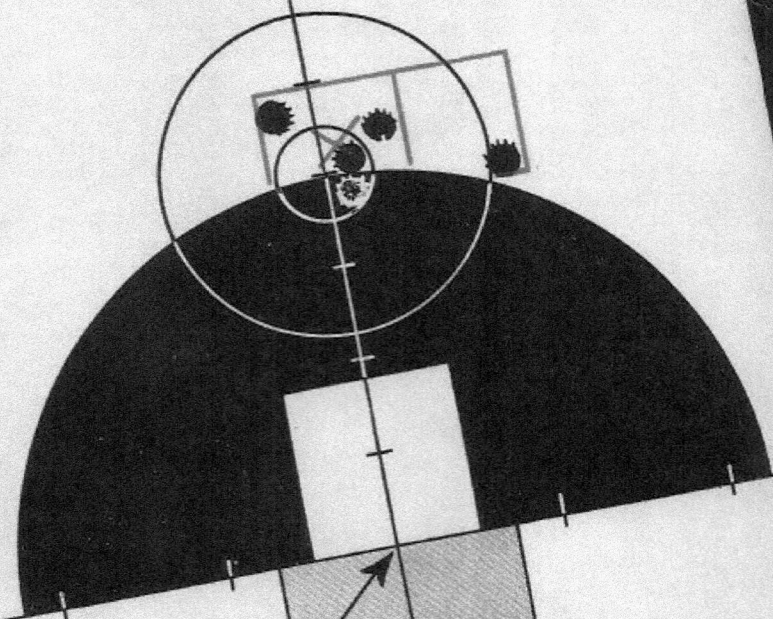

AFTER ZEROING

TARGET No. 2

VERTICAL
ADJUSTMENTS
SIGHT SCALE

.565"

AFTER

PHANTOM
FORESIGHT

AIM HERE

196

ACCURATE ZEROING AT 100 YARDS

THE second method of accurately zeroing the .303 rifle would be to use the standard 100-yard range. Here, we use the standard four-foot target with the hour-glass figure and a centrally-located auxiliary aiming mark shown as a white square.

Because this type of target cannot be taken down from its frame and thus marked like the Standard Zeroing Target for 30 yards, the coach may visually determine the adjustments that are necessary, keep a record of them together with the soldier's rank, name, number and platoon and rifle numbers, so that the soldier can report to the armourer with accurately-recorded sight adjustment instructions.

To determine the adjustment necessary when using the 100-yard target, the zero is placed 8.5 inches above the centre of the Point of Aim. It is on that point the MPI of the Capability Group should rest. If accurately shot, the group's MPI will be dead upon the zero point and the bullet holes in a compact cluster around it.

This new zero is as correct for the 100-yard target as the one which was 2.25 inches above the aiming point of the Standard Zeroing Target for 30 yards. In fact if the bullet were to puncture the latter target and then continue its flight for another 70 yards it would strike the zero of the 100-yard target 8½ inches above the aiming point.

And if that same bullet were to continue its flight for another 200 yards to a target 300 yards from the firer it would land dead upon the aiming point. Yet the aiming points for all three targets were identical.

The zeroing done with the Standard Four-Foot Target at 100 yards is probably the more accurate of the two methods offered but because of the number of firing points available and the number of men whose rifles must be zeroed, it is sometimes necessary to use both methods.

Coaches should study the illustrations opposite as they demonstrate the zeroing methods for the 100-yard target.

197

ACCURATE ZEROING AT 100 YARDS

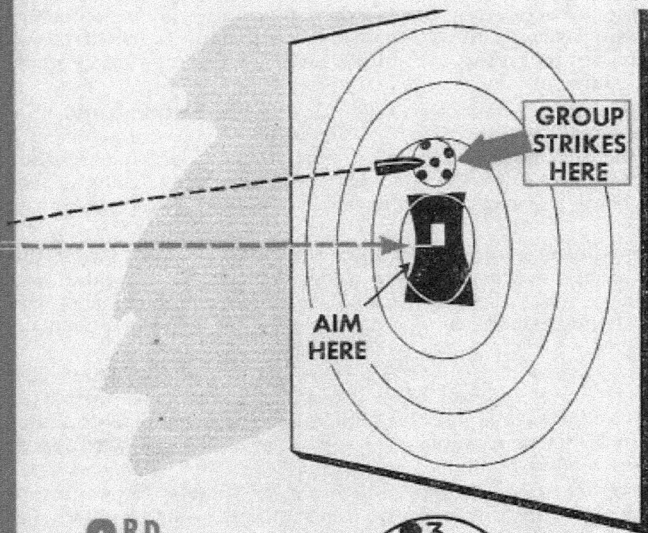

GROUP STRIKES HERE

AIM HERE

3RD STEP

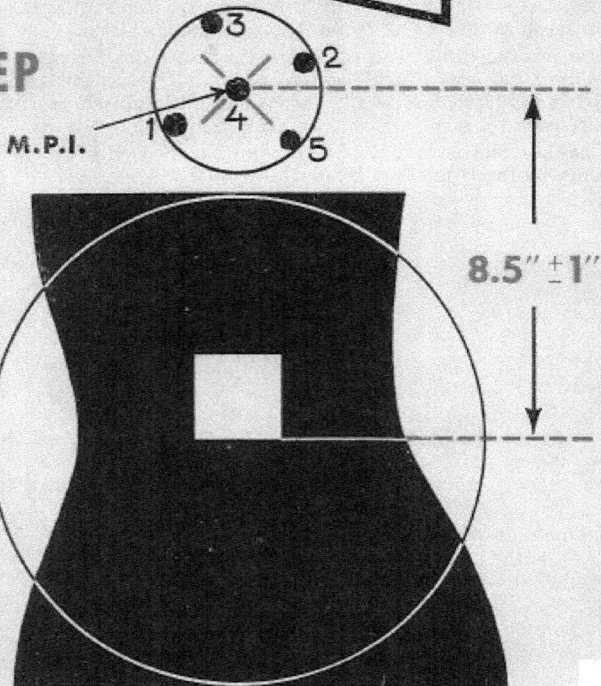

3

2

M.P.I.

1

4

5

8.5″ ±1″

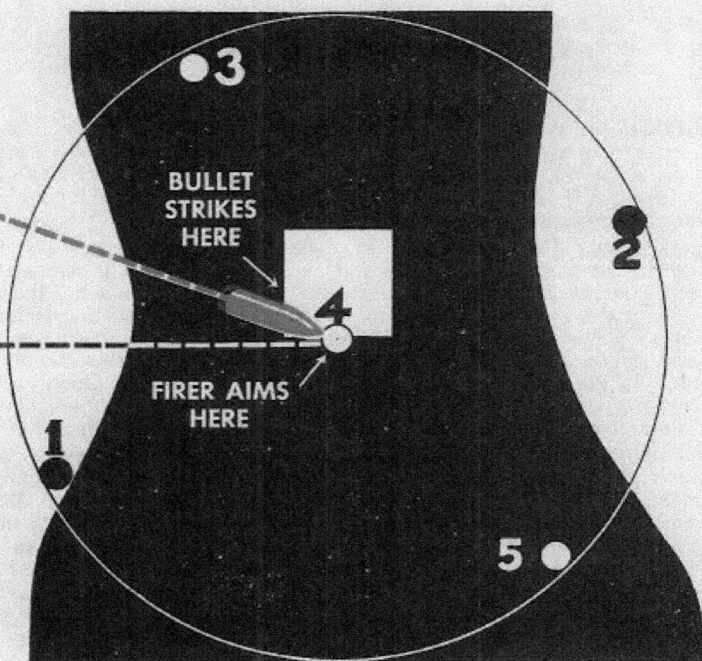

THE PROPERLY-ZEROED RIFLE AT 300 YARDS

BULLET STRIKES HERE

FIRER AIMS HERE

THE ZEROED RIFLE

THE illustration above, shows what the result of your accurate zeroing will do to the soldier's rifle when it is fired at a target 300 yards away. The line of vision has been straight to the aiming point and the correctly-zeroed rifle with its sights adjusted to fit the firer has sent the bullet on its natural trajectory so that it punctures the target at the same point.

In other words, the straight line of vision and aim and the curved line of the bullet's course have come together at the point which you wanted to hit.

The illustration shows the enlargement of the group which has thus been fired from a correctly adjusted rifle. Although shots 1, 2, 3 and 5 are not dead upon the aiming point like Shot 4, they are nevertheless close enough to do a great deal of damage either individually or collectively to an enemy.

CHAPTER ELEVEN

Coaching Technique

SCIENCE will doubtless continue to develop new, amazing and terrible implements of warfare but the skilled infantryman with his trusted rifle will ever be the No. 1 fighting man of any army. The defence of Canada can only be assured, if our soldiers are of sharp-shooting calibre and it takes expert coaching to produce such skill in troops.

It may appear that some branches of the service call for more technical training on the part of those employed as instructors, than is necessary for musketry coaches but such is not the case. The man who teaches the Morse Code to signallers, or motor maintenance to drivers, or knots and lashings to engineers, is surely doing an important job but those keen men who teach raw recruits how to accurately shoot a rifle are providing the means for taking the enemy out of battle and that is the top job of any army. Good coaching develops the usefulness of the individual soldier and a regiment of expert shots is worth several made up of only mediocre performers with a rifle.

Remember that every begrimed, tired, hungry infantryman may be just one of a vast army but he has to fight his own battle, all by himself. Historians and war correspondents may write gripping prose of how an army, or a division, or a regiment or even a platoon fought but it is impossible to describe the hell which a common PBI goes through when he is facing a ruthless enemy. His only comfort, his only friend, is the .303 rifle in which he has utmost confidence. His only solace is his fervent prayer. The confidence he has in his rifle and the confidence he has in his ability to use it, were instilled by the musketry instructor. If the instructor failed to build up this confidence, then the soldier will fail in battle.

The soldier in training cannot capture interest in his rifle if you, the coach, do not thoroughly know what you are teaching. You cannot stand up and recite the contents of this book by heart, like a child at a school concert. You might just as well ask for enough copies to pass around to your class while you go fishing. You must be imaginative enough to use the material herein and present it in your own words, backed up by your own personality and enthusiasm.

It required 75,000 rounds of ammunition to produce one casualty in the Great War of 1914-18, yet that same casualty could have been accounted for with ONE, PROPERLY-DELIVERED SHOT and it is the ratio of one bullet per enemy casualty that is the goal of the Canadian Army.

Look at the matter this way. If the same tremendous figure of ammunition expenditure prevailed while you were on the battlefield, facing an enemy soldier before he became a casualty, you would be giving him—alone—74,999 opportunities to kill you and more than likely he would have succeeded before he fired that many bullets. Surely you now have the proof that accuracy on every shot is more important than volume of fire.

The coach's skill in teaching the basic principles of musketry in a logical order with the constant reminder that it will produce superb shooting skill, will command interest and create a contagious enthusiasm. This enthusiasm will be virtually unbounded if the coach carries a high spirit of interest in his

COACHING is but 1/9th visible above the surface (Range results). — 8 9ths are hidden in the patient, thorough teaching, proving and applying of Basic Principles of Musketry.

COACHING TECHNIQUE—Continued

men from the classroom to the range or from the study of the basic principles to the dress rehearsals at the firing points.

Floating around on the North Atlantic are gigantic icebergs which, although beautiful to see on a clear day, are a serious menace to navigation because only one-ninth of each 'berg shows above the waterline. The hidden eight-ninths are much like musketry coaching because about that much is hidden in the preliminary instruction, the patience, the knowledge, the understanding and the high standard of ability of the trained coach.

The coach must be enthusiastic about his course and he must constantly and convincingly reaffirm that nothing short of expert marksmanship is good enough. Not only will it be apparent in excellent target scores but it is the only reliable assurance of saving the riflemen's lives.

Unadulterated accuracy plays a major role in good coaching. It does not mean that you insist every man do perfectly, the first time, everything you have taught him. But it does mean that you have TAUGHT HIM THE RIGHT WAY and have PROVIDED HIM WITH ENOUGH PRACTICE OPPORTUNITIES to acquire good shooting habits and skill. In other words you can give him a sight of the goal he should seek and will want to reach.

Your recruit must be convinced that only a properly-fired rifle will produce holes in the centres of targets or in the most vulnerable areas of an enemy's anatomy. You can show him that inaccurate shooting has no place in either his life or yours. You can prove to him that exactness in proper position, breathing, holding, aiming and trigger control will produce perfect results.

Mr. Instructor, you must keep yourself up-to-date with new ideas. Develop your own ideas or encourage them from the class. Many of the tricks of good coaching and shooting came from people whose enthusiasm, while taking this coaching course, inspired them to offer valuable suggestions. However, make every new idea prove its merit as a definite improvement to the course before adopting it.

Use pictures, diagrams, blackboards and anything else you can scrounge. You should be a good scrounger in order to have all the required materials for a successful course. You don't have to be an artist to draw suitable sketches.

Teach your class in small doses. Strive for perfection in each step before going on to the next phase. They will practice between sessions to perfect each little trick if you have inspired them.

202

Give your men a preview of what you are about to teach, stressing the fact that it is only one item toward shooting perfection. As you commence each Basic Principle or phase, outline it briefly when you introduce it. In other words give them an insight of Trigger Squeeze, the Scaffold of Bones or the Optical Centre before going into details.

As each phase is unfolded, tie it back to what has been previously taught. This method usually revives the memories of the men. You must remember that you know what it is all about and they don't know and there may be a tendency not to connect up the phases unless you give them tie-backs. For instance the position of the left elbow has not nearly as much appeal by itself as it has when you tie it in with solid holding. Keep reminding them that the link, just taught, strengthens the chain of facts previously revealed.

Erroneous ideas in shooting are far too common. Every recruit has his own viewpoints about shooting and these must be expelled from his mind before he can become a marksman. They are usually a combination of ignorance as to the basic principles coupled with fear of recoil. Scientific instruction, demonstration and leadership on your part will erase these faults from his mind.

If the men are allowed to follow their own instincts they will jerk the trigger instead of squeezing it and flinching will doubtless result. It may take years to overcome these mistaken viewpoints if you do not give your recruit proper coaching and confidence. NO AMOUNT OF RANGE PRACTICE ALONE WILL PRODUCE A GOOD SHOT unless your soldier has been taught the correct way to shoot before going to the range. Start right, continue right and the product will be right.

Musketry drill by numbers is definitely taboo. It is as old-fashioned as hoop skirts. You must have control and full co-ordination of mind and body to be a good shot. There are drill practices, however, where the recruits practice position, holding, and placing of the rifle so that their arm muscles will be strengthened. There are drills for the all-important pre-firing sigh, for aiming precision and for trigger control. But five minutes twice a day, is more valuable than 45 minutes' practice every other day.

The practice of calling of shots is most important as it causes the recruits to be observant of what happens when the trigger is squeezed and provides you with a constant opportunity to check your man's application of the basic principles. Men who do not measure up in these practice periods should be returned for further training.

It should be remembered that every man cannot take the same position in shooting. But by conscientious approach you can bring him up to a point where he will be as close as possible to perfection and still be comfortable and relaxed in keeping with his physical characteristics. As long as he can shoot small groups every time he faces a target, there will not be much wrong with his position.

When your recruit is on the range he MUST HAVE A TRAINED COACH who will watch the firer's two-foot circle for clues. The coach cannot watch the target and expect to aid the pupil. He must constantly check for comfortable, relaxed position, correct and steady trigger squeeze. He must see that the front sight is the object of vision, that the firer calls his shots, has follow through, correct breathing, solid holding and doesn't flinch.

If your recruit follows your teaching, then all of his shots will hit the bull's eye but if there are stray bullet holes they will be caused by some basic principle or combination of several basic principles, not being properly executed. Your job is to find out what is wrong and then make the necessary corrections.

Some recruits have difficulty with their precision of aim, despite all the instruction and practice provided. Such soldiers should be privately and individually interviewed to ascertain if they see the same sight picture for every shot. If not, it may be because they don't quite understand what is wanted. Patient help on this point will prove helpful.

Your recruit may be proficient with one or two basic principles and lax with the rest. Check his position with the charts in this book, looking for either a high or low vertical triangle. His left hand may be either too far forward or not far enough. He may have a twist in his back or his feet may not be far enough apart to form solid contact with the ground. He may not have adopted automatic alignment so that his rifle points toward the target correctly. These are just a few of the common faults.

Should a soldier's bullet hole group be vertical but narrow with the holes strung from top to bottom, it may be that his breathing is to blame. Some boys think they have given the pre-firing sigh when they haven't. You can check the recruit's breathing rhythm by placing your hand lightly upon his shoulder.

Faulty trigger squeeze is common and is usually not admitted by the pupil and not too readily seen by the coach. Several wild shots to the left of the aiming point might be caused by erratic trigger squeeze. More dry practice or another whirl at the coin games should remedy this. The coach should carefully watch the trigger squeeze at all times. It pays.

Flinching can sometimes be overcome by having the recruit close his eyes during the loading process. You can insert an empty shell case or you can insert a live round alternately; or you can make a noise as if you had inserted a round. When your recruit proceeds to fire and discovers that he flinched when there was no bullet to be fired, he will feel a bit foolish. This should gradually break down his fear because he will not know when there is a live round in the chamber.

The recruit with no previous rifle experience should commence his firing upon a large bull's eye. There is a great opportunity with large targets to encourage a man to score. He can usually hit a large bull's eye and immediately has confidence in himself. He will not lose this confidence as the size of the targets diminish or the length of the range is increased. The .22 miniature range should be the initiation point for the recruit because all phases of good shooting, as taught in the classroom, can be put into effect here. There is no recoil from the .22 yet it resembles the .303 and the confidence gained on the miniature range will never be lost when the service rifle is used.

Some skeptics rate the .22 as a toy and not too worthy a piece of equipment. This is erroneous. The United States Marine Corps, one of the finest military shooting organizations, takes all basic rifle training on the .22. If it will produce Leatherneck marksmen, it will do equally as well for Canadians. Its chief value is in bringing the recruit close enough to a large bull's eye so that he can capture the psychological effect of good scoring in his preliminary firing exercises.

204

Field glasses, binoculars or telescopes have no place upon the range during recruit training. A coach peering through glasses to watch the shot land upon the target cannot watch his pupil's shooting style as revealed within the two-foot circle. The results registered upon the target are based upon what the firer does, hence what causes the shot is more important than where it landed. The target can be examined later to prove your diagnosis of any shooting ills.

While a man is firing he should be encouraged to put all five bullets into the bull's eye. If he put them there in the first target he fired, you should encourage him into registering a smaller group on his second target. Telling a recruit that he fired a shot at 2 o'clock will only mean that he will aim off the aiming mark for the second shot and land probably at 8 o'clock. Watch the recruit's every movement and help him. The target can take care of itself.

Aiming off for wind is a bugbear to good shooting because it does not apply to normal service combat conditions. A bullet is not like a light football which has to be booted with regard to wind. It is a lead pellet discharged from a rifle with terrific velocity. It should only be fired straight at the target centre and nowhere else.

A Kansas tornado might throw a bullet 15 inches off a 300-yard target but you won't be doing much shooting in tornadoes. Solid holding as taught here will take care of the average breeze. Incidentally a poll of top-notch Canadian marksmen has revealed that wind has little or no effect upon a bullet at ordinary combat distances therefore its effect from a soldier's point of view is negligible.

Aiming off for movement is sometimes misunderstood. Although you aim slightly ahead of your target (the amount being gauged by the distance the target is from you and the speed it is travelling) you nevertheless MUST MOVE YOUR RIFLE IN TEMPO WITH THE TARGET. You don't just aim ahead and fire. Your aim travels with the target. Don't stop the swing to squeeze the trigger. Squeeze and swing together.

Canting is a bogey that is as valueless as spitting on a fish hook hoping to catch the biggest bass in a lake. It is a show-off stunt which has NO PLACE IN A FIGHTING ARMY AND MUST NOT BE TAUGHT. THE ONLY SURE WAY IS TO PLACE THE AUXILIARY AIMING MARK SQUARELY ON TOP OF THE CENTRE OF THE SQUARE, CLEAR, BLACK, KNIFE-EDGED TIP OF THE FRONT SIGHT.

Twisting the rifle off such an aim would be as foolish as changing the pictures on a wall so that they hung crookedly. However some men have a minor defect of eyesight known as astigmatism which occasionally plays tricks with them. They should be sent for an eye test and their rifles should be carefully zeroed to fit their eyes.

Never overlook the value of dry practices because they are the full dress rehearsals for the range. Experienced shots practice this way every day, never failing to call their shots while doing it. Dry practice perfects the co-ordination between the eye and the trigger finger and synchronises all the basic principles.

205

The value of dry practice will show up most in battle where men who have used it will be able to automatically aim their rifles and account for an enemy casualty with one well-aimed, well-timed, perfectly-fired shot—and that is what your entire coaching effort has been directed towards.

Remember, however, that practice must be sincere and whole-hearted. Men cannot obtain the results of dry practice if they do not keep their minds on it. They can easily become as disinterested as a twelve-year-old who is more concerned with getting out to play ball than taking his piano lessons. Supervise practice periods to guard against mediocre response by your recruits.

Recruits having preliminary training in the elementary principles of musketry will not wear steel helmets, web equipment or anti-gas equipment. This is established in DMT Circular Letter No. 1376 (HQ 6974-G1-7) (Trg 2b) dated 29 June '44, which read as follows:

1. "I am directed to advise you that effective immediately, steel helmets, web eqpt and anti-gas eqpt will NOT be worn by recruits receiving instruction during Basic Training in the principles of rifle firing, i.e. Position, Holding, Breathing, Aiming and Trigger Control and during the preliminary firing practices on the miniature or 30-yard ranges.

2. Experience has shown that recruits wearing such eqpt are handicapped. It has been found that after a recruit has mastered the basic principles of rifle firing and has completed the preliminary firing required in basic training, less difficulty is experienced in completing range classifications during the advanced training wearing battle order.

3. This information is applicable to the Reserve Army."

Instructors should be very careful to observe the rules respecting overloading of range capacities or of trying to impose too much firing practice upon a class. Range classification MUST BE DONE IN THREE PERIODS OF ONE HALF DAY EACH but these periods MUST NOT BE CONSECUTIVE.

The following direction is reproduced for your guidance: "In order that interest may be maintained throughout the rifle course, a man should NOT be engaged at it for more than a half day at a time."

Range facilities differ throughout the training centres of Canada. Some .303 ranges can accommodate relatively large numbers of firers at one time while others can only handle a few. In time of war there is usually a desire upon the part of instructors to rush the recruits through the range training and in order to do this overcrowded conditions prevail and while one relay of firers are struggling through overdoses of range practice, others are bored by the long wait to take their turns at the firing points.

Range organization can be the means of either cinching the recruit as a top notch marksman or it can develop within him a loss of interest. The training staff which makes provision to insure against the latter, is the progressive staff which keeps every man of the range party interested and that means busy.

If the reader will frequently refer to the accompanying illustration he will more readily follow this method of range organization which has been proven successful in obtaining the highest standard of performance from all members of the range parties which have employed it.

206

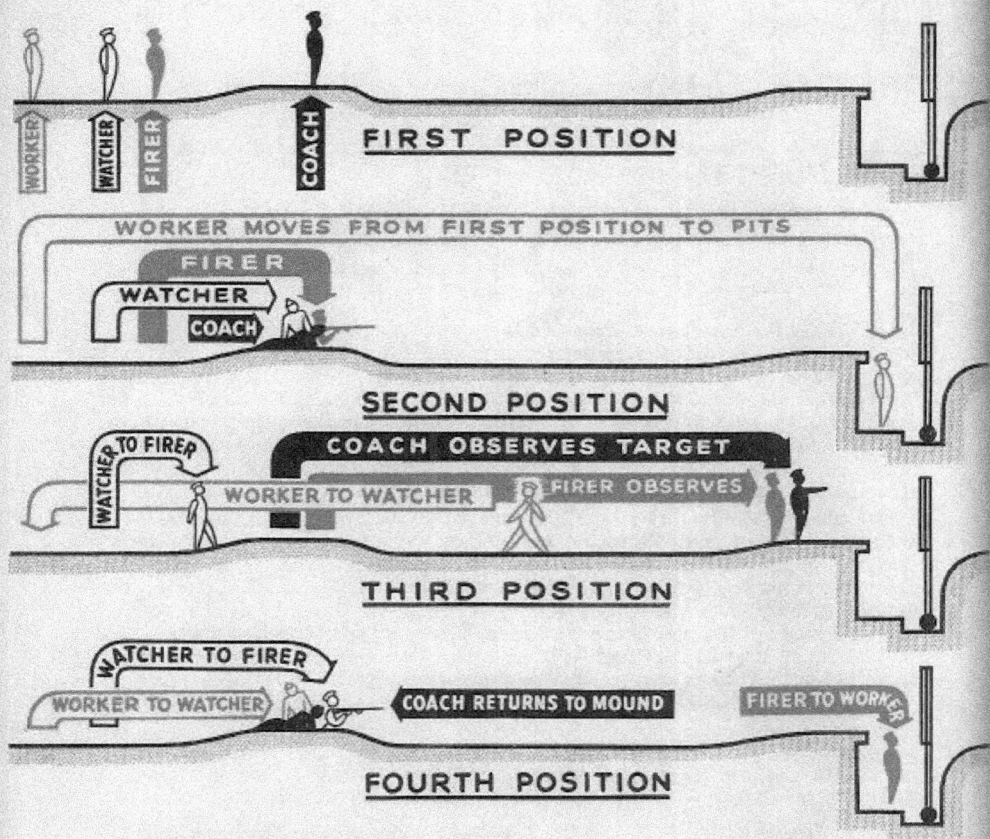

FIRST POSITION

WORKER · WATCHER · FIRER · COACH

WORKER MOVES FROM FIRST POSITION TO PITS

FIRER · WATCHER · COACH

SECOND POSITION

WATCHER TO FIRER · COACH OBSERVES TARGET · WORKER TO WATCHER · FIRER OBSERVES

THIRD POSITION

WATCHER TO FIRER · WORKER TO WATCHER · COACH RETURNS TO MOUND · FIRER TO WORKER

FOURTH POSITION

COACHING TECHNIQUE—Continued

Provide for three men for each target available. See that each firing point has a trained coach. Assuming you have 20 targets at your disposal that would mean you would have 20 trained coaches, No. 1 relay of firers would consist of 20 men, No. 2 relay with another 20 and No. 3 relay 20 more.

No. 1 relay would take the firing position alongside the coaches. No. 2 relay would sit to the side of the coaches and observe the coaching and firing. The third relay would be detailed to work at the butts. In this way each man is concerned with what happens on his own target.

When the No. 1 relay has fired its first practice, it moves up with the coaches to examine the target result; the second relay takes over the firing points and the third relay returns to the firing points as watchers. The first relay then assumes the details at the butts after the targets have been examined. The coaches return to the firing points and the second relay fires and the process is repeated with the No. 3 relay moving up to fire and others shifting the duties to correspond. In this way, everyone is kept busy and interested and firers get their proper rest between turns on the firing points.

Use of each relay as watchers at the firing points in their proper turn so benefits these watchers that their shooting usually shows a vast improvement. Experience has proven this factor.

214

CHAPTER TWELVE

Rapid Fire and
Snap Shooting

THUS far the instruction given in this book has been directed toward the training of a soldier to shoot accurately and with relaxation and confidence always. The ground work of teaching him the basic principles of good shooting have all been thoroughly gone into and if he has been given careful coaching he should, by now, be so proficient in registering consecutive high scores that he can proceed to the advanced stages of shooting. However, he can only be permitted to advance if the coach is satisfied that he and his zeroed rifle are one perfectly co-ordinated machine of precision.

Use of targets in training is only a convenient way of teaching accuracy in shooting. When men get to the battlefields the enemy becomes the target. But the enemy is not placed on range-like platforms. He is seeking concealment from you while he gets into position to kill you. Therefore, you must be prepared to shoot with deadly accuracy on the spur of the moment that you suspect his menacing presence. He may even be fleeing between buildings, or scurring through a brief section of open terrain. The kind of shooting, which takes care of this, is known as SNAP SHOOTING.

In addition there are many occasions in which a soldier is faced with more than one enemy. Here he cannot take his leisurely time between shots but must quickly "erase" all with quick, accurate firing before the enemy has a chance to get into position to retaliate. This style of shooting is known as RAPID FIRE.

Rapid Fire is most effective if the five basic principles of good shooting are followed carefully and put into rhythmic operation. Remember, the Canadian soldier, with his zeroed rifle and with thorough practice in these basic principles, can out-shoot a whole squad of the enemy. He ties an obituary notice on every bullet he fires—and he delivers every one. This is because he is personalizing his fire, by means of the expert training he received from his musketry coach, during his basic and advanced training.

The soldier, who commences to learn rapid fire and snap shooting, is entering the big league of the game. Like the promising rookie of the major baseball team, he may look good in the tryouts but when he gets into the mammoth ball park and sees that every play is being studied by thousands, he becomes crowd conscious and unless he remembers to make every play automatically and perfectly and to keep cool and rhythmical in his work, he will find that he has missed his big chance.

No soldier can approach rapid fire and snap shooting unless and until he has been thoroughly seasoned in all the basic principles. He must make every movement of shooting appear as automatic as the automobile driver who co-ordinates the clutch, the accelerator, the gear shift lever and the steering wheel all into one combination of synchronised movements. Yet the speed, accuracy and split-second timing of rapid firing and snap shooting is no different than changing gears of a car while driving down a busy street.

The basic principles of good shooting as adhered to in preliminary range practice are just as important in rapid fire as they are in gaining top scores on targets. They are just the same principles with nothing added but rhythm. Just because the tempo is increased, is no reason for any relaxation of anything that has been taught in the preceding chapters. True, there is a certain amount of excitement and urge attached to this speeding up. There is a strong desire to hurry the shots. But this robs the soldier of his precision of aim and his cumulative building up of trigger squeeze.

The squeeze of the trigger may be somewhat faster than in ordinary range firing but it is still the SAME SQUEEZE. It can be much more deliberate and longer if some planning is given to the entire rhythmic operation of rapid fire. In no event, should the trigger movement be jerky or hurried. Instead, keep it smooth.

Rhythm is the secret of rapid fire. The kiltie band with its moving kilts demonstrates rhythm. The bass drummer of the regimental band cannot play many fancy tunes on his drum but he keeps the band in time or in rhythm.

Shooting rhythm is much like the smoothly working automobile engine, because each cylinder of your car fires in its properly-spaced interval. Supposing your car has eight cylinders, each one fires in its proper time, eight spaces apart from the last time it fired. The intervening time is taken up with expelling the exhaust, sucking in fresh fuel, taking up the slack by moving up to the firing point, building up the compression and then firing again.

The soldier starts his "motor" by taking correct position and holding it with automatic alignment for his first shot. After it is fired, he uses a regularly-spaced interval for discharging the empty shell and bringing a live round into place. This is his bolt manipulation. Then he takes up his trigger slack and lets out his pre-firing sigh while he places his front sight directly on the point he wants to hit. His "motor" is now nearing the firing point. As the trigger squeeze is slowly and steadily increased, like the compression of his car's engine, the firing pin is disengaged and the rifle is fired but his eye continues the follow through by mentally calling the shot before the process is repeated.

In comparing the firing rhythm of an automobile with that of a rifle, it will be seen that if one cylinder of a car was to be fired ahead of its proper place it would be so far out of rhythm or time that it would damage the motor. A soldier who has no rapid fire rhythm cannot expect to have accuracy, which this type of shooting demands.

Furthermore, your car is the product of thousands of man hours of labor. It has been precisely designed, built, adjusted and timed. The rifleman must be just as painstaking in developing his rhythm or timing by diligent practice. Much of it will be dry practice so that he can acquire that smoothness and accuracy slowly at first and then gradually increase the speed.

Accurate snap shooting and rapid fire have been the objective of this book. The old story of teaching a child to crawl before it walks, walk before it runs, run before it dances, holds good still. The recruit has now arrived at the final or dancing stage. If he is not thoroughly qualified to move into the higher brackets of shooting he should not be permitted to proceed. If he is qualified to advance, then he should not sacrifice nor neglect the basic principles he has hitherto been taught by your patient coaching.

209

There may be a temptation on the part of instructors to rush their men through the rapid fire and snap shooting drills. It may be sponsored by the feeling that if the recruit has mastered slow fire then he should be able to pick up rapid fire in the space of a few hours. The answer to this, is that the gangling kid who could win all the races at the school picnics, found himself a dismal failure when he first started out to dance. The tricky footwork had him worried at the start because the rhythm confused him and he was treading on the dainty toes of his sweetheart-instructress.

But practice, and lots of it, plus good grounding in the fundamentals of dancing, and determination, cured him of all his dancing problems and if you were to watch him at the next canteen dance you would see that he is an expert of the ballroom art.

So it is in rapid fire. A substantial amount of dry practice in the fundamentals of rapid fire and snap shooting before your recruit tests his skill on the range, is essential. Then a half-day's work on the rapid fire range is just like the first dancing lesson. It is not enough and frequently sufficient grounding instruction has not been given.

Coaches should not try to rush their men through the rapid fire practices without regard for scoring. They should watch for any appearance of faulty shooting habits or ills. You cannot put raw recruits who have just grasped slow firing into a race against time. Build them up to perfection the slow, sure and easy way.

For the benefit of coaches who will be teaching rapid fire to their classes, a number of valuable suggestions are presented below. They are practice proven and their presentation to the classes will produce results. Instead of sending men out to shoot in rapid succession in the hope of having some sort of a record established, you will find that, if your men are trained slowly at first, their perfection in all the steps will develop speed but the coach must guard against the enemy of rhythm—hurrying. This usually develops on the range when the recruits become over anxious or excited and lose their sense of shooting rhythm even though they employ it in dry practice. REMEMBER! YOU HAVEN'T TIME TO HURRY!

1. Train your men to take up automatic alignment with their target by shifting their bodies around until they are comfortable and each rifle is pointing directly toward the place where each target will appear.

2. On the command "Watch your front!" your men should concentrate upon their OWN targets. A man cannot shift his sight all over the range area or be continually looking into the magazine or bolt mechanism. Supposing an enemy sniper was in the grass, 200 yards distant and your recruit could barely see the curve of the enemy's helmet. And then suppose your man took his eyes of that target for even a brief moment. What would happen? He would lose sight of the enemy and lose his golden opportunity. No one can watch the bolt action and keep his eye directed toward the target at the same time. The bolt will take care of itself.

210

3. In both rapid fire and snap shooting there is a definite, easy but necessary routine in raising the rifle into firing position. Having attained automatic alignment so that your firing position will be correct, the rifle can be swung onto the target from the ground by the hinge-like action of the two elbows and arms. It is an easy, simple, fool-proof movement.

4. Observe the sequence from top to bottom of Figures 1, 2 and 3 opposite, and the logical manner in which the rifle is raised from ground level to the firing position while the eyes are upon the target. To lower the rifle as in snap shooting, the reverse procedure is all that is needed. These movements provide for a minimum of effort without waste motion.

5. The rifle MUST ALWAYS BE RELOADED AT THE SHOULDER IMMEDIATELY AFTER IT HAS BEEN FIRED. This applies equally to Rapid Fire and Snap Shooting and whether with live rounds or as dry practice. For instance, if you are engaged in Snap Shooting your sequence will consist of fire—reload immediately after firing while the rifle is at the shoulder and the muzzle points toward the target —then return the rifle to the rest position on the ground. If, on the other hand, you are engaged in Rapid Fire, the order will consist of firing—reloading at the shoulder—firing and reloading at the shoulder again and so on.

6. To avoid confusion it is explained that the terms "loading" and "re-loading" are given to the manipulation of the bolt.

7. Bolt operation is simple, yet more soldiers can grimace, squirm, sweat, grit their teeth and otherwise make a hard job out of it than is necessary. The bolt operates smoothly and doesn't require any superhuman strength because it will do its job easily. If soldiers would only work as well as the bolt there would be less rapid fire troubles in the Canadian Army.

8. To efficiently operate the bolt during rapid fire, the recruit MUST KEEP HIS RIFLE BUTT UPON THE SHOULDER MUSCLE PAD. He should not shift his elbows or otherwise he will throw himself out of alignment with the target. There are some types of men with short forearms who may have to raise their right elbows from the ground but in most cases this should not be necessary if they have been issued with correctly-fitting rifles. Under NO circumstances should the LEFT ELBOW be MOVED.

9. Observe the series of seven photographs on pages 220 and 221 and note carefully each individual movement in bolt operation.

212

1. A shot has been fired

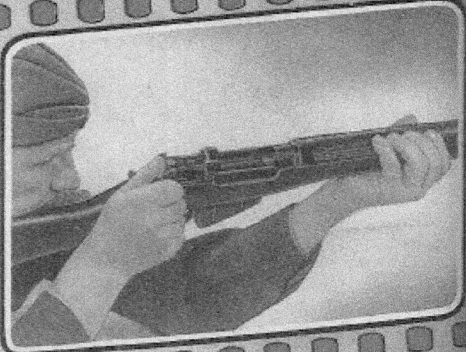

2. Tilt the rifle with the left hand, toward the right, as the right hand takes hold of the bolt handle.

5. Then the bolt is moved forward again. This whole operation involves two movements, which with practice, become one.

6. When the operation has been completed the left hand tilts the rifle back to the left, to its normal firing position.

213

SEQUENCE SHOWN BELOW

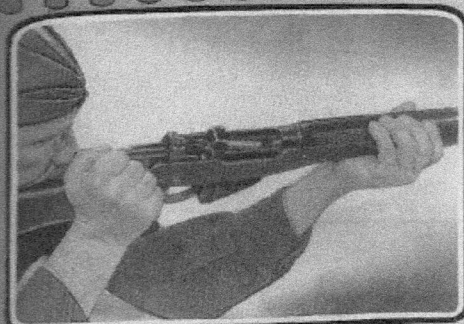

3. The bolt is unlocked with the tilt to the right and, because of this, spent rounds are more easily thrown from the chamber.

4. This tilt makes it easy to move the bolt backwards without striking the face. Note the chin pressure on the butt and the forward direction of the eyes.

7. The tilting has automatically locked the bolt handle and the right hand is around the small of the butt again, and the finger is on the trigger all ready to fire.

214

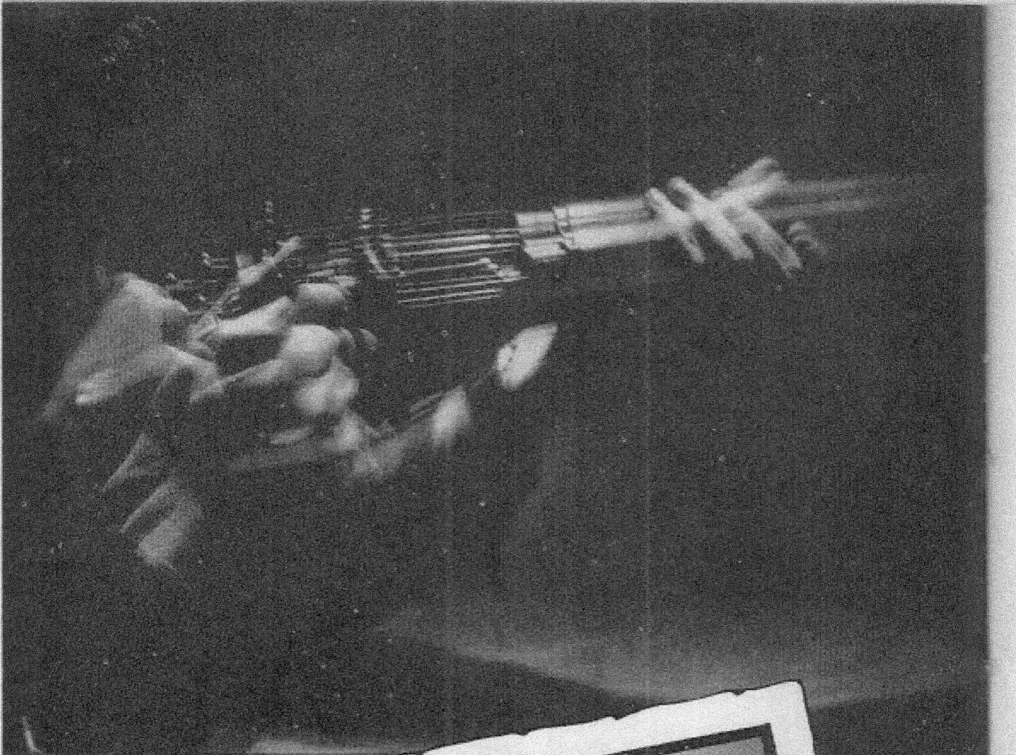

FIG. 1

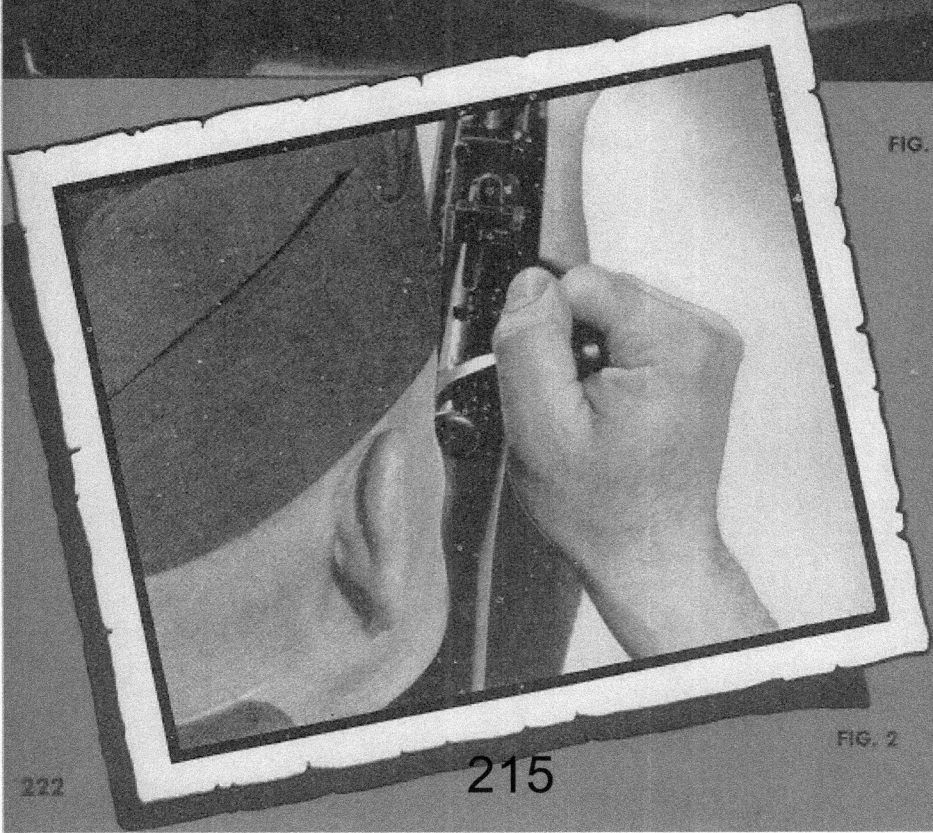

FIG. 2

222

215

The head should remain in contact with the butt and the eyes should stare forward to the target. The chin pressure is increased to its normal amount as the rifle is tilted back into its normal position. Then the trigger slack and the pre-firing sigh are taken. The front sight is placed upon the point of aim and the steady cumulative trigger squeeze is applied and the rifle is fired.

To develop this movement of the bolt down to the point where it is a smooth, easy, co-ordinated series of several motions blended into one, requires much practice. The series of pictures on the preceding pages should be closely followed and as each one is studied and practiced in sequence they should be combined to become one quick movement.

The high speed of each of the phases of this movement, when combined into one whole, is illustrated at Figure 1, opposite, which also portrays the lack of wasteful motion.

Figure 2, shows that when the rifle is tilted to the right it permits the bolt to be drawn back without striking the face. If there was no tilt, the rifleman would have to remove his head from the proper keystone position against the butt or be struck by the bolt or thumb. This threat is eliminated in the time-saving bolt action by the left hand.

Figure 3 shows the correct way for the bolt to be grasped by the right hand when the rifle is tilted. The hand moves from the butt grip and takes a firm hold of the bolt handle.

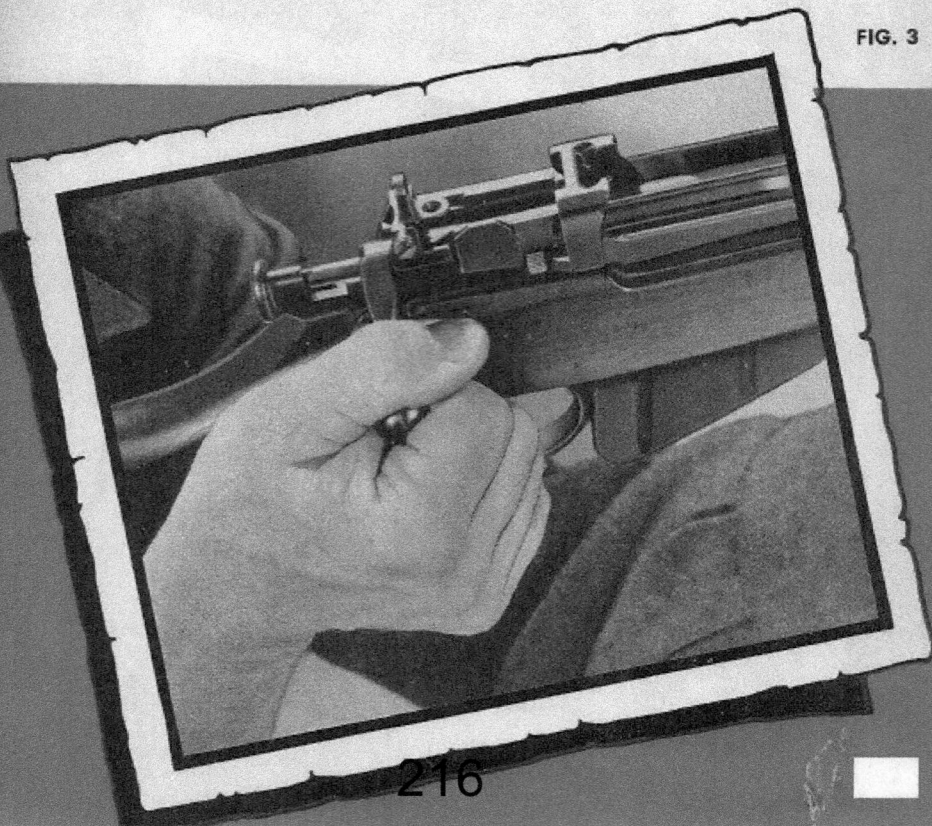

FIG. 3

216

RAPID FIRE AND SNAP SHOOTING—Continued

Count out a five-second rhythm for your recruits such as "1-2-3-4-Bang!" so that on "1" the left hand tilts the rifle toward the right hand which then manipulates the bolt and the rifle is returned to the firing position. In "2," the right hand takes its butt grip position as the slack is taken up and the pre-firing sigh is given. On "3," the front sight is brought up to the aiming mark and on "4," the trigger squeeze is commenced. With one whole beat left for careful trigger control the rifle will probably be discharged on or about the count of "Bang!" Anything sooner than this might indicate a hurrying of the trigger squeeze. In other words, the proverb "Maketh haste slowly" applies here.

Dry practice brings rich dividends. Step by step, each phase of rapid fire can be developed in strict conformance with the basic principles of slow fire until each man can attain an easy, swingy tempo of "1-2-3-4-Bang!, 1-2-3-4-Bang!, 1-2-3-4-Bang!," with each Bang! being the drum beat of a funeral march for an enemy as the bullet goes winging on its way.

THE CORRECTLY-LOADED CHARGER

There may be many ways in which five cartridges can be placed into a charger or clip but there is ONLY ONE CORRECT WAY in which the loading can be done so that the rifle will operate without jamming. Instructors should study the illustration below and then demonstrate carefully to the recruits.

Occasionally, recruits find it difficult to properly insert the charger into the magazine. With the bolt drawn back, the charger is placed as in Figure 1, opposite. Then, with the fingers resting underneath the woodwork alongside the magazine, the ball of the thumb should be placed upon the top round and just ahead of the frame of the charger as in Figure 2. Firm pressure of the thumb should now be applied downward. The first charger's load should be pushed well down into the magazine as in Figure 3 and the empty clip removed by hand. The second charger of five cartridges can now be placed on top of the first five and the action repeated except that you will not have to remove the clip from the magazine. As shown in Figure 4, the closing of the bolt will throw the charger clear of the magazine. This is helpful in battle as it is a time-saver.

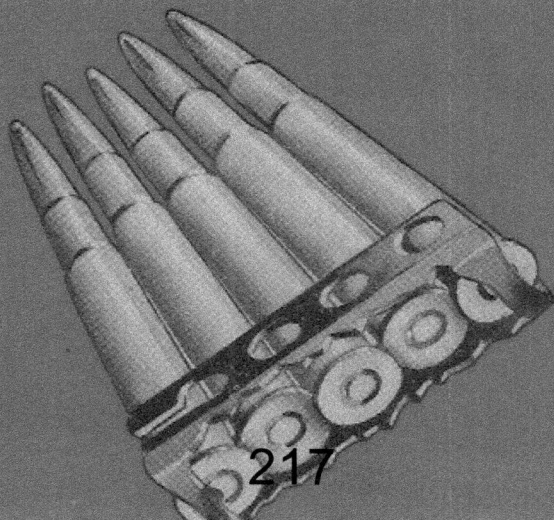

217

FIG. 1

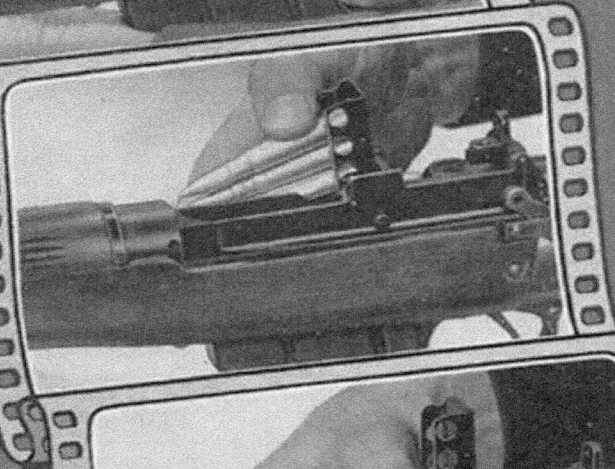

FIG. 2

FIG. 3

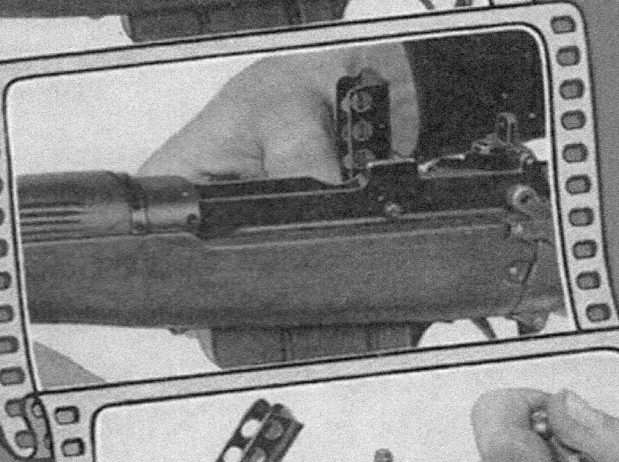

FIG. 4

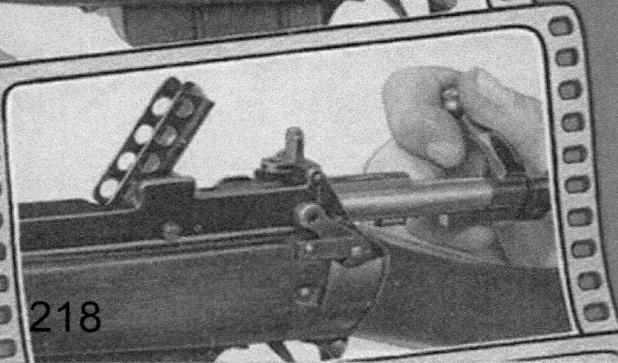

CHAPTER THIRTEEN

Psychology of Coaching

WHEN you were selected to teach musketry to young Canadian soldiers, you were given one of the Army's most responsible jobs. Upon you, and you alone, rests the onus of developing fighting skill in all the recruits who report to you for training. That skill will represent lives saved for Canada, hence never in the history of the world did such an obligation rest upon musketry instructors.

The manner in which you teach the mechanics of expert marksmanship will determine whether the recruits you handle will become good soldiers or poor ones. You receive the raw material and you alone turn out the finished rifleman from the assembly line of efficient coaching.

The recruits who come to you, today, were civilians only yesterday. They still think and act as civilians even though they wear crisp new battle dress. Some will be volunteers and some will be in the Army because of war's emergency. The vast majority of them will want to get back to their civilian pursuits as quickly as possible.

Probably, if you are teaching musketry to the Reserve Army or to the Royal Canadian Army Cadets, you are dealing with men who are more civilian-minded than those on Active service. Their civilian viewpoints must be

219

respected and you must be prepared to make your instruction attractive, clear, interesting and scintillating with gems of learning which will captivate their interests and ambitions.

The age of your recruits may vary from 12 years for cadets to men of 50 in Reserve units or in the Veterans' Guard of Canada. They will represent a variety of backgrounds ranging from bank presidents, lawyers and machinists to dentists, laborers, truck drivers and teachers. Some will be married with families and others will still be in school or university.

They will come from all parts of the country and will have widely-differing provincial viewpoints. Some will have plenty of money and others will lack financial independence. Some will have college educations, while others will have trouble writing their own names. Some will have mechanical abilities which will be receptive to much of your teaching, yet others will find the course more difficult to comprehend.

There will be those with keen intellects, who will work hard and whose enthusiasm will keep the class closely knit together. But there will also be those work-dodging smart Alecks who will try out easy ways of beating the game. No two will be alike and your patience and personal interest in every one of them will be constantly demanded.

They will fear the rifle's recoil but the coach by his methodical practice and preaching of Safety First and his confidence-inspiring approach to all phases of the course will dispel fears and yet encourage shooting perfection. He will develop a confidence in the service rifle and utter accuracy in its use.

Training a recruit to be a good shot has to be done in just a few days because there is not time for lengthy instruction. In fact, there is just time enough for you to teach the fundamentals with logic and punch so they will stick with the recruit. Hence every minute of your instruction must count because time is short and men's lives depend upon it and YOU.

You won't be able to guess what assignments await the men whom you teach. As long as you can be satisfied beyond a doubt that they will acquit themselves ably on a battlefield you will be able to feel that your contribution has been merited.

You don't have to preach anger, hatred or fanaticism in teaching a fighting attitude. Your men must have a calm, clear understanding of the job to be done which is the hunting down and destroying of the enemy.

Teaching musketry must be methodical and logical. It cannot be haphazard. It must be military and yet not stiff. It must be humanized and not presented as if to automatons. You can't recite stiff, military manual jargon and expect it to click. The lawyer in court may use tricky legal phraseology but the newspaper report of the trial is written in language which the layman can understand. Therefore, you should know the technical aspects of good teaching and good shooting but present them in the soldier's language. Your recruit must know what you are talking about in order to learn.

We have all been instructors at one time or another whether it was in directing someone to the correct street address, helping with an income tax return or giving Junior a hand with his homework. You did the instructing automatically and clearly. When teaching marksmanship you need the same kind of horse sense. It is the most important task you ever had.

If you are going to be a good instructor you must want to be good. You should be a first class shot yourself so that you can shoot as good as you can talk about it.

You cannot "hog" the laurels but should encourage each pupil to shoot as well—if not better—than you. It won't hurt your prestige but, instead, will improve it. Incidentally, don't take yourself too seriously. Take your job seriously, instead.

When Knute Rockne was coach of the University of Notre Dame's fighting Irish football eleven he was frequently cheered by his gridders, who worshipped him because he was the genius which spark-plugged them to victories. You can be the Knute Rockne of marksmanship by having each class become so enthusiastic and so confident of success that they will sweep along to perfection in the greatest contest of human endeavour—modern war.

In order to acquire this kind of response from each class you teach you must merit it. You must be able to analyze their mistakes, dispel their false notions; persevere; be sympathetic; be encouraging and not a soft-soaper. You cannot go around bellowing like a cartoon model of a so-called "tough" sergeant-major. Crack a joke in the middle of a lecture, to relieve any tension there may happen to be.

A group of community leaders and military authorities were invited to watch the manoeuvres of an advanced training centre. A drill sergeant shouted and cursed and confused his men so much that they missed their objective. The assault group which got the "nod" from the umpires was LED, NOT DRIVEN, by an instructor who encouraged as he criticised. He knew how to get results. You cannot bludgeon troops into being expert shots but your teaching and personality can certainly MAKE THEM WANT TO BE MARKSMEN.

The expert shot has no pipeline to hidden information. He has merely studied, practiced and applied that priceless gift known as common sense. Encourage its use in your class.

There is no place in musketry coaching for monotony. Cultivate your voice so that it is conversational and not harping. Give the class a bird's eye view of what you propose to teach before you begin teaching it—then be graphic. Use the illustrations, the blackboard or a model but by all means use your imagination. You are the salesman and you have a top-notch product to sell. Don't be guilty of letting your "customers" become lukewarm to your course.

You don't have to grimace, squirm, dance or otherwise act like a character player in the movies. You don't have to lean over backwards with wishful thinking when all along cold, plain facts will sell the story if logically presented in interesting sequence. It never hurts a class to be reminded that a new phase ties back to one previously given. DON'T USE REPETITION WHEN RECALL WILL DO THE JOB BETTER.

One of the most contagious driving forces possessed by humans is that quality known as enthusiasm. If given a chance it can spread like wildfire. Love may be able to move mountains but enthusiasm is the foreman of the moving gang. It was the enthusiasm of General Bernard Montgomery which started the drive which ousted the Germans from North Africa. It was enthusiasm which sparked our First Division at Ortona in Italy; our Third Division at Caen and our First Army at Walcheren Island, at Groemingen and on the Rhine. Enthusiasm in musketry can come from the instructor's positive thinking, determination and personality.

PSYCHOLOGY OF COACHING—Continued

The purpose of military manuals has always been to lead instructors by providing the foundation for their lectures and demonstrations. Instructors must therefore be imaginative enough to use their own language and tie it in with training equipment to present one complete story.

When the coach takes his men to the RANGE he must remember that the men are trying to put into practice what has been taught in the CLASSROOM. He must analyze targets quickly yet accurately. He must observe the actual shooting performance of each man, yet do it quietly, efficiently and promptly. You cannot bawl a man out to the extent that he will get mad. He not only loses that needed relaxation when he is mad but he defeats everything you should be doing for him. Anger and damaged pride can upset your whole course. Never show anger, yourself, in front of your class and don't give it an opportunity to creep into the minds of your recruits. A big, happy shooting family is what you should try to establish.

You have been told to avoid bad shooting habits. Make it a hard and fast rule but don't fall for the old trick of showing a man the wrong way of doing something in order to prove the right way. Show the CORRECT way, FIRST, LAST and ALWAYS. Then it will stick.

There is much psychological value in convincing your men that the weapons they will take into battle are still the best that have ever been devised. In the clinches, the rifle and bayonet represent a personalized threat to any enemy and is more feared when it is in the hands of men skilled in its use. The training is based upon the natural considerations of the five basic principles and is not an involved or hard-to-learn process. The chief requisite is in knowing what steps are needed to produce high scores and then perfecting that knowledge through diligent practice.

So far we have exhorted you to be a specialist who commands the interest, respect and attention of the class without preaching; who LEADS rather than drives his men; who is helpful to all without favourites; who with Job-like patience takes time to supervise and guide his class; whose personality is reflected in his work to inspire the recruit and whose creed is not "Have I covered the ground?" but "Does every man know what I have tried to teach?"

We have told you to keep your lectures speeded up without skipping rough shod over fundamentals. We don't want you to use rusty, dry repetition in your presentation nor do we want you reading text books to your classes. We want you to know your subject and not expound theory. We want the recruit to feel that he is making steady progress because nothing is so progressive nor contagious as success. Keep the challenge always before you that the recruit MUST SUCCEED.

War brings out some startling facts. Usually when the omnious dark clouds of battle appear we have a tendency to seek from our manuals and text books the easiest way of training men to fight. But sometimes, between wars, the methods of teaching have acquired the mildew of age.

In this war, for instance, our training methods were analyzed and it was revealed that:

10% of lectures HEARD are remembered and 90% of them are forgotten.

30% of demonstrations SEEN are remembered and 70% of them are forgotten.

BUT 60% of DOING or ACTUAL PRACTICE is remembered and only 40% forgotten.

Hence, if the smart instructor is going to completely sell good shooting, he must make certain that his lectures are *simple* and *logical*, that his demonstrations are *clear* and *graphic* and the periods for *doing* are ample enough so that when the results of each phase are totalled, every man in the class will have learned a full *100 percent*.

Some instructors are naturally shy. They seem to develop a self-consciousness when standing before a class. If you are sold on a course your shyness will bury itself. If you were on a battlefield with a recruit to teach (which you won't be) you would cast shyness aside and teach him to shoot so well that he would save his own life. If you could do it on the battlefield then you can do it in the classroom or on the range. You must know your subject and your job. You can save the recruit's life in the training stage by teaching good shooting just as easily as you could teach it in the emergency of the battlefield.

223

No course can be a success if it has not been carefully planned beforehand. You cannot command interest from your men if you haven't chalk, laths, charts, ammunition or any of the other implements of coaching readily available. Organize your material before the class assembles then STUDY - - - PRACTICE - - - PLAN.

You do not have to be a glamour boy to be a good instructor. But you can be friendly because your attitude toward your men will be, in a large measure, their attitude toward you. Be courteous because they are men and not an annoyance to put up with. Be fair without favouritism and be enthusiastic.

Be direct. Talk to your class and not to the charts, blackboard or floor. Look them in the eye because it is more personal that way. Develop a good voice by adopting the right pitch to command attention. Be military because your demeanour should command respect, but remember, being military also means being a gentleman.

Let the men discuss the training with you in rest periods. You may be able to iron out a few kinks that way. Praise them for good work but under no circumstances reprimand them collectively or individually in public. You cannot teach if there is anger or resentment. Respond to their good emotions and create enthusiasm wherever you can. And it is well to remember that soldiers like man-to-man advice. They will seek it, so be their kindly advisor.

This course is not impossible. It is simple and you can sell it if you put your mind to it because it is only based upon logic. Apply the Golden Rule of Training:

"Teach your recruit good musketry as you would have him teach it to you."

224

CHAPTER FOURTEEN

Conclusion

THERE you are, Mr. Musketry Coach, the story of "Shoot to Live" has been told. You have been given the full details of how to teach good shooting to your troops and also of how to encourage it. All the facts have been presented in words and pictures and you are on your own from here in. You can either be successful in instructing men to become ace marksmen or you can be a dismal failure. You must decide that point because there are no half-way gradings when it comes to musketry coaching. You will either be a good coach or a poor one.

As you complete successive classes you should find that you are improving your presentation of the course. If it doesn't improve it will be because you have not put your whole determination into the task.

A self-evaluation test has been prepared here and only your own conscience can honestly answer the questions. If you cannot truthfully answer all questions in the affirmative then you have some polishing up to do on your coaching technique. The test follows:

1. *Do I keep myself smartly groomed and do I act like a good soldier?*

2. *Do I select good locations for my classes and demonstrations?*

3. *Do I consider the comfort of my men such as to heat, light, ventilation, seating accomodation etc.?*

4. *Do I plan my instructional periods carefully so that every phase takes its proper place and do I always have the tools with which to teach?*

5. *Do I command and maintain the interest of the class?*

6. *Do the instruction periods and demonstrations run smoothly?*

7. *Do I give a brief outline of what I start out to teach and do I conclude with a brief resumé?*

8. *Do I demonstrate each phase convincingly? Do my lectures and demonstrations appear logical to the men and do they tie back to previous instruction?*

9. *Can the recruits do what I teach or show them?*

10. *Do I set a good example? Am I enthusiastic and cheerful? Am I fair?*

11. *Do I praise good work publicly but reprimand poor work privately?*

12. *Do I use a clearly understandable language? Do I talk "on the level" with the class? Have I developed a good speaking voice?*

13. *Do I prepare my work in advance of the class sessions?*

14. *Do I encourage better musketry?*

15. *Am I absolutely accurate in my coaching and target analysis?*

16. *Do I continually seek new ways of improving?*

17. *Do I know what I am talking about?*

After reading this book you may entertain the opinion that in theory the methods outlined herein sound good but because they may appear to be radically new they may not be practical.

The co-author of this book is a civilian who at first was not conversant with the fine points of musketry and who doubted whether the coaching methods as outlined could produce the results which the Army desires and requires. It became his good fortune to observe 24 officers and NCO's take the instruction as presented in this book. At the conclusion of the course, these officers and NCO's took 24 new recruits who had not had any previous shooting experience and in TWO AND ONE-HALF HOURS they taught those recruits how to improve their scores from a pre-coaching average of 7.2 percent out of a possible 100 to an average of 77.74 percent after coaching.

If, under high pressure and limited time, that much improvement is possible then you, with more teaching and coaching time at your disposal and with opportunities for class practice should be able to establish a much higher rate of improvement. Remember, one group of repatriated soldiers who trained in Canada and Overseas early in the war, found this way of shooting upped their scores from 41.2 percent to 84 percent in just 2½ hours of coaching.

The Canadian Army needs expert marksmen at all times. Its shooting performance in the past has had much room for improvement. If the Canadian Army in war or in peace, can top the world with good shooting performance then the nation's defence is assured because the sniper with a rifle is still the top fighting man of any army.

Of course there will be some views expressed that this method of teaching musketry is radical —unorthodox—and that the old methods having done a fair job in the past should be retained as the basis for Army musketry teaching.

Having this in mind, the Canadian Army should probably never have adopted the khaki battle dress but instead should still use the brightly coloured outfits similar to the one illustrated here.

War has been modernized with mechanical weapons while until recently the basic weapon, the infantryman's rifle got only a smattering of attention. We were content to teach the hand-me-down methods. The teaching and coaching system as outlined herein is as modern as radar although it took 20 years to develop.

The life of one Canadian soldier is a billion times more important than ill-advised opinions of the merits of the course. If any would-be instructor is too unconcerned to apply himself to the course or whose mind is not receptive to new ideas, he should either not be an instructor or he should read this book again and AGAIN.

So, Mr. Instructor, the job is now yours. The methods herein are commended to you by all ranks of the Canadian Army who have studied them and have seen the results their application produces.

May every man you coach "Shoot to Live" and "Live to Shoot".

THE END.

. . . AND THE GREATEST OF THESE IS TRIGGER SQUEEZE!

227

. . . AND NOW WE'VE *TAUGHT* YOU HOW TO SHOOT!

GLOSSARY OF TERMS

ACCURATE ZEROING - Final adjustment of a rifle's sights to fit the eyesight of a soldier.

ACTUALITY GROUP - The area of a target occupied by five bullet holes.

ADJUSTMENTS - Major or minor alterations of the body's position and or the left hand to correct the rifle's aim for elevation.

AIMING - The process of steering a bullet to as target.

AUTOMATIC ALIGNMENT - The ability of a soldier to accurately, and habitually, adopt a position which will bring his rifle's aim upon the bull's eye.

AUXILIARY AIMING MARKS - White squares on target centres to assist the firer in attaining correct aim.

BACKWARD PRESSURE - The drawing of a rifle butt toward the protective muscle pad of the shoulder.

BLACKENING SIGHTS - Applying a dull, lampblack finish to cleaned sights to improve the aiming facilities.

BODY SLOPES - The natural curve body takes when in. proper and relaxed firing position.

BREATHING - The ability to control the breathing with a natural, audible sigh immediately prior to squeezing the trigger.

BRIDGE TRUSS - The bridge-like use of bones instead of muscles with which to support a rifle.

BUTT GRIP - The proper method of using the right hand in holding the rifle.

BUTT LENGTHS - Rifle butts come in four, correctly marked, lengths to fit the varying arm-lengths of soldiers.

BUTT PLATE - A metal strip across the butt end of a rifle.

CALL AND CHECK CARD - Coaches' method of recording the shooting style and faulty application of the basic principles of his pupils as observed in the two-foot circle.

CALLING THE SHOTS - The ability to correctly state the movement of the front sight upon the release of the firing pin in dry practice or upon firing a live round.

CANCER OF MUSKETRY - Flinching when the rifle is tired.

CAPABILITY GROUP - The area occupied upon a target by the four, most closely-clustered, shots of a group of five shots.

COIN GAMES - A practice method of developing trigger squeeze and co-ordination of all basic principles of good shooting.

COORDINAT1ON - The perfect, automatic application of all basic principles in the firing process.

DOTTING PRACTICE - A method of teaching accurate sighting in using the Winter's Sighting Device.

DRY PRACTICE - Following al1 the basic principles of firing without a live round in the chamber.

EQUIPMENT OF AIMING - Sighting bars and devices designed to improve the aiming precision of recruit marksman.

EYE DISTANCE - The correct space between the pupil of the eye and the rear sight of the rifle, or aperture sight of a rifle.

FLAT HAND METHOD - The procedure of checking the position of the left elbow by raising and lowering the open left hand while keeping if before the vision of the firer.

FOCUS - Concentration, of vision upon one object.

FOLLOW THROUGH - Continuing the squeeze of the trigger after the bullet has been fired.

GROUPS - The shapes and sizes of the clusters of bullet holes upon a target.

HALF ROLL - The practice of partially rolling over upon one's right side while the rifle is pointed upward, so that the left elbow can be brought down into its correct position directly beneath the rifle.

HEEL OF THE HAND - The muscled portions of the hand closest of the wrist.

HIGH RIGHT HAND - A condition of the right shoulder caused by the improper placing of the right elbow raising the vertical triangle and creating unsteadiness of the rifle,

HOLDING - The term given to the correct support and solidness of a rifle in the hands of a trained marksman.

HORIZONTAL TRIANGLE - An imaginary, even-sided, triangle formed by the centre of the body and the two elbows, when viewed from above.

LANGUAGE OF BULLET HOLES - The advanced study of bullet holes in targets and the merits, or faults, of each.

MAJOR ADJUSTMENT - The forward or backward inching of all the body, except the two elbows, to correct the rifle's aim for elevation.

MASTER EYE - The most-used eye.

MEAN POINT OF IMPACT - The dead centre of a bullet-hole group.

MINIATURE RANGE - A 25- or 30-yard range for the use of the .22 calibre rifle.

MINIATURE RIFLE - A .22 calibre rifle, similar in design and operation to the standard service rifle but used for preliminary training of marksmen.

MINOR ADJUSTMENT - The forward or backward adjustment of the left hand to correct the rifle's aim for elevation.

MUSCLE PAD - A shock-absorbing concentration of muscles directly below the collarbone.

OBLIQUE BODY ANGLES - The angle at which the trunk of the body points in relation to the direction of the rifle's aim.

OPTICAL CENTRE - The distinct clear core of the line of vision when funneled through the rear or aperture sight.

ORPHAN ANNIE - The stray shot.

PEEP SIGHT - The finely drilled hole in a rear sight through which the target and front sight are lined up.

POINT OF AIM - The place where the firer's shots should strike if the principles of musketry are followed.

POSITION - The comfortable, lying-down, state of a soldier whose body and rifle are a unit pointing naturally toward the target.

POSITION CHARTS - Instructional diagrams to assist is teaching correct firing position.

PRECISION OF AIM - Unqualified exactness in steering bullets.

PRONE - The lying-down firing position.

ROLLING WITH THE SHOVE - Allowing the head to ride with the butt during recoil.

ROUGH ZEROING - Preliminary sight adjustment of a rifle.

SCAFFOLD OF BONES - Use of bones as a structure of solid support for a rifle.

SERVICE TARGET - The enemy.

SIGHT CORRECTION - The indication upon targets of the extent of adjustment necessary to fit the rifle's sights to the eyesight of the soldier.

SIGHT PICTURES - The uniform view seen for each aim.

SNUBBING EFFECT - Hands used as shock absorbers to arrest the rifle's recoil.

SOLID HOLDING - Rigid support for the rifle.

TARGET ANALYSIS - The study of targets to determine and measure the shooting ability of the firer and the clues from which the correction of faults can stem.

TRIGGER. CONTROL - The calculating steady, cumulative, squeeze of a trigger.

TRIGGER SOLITAIRE - Practice of the trigger-squeeze game.

TWO-FOOT CIRCLE - The position which the coach takes to check and advise the recruit upon the range.

VERTICAL TRIANGLE - Imaginary, even-sided, oblique triangular formed by the two elbows and the contact points of the hands upon the rifle, when viewed from in front of the muzzle.

VIBRATIONS AND TENSIONS - Unwanted movement imparted to the rifle when the body is not relaxed.

ZEROING - The application of correct sights to fit the eyesight of the firer.

INDEX

A

ACCIDENTS - 163
ACCURACY - 203
ACCURATE Sight - 76
    Zeroing at 30-yards - 293
    Zeroing at 100-yards - 197
ACTUALITY Groups - 168
ADJUSTING Positions - 29
    ADJUSTMENTS for
elevation - 31
    Major and Minor - 31
ADVICE Encouragement and -
79
AIM, Precision of – 109
    Service Targets and - 109
AIMING and eyes - 81
    Breathing and - 71
    Chapter on - 74
    Equipment of -114
    Exercises - 122
    Mark - 95
    Auxiliary - 95
    New rules of - 127
    Off for movement - 205

Wind - 205
    Perfect - 79
    Points of - 107
    Value of - 79
ALIGNMENT Automatic - 73
    Sight - 122
AMERICAN Sighting bar - 115
AMOUNT of butt on shoulder -
53
ANALYSIS. Target, chapter on -
164
ANGLES, Body - 29
APERATURE Sight - 29, 74
APPLICATION of Trigger
Control - 141
AUDIBLE Sigh - 72
AUSTRALIAN Sight Bar - 117
AUTOMATIC Alignment - 73
AUXILIARY Aiming marks - 105
AXIS of rifle - 29

B

BACK Sight - 84
BACKWARD Pressure - 18
    Checking - 55
BAG, Sand, Use of - 157
BAR, American Sighting - 115
    Australian Sight - 117
    Johnson Sighting - 119
BASIC Principles - 3

U

V

W

Z

www.ingramcontent.com/pod-product-compliance
Lightning Source LLC
Chambersburg PA
CBHW060011050426
42448CB00012B/2699